THE
COLLEGE
PRESS
NIV
COMMENTARY

ESTHER & DANIEL

THE COLLEGE PRESS NIV COMMENTARY

ESTHER & DANIEL

MARK MANGANO, PH.D.

Old Testament Series Co-Editors:

Terry Briley, Ph.D.
Lipscomb University

Paul Kissling, Ph.D.
Great Lakes Christian College

 COLLEGE PRESS
PUBLISHING COMPANY
Joplin, Missouri

Library of Congress Cataloging-in-Publication Data

Mangano, Mark, 1958–
    Esther/Daniel / Mark Mangano.
       p.   cm. — (The College Press NIV commentary. Old
  Testament series)
    Includes bibliographical references.
    ISBN 0-89900-885-2
    1. Bible. O.T. Esther—Commentaries. 2. Bible. O.T.
  Daniel—Commentaries.   I. Title. II. Series.
  BS1375.53.M26 2001
  222'.9077—dc21

                                    2001047688

A WORD
FROM THE PUBLISHER

Years ago a movement was begun with the dream of uniting all Christians on the basis of a common purpose (world evangelism) under a common authority (the Word of God). The College Press NIV Commentary Series is a serious effort to join the scholarship of two branches of this unity movement so as to speak with one voice concerning the Word of God. Our desire is to provide a resource for your study of the Old Testament that will benefit you whether you are preparing a Bible School lesson, a sermon, a college course, or your own personal devotions. Today as we survey the wreckage of a broken world, we must turn again to the Lord and his Word, unite under his banner and communicate the life-giving message to those who are in desperate need. This is our purpose.

ABBREVIATIONS

AJSLL . . . . American Journal of Semitic Languages and Literature
ANET . . . . Ancient Near Eastern Texts
AUSS . . . . Andrews University Seminary Studies
BA . . . . . . Biblical Archaeologist
BAR . . . . . Biblical Archaeology Review
BBR . . . . . Bulletin for Biblical Research
BDB . . . . . A Hebrew and English Lexicon of the Old Testament by
         Brown, Driver and Briggs
BSac . . . . . Bibliotheca Sacra
BT . . . . . . The Bible Translator
CBQ . . . . . Catholic Biblical Quarterly
EvQ . . . . . The Evangelical Quarterly
ExpTim . . . The Expository Times
HAR . . . . . Hebrew Annual Review
ICC . . . . . . International Critical Commentary
JBL . . . . . Journal of Biblical Literature
JES . . . . . . Journal of Ecumenical Studies
JETS . . . . Journal of the Evangelical Theological Society
JNES . . . . Journal of Near Eastern Studies
JR . . . . . . Journal of Religion
JSOT . . . . Journal for the Study of the Old Testament
JTS . . . . . Journal of Theological Studies
LB . . . . . . Linguistica Biblica
LXX . . . . . Septuagint
RQ . . . . . . Restoration Quarterly
SBLDS . . . Society of Biblical Literature Dissertation Series
TynBul . . . Tyndale Bulletin
VT . . . . . . Vetus Testamentum
WTJ . . . . . Westminster Theological Journal
ZAW . . . . . Zeitschrift für die alttestamentliche Wissenschaft

Simplified Guide to Hebrew Writing

Heb. letter	Translit.	Pronunciation guide
א	ʾ	Has no sound of its own; like smooth breathing mark in Greek
ב	b	Pronounced like English B *or* V
ג	g	Pronounced like English G
ד	d	Pronounced like English D
ה	h	Pronounced like English H
ו	w	As a consonant, pronounced like English V or German W
וּ	û	Represents a vowel sound, pronounced like English long OO
ו	ô	Represents a vowel sound, pronounced like English long O
ז	z	Pronounced like English Z
ח	ḥ	Pronounced like German and Scottish CH and Greek χ (chi)
ט	ṭ	Pronounced like English T
י	y	Pronounced like English Y
כ/ך	k	Pronounced like English K
ל	l	Pronounced like English L
מ/ם	m	Pronounced like English M
נ/ן	n	Pronounced like English N
ס	s	Pronounced like English S
ע	ʿ	Stop in breath deep in throat before pronouncing the vowel
פ/ף	p/ph	Pronounced like English P *or* F
צ/ץ	ṣ	Pronounced like English TS/TZ
ק	q	Pronounced very much like כ (k)
ר	r	Pronounced like English R
שׂ	ś	Pronounced like English S, much the same as ס
שׁ	š	Pronounced like English SH
ת	t/th	Pronounced like English T *or* TH

Note that different forms of some letters appear at the end of the word (written right to left), as in כָּפַף (*kāphaph*, "bend") and מֶלֶךְ (*melek*, "king").

Vowels in Hebrew (except where the ו is used to represent a vowel sound), are represented by "vowel points" added to the consonant. For example: הַ (*ha*, "the"). The letter *yod* (י, y) also becomes a *part of* certain vowel sounds, as in the conjunction כִּי (*kî*, "that"). Originally, Hebrew was written as "unpointed" text, with just the consonants. For convenience, the different vowel points are shown below on the letter Aleph (א).

אָ	ā	Pronounced not like long A in English, but like the broad A or AH sound
אַ	a	The Hebrew short A sound, but more closely resembles the broad A (pronounced for a shorter period of time) than the English short A
אֶ	e	Pronounced like English short E
אֵ	ē	Pronounced like English long A, or Greek η (eta)

א	i	Pronounced like English short I
א	î	The same vowel point is sometimes pronounced like אֵ (see below)
א	o	This vowel point sometimes represents the short O sound
אֹ	ō	Pronounced like English long O
א	u	The vowel point ֻ sometimes represents a shorter U sound and
א	ū	is sometimes pronounced like the וּ (û, see above)
אֵ	ê	Pronounced much the same as א
אֵ	ê	Pronounced much the same as א
אֵ	î	Pronounced like long I in many languages, or English long E
א	ə	An unstressed vowel sound, like the first E in the word "severe"
א, א, א	ŏ, ă, ĕ	Shortened, unstressed forms of the vowels א, א, and א, pronounced very similarly to א

PREFACE

Why should Esther and Daniel be placed side by side in the same commentary? Here are some reasons.

First, both books share the same setting: the exile. In 586 B.C. the Babylonians destroyed the city of Jerusalem and deported her citizens. Second Kings 25:10-11 establishes this truth: "The whole Babylonian army, under the commander of the imperial guard, broke down the walls around Jerusalem. Nebuzaradan the commander of the guard carried into exile the people who remained in the city, along with the rest of the populace and those who had gone over to the king of Babylon." God's people were now living in a strange land. When we first encounter Daniel, he is in Babylon, in training for a life of service in the king's palace (Dan 1:4). When first we meet Esther, she is living in Susa, a prominent Persian capital, and soon to be King Xerxes' queen. The Persians had conquered the Babylonian Empire; Xerxes continued Persian rule from 485 to 465 B.C.

Additionally, both Daniel and Esther assume prominent roles in the palaces of foreign kings. Daniel became a trusted advisor to both Babylonians and Persians: to Nebuchadnezzar, Belshazzar, and to Darius/Cyrus. In fact, during the co-regency of Belshazzar, Daniel was promoted to the position of third highest ruler in the land (Dan 5:29). Esther was, as has already been noted, queen of the entire Persian realm.

The Old Testament Scriptures do not give us any hint that either Daniel or Esther resided in Palestine after the Exile had officially ended. In 539 Cyrus, king of Persia, brought Israel/Judah's exile to an end, when he decreed, "The LORD, the God of heaven, has given me all the kingdoms of the earth and he has appointed me to build a temple for him at Jerusalem in Judah. Anyone of his people among you—may the LORD his God be with him, and let him go up" (2 Chr 36:23).

More importantly, this man, Daniel, and this woman, Esther, use their exalted status for the benefit of God's people (like Joseph who lived long before) and for his glory.

When Daniel had completed his interpretation of King Nebuchadnezzar's dream of the colossus, the King said to Daniel, "Surely your God is the God of gods and the Lord of kings and a revealer of mysteries, for you were able to reveal this mystery" (Dan 2:47). When God had delivered three of Daniel's friends from a fiery furnace and a certain death, Nebuchadnezzar said, "Praise be to the God of Shadrach, Meshach and Abednego, who has sent his angel and rescued his servants!" (3:28). Such praise for God! and on the lips of a foreign king. In another context, Nebuchadnezzar wrote of the Most High, "His dominion is an eternal dominion; his kingdom endures from generation to generation. All the peoples of the earth are regarded as nothing. He does as he pleases with the powers of heaven and the peoples of the earth. No one can hold back his hand or say to him: 'What have you done?'" (Dan 4:34-35).

The story of Esther is well known. She risked her position and life to intervene on behalf of God's people — to deliver them from the maniacal hatred of Haman. Her story is told and retold, to the praise of her God!

The Books of Daniel and Esther remind their readers that the forces of evil may prevail for a time or a season, but ultimately God will be victorious. The hatred of Haman for Mordecai and for the Jews mirrors Satan's disregard for mankind and his contempt for God's people. If Haman's plan to exterminate all God's people had come to pass, then Satan would have prevailed over God and his plan to free humanity from the powerful clutches of the Evil One (Gen 3:15). But Haman's plan failed. No Jew lost his or her life as a direct result of Haman's hatred. God had delivered his people! God had vanquished his foe! Haman died, as did his sons.

The Book of Esther recounts a recent threat against God's people. The Book of Daniel predicts a future threat. The maniacal hatred of Satan for God and his people will manifest itself in the person of Antiochus Epiphanes. Daniel predicts of him: "He will destroy the mighty men and the holy people. He will cause deceit to prosper, and he will consider himself superior. When they feel secure, he will destroy many and take his stand against the Prince of princes" [that is, God] (Dan 8:24-25).

The hatred of Haman would be incarnated in the person of Antiochus, who would bring intense persecution against God's people. But like Haman, Antiochus will be defeated and destroyed (Dan 9:25). No one, as Jesus said, not even Satan himself, can eclipse the power of God (Matt 16:18).

Every generation has known or will know a Haman or an Antiochus. The people of God have endured and will continue to endure persecution. But it is only for a "time, times, and half a time" (Dan 7:25). In God's time "the sovereignty, power and greatness of the kingdoms under the whole heaven will be handed over to the saints, the people of the Most High. His kingdom will be an everlasting kingdom, and all rulers will worship and obey him" (Dan 7:27).

The Books of Daniel and Esther point to a lifestyle of faith at all times, but especially during times of distress. When faced with the prospect of death in the fiery furnace, Shadrach, Meshach, and Abednego entrusted themselves to the sovereign and holy will of their God. "If we are thrown into the blazing furnace, the God we serve is able to save us from it, and he will rescue us from your hand, O king. But even if he does not, we want you to know, O king, that we will not serve your gods or worship the image of gold you have set up" (3:17-18). When faced with the threat of death, Esther entrusted herself to the Lord for "relief and deliverance" (4:14).

Each book is integrally related to an important Jewish festival. The Book of Esther served to establish and authorize within Judaism the Festival of Purim. It is a time of joy, of the exchanging of gifts, and of the celebration of freedom from oppression. In the course of the celebration, from ancient times into the present century, the story of Queen Esther is told and retold to each generation.

As has been noted, the Book of Daniel predicts the persecution of God's people by Antiochus Epiphanes. But in time Antiochus's hatred would be overcome by the power of God and a Jewish revolt. The Jews were then able to again take control of the temple. They tore down the altar that Antiochus had desecrated, built a new one, dedicated it, and began to offer burnt offerings with gladness. The Jews then "determined that every year at that season the days of the dedication of the altar would be observed with gladness and joy for eight days" (1 Macc 4:59). The celebration is known as Hanukkah.

Esther was clearly a beautiful woman. According to the Rabbis she was one of the four most beautiful women in the biblical world (Sarah, Rahab, and Abigail are the other three [Megillah 15a], in case you are interested!). As a young man, Daniel was "without any physical defect, handsome" (1:4). Their respective beauty was an essential element to their entree to life in a foreign court.

The Bible teaches us, however, not to be duped by outward appearance. After all, beauty is fleeting (Prov 31:30). Rather, like God, who looks at the heart (1 Sam 16:7), we should be captivated by the enduring work of God in the human heart (1 Tim 2:8-10). Esther and Daniel are enduring characters because of the providence of God in their lives. God blessed Daniel with knowledge and understanding (1:17). He was a man highly esteemed by both man and God (9:23). The beauty of God's presence in the life of Queen Esther is forever remembered in the timeless question, "And who knows but that you have come to royal position for such a time as this?" (4:14).

Through fasting (Esth 4:16; Dan 9:3), prayer, and confession (Dan 6:10; 9:4-19), both Esther and Daniel discovered the tenacious resolve of faith, its uncompromising purity, and the security of its shelter. These are a man and a woman of faith. They challenge us to follow their lead.

THE BOOK OF
ESTHER

INTRODUCTION

In the Hebrew Bible (the Old Testament) the Song of Songs, Ruth, Lamentations, Ecclesiastes, and Esther are together called the five *Megilloth* ("Scrolls"). Jews read these books during their great religious festivals: the Song of Songs during Passover, Ruth during Pentecost, Lamentations on the anniversary of the destruction of Jerusalem, Ecclesiastes during Tabernacles, and Esther during Purim.[1] Due to the immense popularity of the Book of Esther, it is called "The Scroll."

AUTHORSHIP

The text of Esther nowhere names the author. Josephus (*Antiquities* 11.6.13) considered Mordecai to be the author. Living in Susa, Mordecai would have understood Persian life and customs. As Xerxes' Prime Minister he would have had access to court records (cf. 2:23; 10:2). The Jewish nationalism of the book certainly suggests a Jewish interest. However, it is unlikely he would have written such self-congratulatory words as found in 10:3.

---

[1]In his book *Five Festal Garments: Christian Reflections on the Song of Songs, Ruth, Lamentations, Ecclesiastes and Esther* (InterVarsity, 2000), Barry G. Webb writes that "the book of Esther is indeed a festive garment, a garment to put on when we are astonished, once again, at some unexpected way God has rescued us, and when we are ready to celebrate. But it is also a garment to put on when the forces arrayed against us seem all-powerful, when to laugh may be the only way to stay sane. To put this garment on, however, is not to whistle in the dark, or to pretend that things are other than they are. It is to clothe ourselves with the truth that God is sovereign, and to be reminded that he is always with us, even when he seems most absent, and that nothing can ultimately thwart his purposes. To put on Esther is to affirm that God is our deliverer, and to share in the laughter of heaven" (pp. 132-133).

Baba Bathra 15a proposed that the men of the Great Synagogue wrote the book. The Great Synagogue or Great Assembly was a council of great religious authority that is traditionally linked with Nehemiah 8–10, where its earliest beginnings are suggested. The rabbis regarded Ezra as leader of the Great Assembly.

In short the identity of the author remains unknown.

Is the book the work of one author or is it composite? Alleged differences in vocabulary and style are the principal arguments for a plurality of authors.

DATE

Since the question of authorship is insoluble, there can be no absolute certainty about the date of composition. The *terminus a quo* (the starting point) must be no earlier than the death of Xerxes in 465 B.C. (cf. 10:2). The *terminus ad quem* (the finishing point) is much harder to determine.[2] Scholars generally defer to one of two positions: the early date (450–350 B.C.)[3] or the late date (175–100 B.C.), that is, the Maccabean period.[4]

The early date is much more likely. The author's intimate knowledge of Persian customs, names and loan words;[5] the topography of

---

[2]The colophon to the Septuagint (LXX) version of Esther provides evidence that the LXX translation of Esther must have been made sometime before either 114 B.C., the fourth year of Ptolemy VIII or 77 B.C., the fourth year of Ptolemy XII. That colophon reads: "In the fourth year of the reign of Ptolemy and Cleopatra, Dositheus, who said that he was a priest and a Levite, and Ptolemy his son brought to Egypt the preceding Letter of Purim, which they said was genuine and had been translated by Lysimachus the son of Ptolemy, one of the residents of Jerusalem."

[3]E.J. Young, for example, writes, "It is best to regard the author as having lived sometime during the latter half of the fifth century B.C. But of this we cannot be certain" (*An Introduction to the Old Testament* [Grand Rapids: Eerdmans, 1977], p. 355).

[4]Otto Kaiser, for example, infers "a date in the first half of the second century B.C." (*Introduction to the Old Testament*, trans. John Sturdy [Minneapolis: Augsburg, 1977], p. 203).

[5]H.S. Gehman, "Notes on the Persian Words in the Book of Esther," *JBL* 43 (1924): 321-328; A.R. Millard, "The Persian Names in Esther and the Reliability of the Hebrew Text," *JBL* 96 (1977): 481-488; R. Zadok, "Notes on Esther," *ZAW* 98 (1986): 105-110.

Susa; and the Persian royal palaces argues for a date in the Persian period.[6] Such detail would not likely have survived till the Maccabean period. In fact, "the latest terminus ad quem is prior to 330 B.C. since there are no traces of Greek influence either in language or in thought to be discovered in Esther."[7] Comparison of literary Hebrew of the second century B.C. from Qumran with Esther "would rule out a second-century date for Esther, and make a third-century date unlikely."[8]

Many late-date advocates argue that the anti-Semitism of Haman is historically appropriate *only* after the persecutions of Antiochus IV Epiphanes (175–163 B.C.). A.E. Morris has even suggested that Haman was Antiochus IV in disguise.[9]

PURPOSE

Many interpreters assert that the major purpose of the Book of Esther was to explain and legitimate the feast of Purim.[10] This is unlikely since only chapter 9 deals specifically with the feast.

Clearly, the Book of Esther is written to demonstrate God's providential care of His people. "The book of Esther," writes Young,

---

[6]According to Moore and Clines, the details of Persian life confirmed by extrabiblical sources include: the extent of the empire under Xerxes from India to Ethiopia (1:1); the council of seven nobles (1:14); the efficient postal system (3:13; 8:10); the keeping of official diaries including records of the king's benefactors (2:23; 6:8); the use of impalement as a form of capital punishment (2:23; 5:14; 7:10); the practice of obeisance to kings and nobles (3:2); belief in lucky days (3:7); setting crowns on the heads of royal horses (6:8); reclining on couches at meals (7:8) (Carey A. Moore, *Esther,* Anchor Bible [Garden City, NY: Doubleday, 1971], p. xli; D.J.A. Clines, *Ezra, Nehemiah, Esther,* New Century Bible Commentary [Grand Rapids: Eerdmans, 1984], p. 261).

[7]Gleason L. Archer, Jr., *A Survey of Old Testament Introduction* (Chicago: Moody, 1978), p. 417.

[8]Moore, *Esther,* p. lvii.

[9]A.E. Morris, "The Purpose of the Book of Esther," *ExpTim* 42 (1930–31): 124-128.

[10]Bernhard W. Anderson writes, "It [Esther] is an emphatically Jewish book whose primary purpose is the authorization and regulation of a purely Jewish festival, Purim" ("The Place of the Book of Esther in the Christian Bible," *JR* 30 [1950]: 32).

"serves the purpose of showing how divine providence overrules all things; even in a distant, far country, God's people are yet in His hands."[11]

Berg has noted that the Book of Esther parallels the Joseph story (Gen 37–48) at a number of points. In addition to verbal parallels (Esth 6:11/Gen 41:42-43; Esth 3:4/Gen 39:10; Esth 8:6/Gen 44:34; Esth 2:3-4/Gen 41:34-37), the stories have other similarities: both stories are set at the court of a foreign king; both Esther and Joseph become the means by which the Jews are saved; in both stories the disturbed sleep of the king results in the promotion of a Jew (Esth 6:1-3/Gen 41); the reward of both Joseph and Mordecai includes a gift of garments and a ride through the city; and both Joseph and Esther reveal their Jewish identities at a banquet (Esth 7:1-6; Gen 45).[12]

Like the Book of Esther, the Joseph Story illustrates God's overruling care of his people, even in a distant country. Joseph's words to his brothers express the truth: "And now, do not be distressed and do not be angry with yourselves for selling me here, because it was to save lives that God sent me ahead of you. For two years now there has been famine in the land, and for the next five years there will not be plowing and reaping. But God sent me ahead of you to preserve for you a remnant on earth and to save your lives by a great deliverance" (Gen 45:5-7).

TEXT

The Hebrew version (the Masoretic Text) of Esther contains 167 verses, as does the NIV. The Greek version, the Septuagint (or LXX), of Esther contains six additions totaling 107 verses that supply the religious element that is lacking in the Hebrew text. These verses make frequent reference to God and give prominence to prayer. These verses are collectively called "The Additions to the Book of Esther," and can be found in the Apocrypha. These verses have little or no historical value. The six additions are (1) Mordecai's Dream [11:2–12:6], (2) Text of the King's First Letter [13:1-7], (3) The

---

[11]Young, *Introduction*, p. 358.

[12]Sandra B. Berg, *The Book of Esther: Motifs, Themes and Structure*, SBLDS 44 (Missoula, MT: Scholars Press, 1979), pp. 124-128.

Prayers of Mordecai and Esther [13:8-14:19], (4) Esther Appears before the King Unsummoned [15:1-16], (5) Text of the King's Second Letter [16:1-24], and (6) The Interpretation of Mordecai's Dream [10:4-11:1].[13]

CANONICITY

The great Jewish scholar Maimonides (A.D. 1135-1204) ranked Esther after the Pentateuch, declaring, "When all the rest of the Old Testament passed away in the days of the coming of the Messiah, only Esther and the Law would remain."[14] On the other hand, Martin Luther wrote, "I am so hostile to [2 Maccabees] and to Esther that I could wish they did not exist at all; for they judaize too greatly and have much pagan impropriety" (*Table Talk*, xxiv).

Even though Josephus (A.D. 37-100) regarded Esther as canonical (*Against Apion* 1.38-41), the book was disputed by some Jews and rejected by others. Melito, the bishop of Sardis about A.D. 170, during a visit to the east, ascertained the number and names of the books of the old covenant. His list, derived from a Jewish source, includes all the books of the Hebrew Bible except Esther.

According to Carey Moore, among the Christians in the East, Esther was often denied canonical status, whereas, in the West, Esther was nearly always regarded as canonical.[15] Both the Council of Hippo in A.D. 393 and the Council of Carthage in A.D. 397 recognized the canonicity of Esther.

Jew and Christian may have objected to the book because it "seemed too anthropocentric since it does not even mention God. Moreover, apart from fasting, no distinctively religious practices or concepts seem to be in the canonical version."[16]

To date no satisfactory reason has been suggested to account for the absence of the Book of Esther at Qumran. The absence of Esther from the Qumran library may be an accident of the preservation of

---

[13]Carey Moore, "On the Origins of the LXX Additions to the Book of Esther," *JBL* 92 (1973): 382-393.

[14]Quoted in Joyce G. Baldwin, *Esther*, Tyndale Old Testament Commentaries (Downers Grove, IL: InterVarsity, 1984), p. 51.

[15]Moore, *Esther*, pp. xxv-xxviii.

[16]Ibid., p. xxxi.

manuscripts. It seems more likely that Esther was not found at Qumran because the Essenes did not include Purim in their liturgical calendar.

GENRE

What type of book is Esther?[17] Shemaryahu Talmon classified the book as a *historicized Wisdom tale*.[18] Robert Gordis postulated that a Jewish author undertook to write his book in the form of *a chronicle of the Persian court*, written by a Gentile scribe.[19] W.W. Hallo classifies Esther as a *historical novel or novella*. "It is full of authentic historical memories of the Persian period and the Persian setting of Jewish life after the Babylonian exile, and thus conforms in interesting details with archaeological evidence, but it is not to be read as the authentic record of actual events."[20] Likewise, Carey Moore writes, "We conclude that Esther is neither pure fact nor pure fiction: it is a historical novel."[21] W. Lee Humphreys suggests that Esther is *a life-style tale* for the Diaspora. Esther presents "a style of life for the diaspora Jew which affirms most strongly that at one and the same time the Jew can remain loyal to his heritage and God and yet can live a creative, rewarding, and fulfilled life precisely within a foreign setting."[22] Michael V. Fox argues that Esther is a *historical story*, a self-contained narrative mainly concerned to recount what a particular event was and how it happened, but given contours conceived in the writer's particularizing imagination.[23] Some have labeled Esther a *festival eti-*

---

[17]For an excellent treatment of this question, see Michael V. Fox, *Character and Ideology in the Book of Esther* (Columbia, SC: University of South Carolina Press, 1991), pp. 141-152.

[18]S. Talmon, "'Wisdom' in the Book of Esther," *VT* 13 (1963): 419-455. See also Jonathan Magonet, "The Liberal and the Lady: Esther Revisited," *Judaism* 29 (1980): 167-176.

[19]R. Gordis, "Religion, Wisdom and History in the Book of Esther — A New Solution to an Ancient Crux," *JBL* 100 (1981): 375-382. Baldwin approves of Gordis's suggestion (*Esther*, p. 36).

[20]William W. Hallo, "The First Purim," *BA* 46 (1983): 23.

[21]Moore, *Esther*, p. lii.

[22]W. Lee Humphreys, "A Life-Style for Diaspora: A Study of the Tales of Esther and Daniel," *JBL* 92 (1973): 223.

[23]Fox, *Character*, p. 150.

ology. An etiology is a narrative that explains the origin of some existing aspect of society, religion, or nature.[24]

HISTORICITY

The most serious objection raised against the historicity of Esther is that the only known wife of Xerxes was called Amestris. Persian records mention neither Vashti nor Esther. It may be that Xerxes had more than one wife but that Herodotus[25] mentioned only the most prominent. J.S. Wright has argued that an identification of Vashti with Amestris can possibly be made.[26] Vashti would have been her Hebrew name and Amestris her Persian name.

The four years between the demotion of Vashti (1:3) and the installation of Esther as queen (2:16) coincide with the four years Xerxes was busy with the expedition against the Greeks.

As to the objection that Esther could not have become the queen because Amestris/Vashti wielded power when her son Artaxerxes I came to the throne in 464, Shea responds:

In essence, Herodotus breaks off his account of Xerxes' reign at this point, after the description of these events that took place in Xerxes' 7th year subsequent to the king's return from the Greek campaign. This is an overstatement of the case to say that Amestris was Xerxes' queen between his 7th and 12th years, since we have no further information about her until the time her son Artaxerxes I occupied the Persian throne. In view of this silence of our sources, there is no specific evidence to

---

[24]S.R. Driver, *An Introduction to the Literature of the Old Testament* (Cleveland: World Publishing, 1963), p. 486.

[25]Herodotus (ca. 484–424 B.C.), the "Father of History," an ancient Greek historian, whose *The History* is an important source for the history of the Persian period. For a convenient summary of his life and accomplishment, see William E. Pemberton, "Herodotus," *The Ancient World*, vol. 1, Dictionary of World Biography, ed. Frank N. Magill (Hackensack, NJ: Salem Press, 1999). In this commentary the references to and citations of Herodotus are from Aubrey de Sélincourt, *Herodotus: The Histories* (New York: Penguin Books, 1954).

[26]J.S. Wright, "The Historicity of the Book of Esther," in *New Perspectives on the Old Testament*, ed. J. Barton Payne (Waco, TX: Word, 1970), pp. 40-43. William H. Shea ("Esther and History," *AUSS* 14 [1976]: 236-237) agrees.

indicate whether or not Amestris was Xerxes' chief wife from his 7th year to the end of his reign. This silence at least allows a place in Persian history for Esther, although it does not prove that she occupied it.[27]

Some have objected to Esther, a Jewess, becoming queen, since the Persian queen had to come from one of the seven royal families (Herodotus, 3.84). This objection is historically inaccurate. As J.S. Wright has pointed out, "Certainly Darius married other wives besides one from the Seven; and his son, Xerxes, who succeeded him, was not the son of this wife. Xerxes' wife, Amestris, was the daughter of Otanes; but this Otanes was the son of a certain Sisamnes, while the Otanes who was one of the Seven was the son of Pharnaspes."[28]

THEOLOGY

A remarkable feature of the Book of Esther is the complete absence of the name of God. It is agreed that this feature must have been intentional. There is a veiled reference to the deity in 4:14, "relief and deliverance for the Jews will arise from another place." The omission of God's name does not detract from the book's theological worth, rather it enhances it. The Book of Esther affirms that the God who appears hidden nevertheless remains present.

In the Old Testament God sometimes expressed his displeasure with his people by withdrawal (Ezek 11:23) and silence (Amos 8:11), in short, hiddenness. The absence of God's name from the Book of Esther implies then his displeasure with the sinfulness of his people.[29]

Mordecai and Esther were not blameless. Mordecai advised Esther to conceal her identity (2:10,20) in order to become queen (Lev 19:11). Mordecai's pride led to the confrontation with Haman. J.S. Wright writes, "The Christian judgment of the Book of Esther has been unnecessarily cramped through our feeling that because Mordecai is a Bible character, he must be a good man. Yet, like

---

[27]Shea, "Esther," pp. 240-241.
[28]Wright, "Historicity," p. 38.
[29]F.B. Huey, Jr. explores this theme in "Esther," in *The Expositor's Bible Commentary*, vol. 4, ed. Frank E. Gaebelein (Grand Rapids: Zondervan, 1988), pp. 793-794.

Samson and Jehu he may have been little more than a time-server. The Bible makes no moral judgment upon him, but it expects us to use our Christian sense. He was raised up by God, but he was not necessarily a godly man."[30] Esther was willing to hide her identity to become queen and was not reluctant to indulge the king's sexual appetite (2:15-16; cf. Deut 7:3). Moore has suggested that "Esther's Jewishness was more a fact of birth than of religious conviction."[31]

Clearly, then, the actions of Mordecai and Esther reveal them to be less than exemplary. They both failed in consistently living according to the standard of God's holiness.

In spite of God's displeasure, the Book of Esther still implicitly teaches God's providential care of his people. According to Fox, four types of evidence have been adduced to demonstrate God's presence and activity in the Esther story: allusions, coincidences, reversals, and themes.[32]

Various statements have been thought to allude to God. In point of fact, both Esther and Mordecai believe that their God is present. When Esther instructs Mordecai to "gather together all the Jews who are in Susa, and fast for me" (4:16), she is expressing a belief in the efficacy of prayer. (In the OT fasting is associated with praying.) Mordecai's words to Esther in 4:14 reveal his belief in the certainty of divine deliverance. Additionally, the story of the institution of a festival (Purim) must be, for Israel, a story of a mighty deed of its God.[33]

Esther 9:1 reads, "On this day the enemies of the Jews had hoped to overpower them, but now the tables were turned and the Jews got the upper hand over those who hated them." The verse provokes the question, Turned by whom? The answer is obvious: God.

The "coincidences" reported in the Book of Esther cannot be mere chance; God surely brought them to pass. The coincidences include: the timely vacancy of the queenship at the Persian court, the opportune accession of a Jew to queenship, Mordecai's discovery of the eunuchs' conspiracy, Esther's favorable reception by the king, the king's insomnia, Haman's early arrival at the palace, and Haman's reckless plea for mercy at Esther's feet.[34]

---

[30]Wright, "Historicity," p. 45.
[31]Moore, *Esther,* p. liv.
[32]Fox, *Character,* p. 240.
[33]Clines, *Ezra, Nehemiah, Esther,* p. 269.
[34]Fox, *Character,* p. 241.

The author consistently uses the technique of reversal (peripety) to highlight the providential intervention of God. Take note of these examples.

3:1 After these events, King Xerxes honored Haman son of Hammedatha, the Agagite, elevating him and giving him a seat of honor higher than that of all the other nobles.	10:3 Mordecai the Jew was second in rank to King Xerxes, preeminent among the Jews, and held in high esteem by his many fellow Jews. . . .
3:7 . . . they cast the *pur* (that is, the lot) in the presence of Haman to select a day and month. And the lot fell on the twelfth month, the month of Adar.	9:24-25 For Haman son of Hammedatha, the Agagite, the enemy of all the Jews, had plotted against the Jews to destroy them and had cast the *pur* (that is, the lot) for their ruin and destruction. But when the plot came to the king's attention, he issued written orders that the evil scheme Haman had devised against the Jews should come back onto his own head, and that he and his sons should be hanged on the gallows.
3:10 So the king took the signet ring from his finger and gave it to Haman son of Hammedatha, the Agagite, the enemy of the Jews.	8:2a The king took off his signet ring, which he had reclaimed from Haman, and presented it to Mordecai.
3:11b . . . and do with the people as you please.	8:8a Now write another decree in the king's name in behalf of the Jews as seems best to you. . . .
3:12-15 See the commentary at 8:9-16.	8:9-16 See the commentary at 8:9-16.
4:1 When Mordecai learned of all that had been done, he tore his clothes, put on sackcloth and ashes, and went out into the city, wailing loudly and bitterly.	8:15 Mordecai left the king's presence wearing royal garments of blue and white, a large crown of gold and a purple robe of fine linen. And the city of Susa held a joyous celebration.
4:3 In every province to which the edict and order of the king came, there was great mourning among the Jews, with fasting, weeping and wailing. Many lay in sackcloth and ashes.	8:17a In every province and in every city, wherever the edict of the king went, there was joy and gladness among the Jews, with feasting and celebrating.
5:14 His wife Zeresh and all his friends said to him, "Have a gallows built, seventy-five feet high, and ask the king in the morning to have Mordecai hanged on it."	7:9-10 Then Harbona, one of the eunuchs attending the king, said, "A gallows seventy-five feet high stands by Haman's house. He had it made for Mordecai, who spoke up to help the king." The king said, "Hang him on it!" So they hanged Haman on the gallows he had prepared for Mordecai.

6:6-9 When Haman entered, the king asked him, "What should be done for the man the king delights to honor?" Now Haman thought to himself, "Who is there that the king would rather honor than me?" So he answered the king, "For the man the king delights to honor, have them bring a royal robe the king has worn and a horse the king has ridden, one with a royal crest placed on its head. Then let the robe and horse be entrusted to one of the king's most noble princes. Let them robe the man the king delights to honor, and lead him on the horse through the city streets, proclaiming before him, 'This is what is done for the man the king delights to honor!'"	6:11-12 So Haman got the robe and the horse. He robed Mordecai, and led him on horseback through the city streets, proclaiming before him, "This is what is done for the man the king delights to honor!" Afterward Mordecai returned to the king's gate. But Haman rushed home, with his head covered in grief.

Finally, the presence of religious themes bears witness to God's presence. For example, the deliverance of the Jewish people from Haman's attempted genocide is clear enough, for they are the people of God's covenant.

The Book of Esther also teaches that human initiative and divine action can be complementary. "The story of the loyalty of Mordecai, the courage and cunning of Esther, and the providence of God makes a strong statement about the complementarity, the synergism, of divine and human action in effecting the deliverance of the people of God."[35] "The narrator understandably refrains from any reference to the deity in order to accentuate the role of human responsibility in shaping history, and to indicate the hiddenness of God's control of history."[36] "God's action is indeed involved, but it seems clear that the Book of Esther sees the manner of God's action . . . as strategic help periodically supplied to those who with full awareness struggle for his cause and theirs."[37]

---

[35]Frederic Bush, *Ruth, Esther*, Word Biblical Commentary (Dallas: Word, 1996), p. 334.

[36]Berg, *Esther*, p. 179.

[37]Ronald M. Hals, *The Theology of the Book of Ruth* (Philadelphia: Fortress Press, 1969), p. 52.

STRUCTURE

According to Fox, the structure of the Book of Esther is ordered according to the theme of reversal. The narrated events are organized "as a symmetrical series of theses and antitheses, situations and their reversals. The theses are situations portending disaster for the Jews and success for their enemies, situations which could be expected to lead, in the natural course of events, to the Jews' destruction. But events do not run their natural course, but lead to the antitheses, which are the exact opposites of the result potential in the theses."[38]

If the plot of the book is built and the message conveyed through the technique of reversal, then it is not surprising to find that the ten chapters of Esther are chiastically arranged. Accordingly, Yehuda T. Radday offers the following outline, with 6:1 (the king's insomnia) the turning point in the book.[39]

   I. Opening and Background (ch. 1)
     II. The King's First Decree (ch. 2–3)
       III. The Clash between Haman and Mordecai (ch. 4–5)
         IV. 'On that night, the king could not sleep' (6:1)
       III'. Mordecai's Triumph over Haman (6:2–7:10)
     II'. The King's Second Decree (ch. 8–9)
   I'. Epilogue (ch. 10)[40]

---

[38]Quoted in Berg, *Esther,* p. 106.

[39]Yehuda T. Radday, "Chiasm in Joshua, Judges and Others," *Linguistica Biblica* 27-28 (1973), pp. 9-10. "Chiasm(us)" or "antimetabole" is a "grammatical figure by which the order of words in one of two parallel clauses is inverted in the other" (*Oxford English Dictionary*). A classic example of this is "I do not live to eat, but eat to live."

[40]In *Mastering the Old Testament: Ezra, Nehemiah, Esther* (Dallas: Word Publishing, 1993), Mark Roberts adapts Radday's structure as follows,
  Prelude to the Story of Esther (1:1-22)
    Mordecai and Esther in Relationship with the King (2:1-23)
      A Royal Decree to Destroy the Jews Issued by Haman (3:1-15)
        Esther Responds to Haman's Plot (4:1–5:8)
          Haman's Prideful Obsession (5:9-14)
            The King's Sleepless Night (6:1-3)
          Haman's Prideful Obsession Leads to Shame (6:4-14)
        Esther Defeats Haman (7:1-10)
      A Royal Decree to Save the Jews Issued by Mordecai (8:1-17)
    Mordecai and Esther Establish Purim (9:1-32)
  Epilogue in Praise of Mordecai (10:1-3)

WISDOM IN THE BOOK OF ESTHER

According to S. Talmon, "What the Esther narrative in fact does is to portray *applied* wisdom. The outline of the plot and the presentation of the central characters show the wise man in action, with the covert, but nevertheless, obvious implication, that his ultimate success derives from the proper execution of wisdom maxims, as set forth, e.g. in Proverbs and to a certain degree, in Ecclesiastes."[41] Here are some of the wisdom themes Talmon has detected in the Book of Esther.

King Xerxes is so easily duped that his weakness becomes the source of his courtiers' corruption.	"If a ruler listens to lies, all his officials become wicked" (Prov 29:12).
Unaware of his folly, Xerxes is conceited, irritable and unpredictable.	"A king's wrath is like the roar of a lion; he who angers him forfeits his life" (20:2). "A king's wrath is a messenger of death, but a wise man will appease it" (16:14).
Haman violates all the rules of wise behavior. His hatred and rage eventually overpower him.	"An angry man stirs up dissension, and a hot-tempered one commits many sins" (29:22).
Haman discloses his thoughts before others like any proverbial fool (5:10-13).	"A prudent man keeps his knowledge to himself, but the heart of fools blurts out folly" (12:23).
Haman acts when he is controlled by rage and impatience.	"A quick-tempered man does foolish things" (14:17a; cf. 29b).
Mordecai triumphs over Haman.	"A king delights in a wise servant, but a shameful servant incurs his wrath" (14:35). "A king's rage is like the roar of a lion, but his favor is like dew on the grass" (19:12).
Haman hanged on the gallows he had prepared for Mordecai.	"The righteous man is rescued from trouble, and it comes on the wicked instead" (11:8). "If a man digs a pit, he will fall into it; if a man rolls a stone, it will roll back on him" (26:27; Ps 7:16; Eccl 10:8).

[41]Talmon, "Wisdom," p. 427.

Mordecai plans carefully and never rushes into action.	"Better a patient man than a warrior, a man who controls his temper than one who takes a city" (16:32).
Esther builds her house in wisdom, and were it not for her designs her people would have come to ruin.	"The wise woman builds her house" (14:1a). "For lack of guidance a nation falls" (11:14a).
The victory of the good (Esther and Mordecai) over the evil (Haman) is just cause for celebration.	"When the righteous prosper, the city rejoices; when the wicked perish, there are shouts of joy" (11:10). "The prospect of the righteous is joy, but the hopes of the wicked come to nothing" (10:28). "Misfortune pursues the sinner, but prosperity is the reward of the righteous" (13:21).

ESTHER

Esther was a Jewish orphan who became the queen of Ahasuerus (Xerxes) the Persian king. Esther was brought up in Susa by Mordecai, who was an official in the royal court. After Xerxes deposed Vashti, his former queen, he selected her successor from the most beautiful virgins from all the provinces of his empire. He chose Esther. Her Jewish name was Hadassah.

Soon after Esther's accession Haman, a Persian noble and vizier of the empire under Xerxes, threatened the Jews with destruction. The Book of Esther relates how Haman was destroyed and the Jews were delivered.

Nothing more is known of Esther than is revealed in the book that bears her name.

OUTLINE

BIBLIOGRAPHY

Albright, W.F. "The Lachish Cosmetic Burner and Esther 2:12." In *Old Testament Studies in Honor of Jacob M. Myers*, pp. 25-32. Edited by H.N. Bream, R.D. Heim, and C.A. Moore. Philadelphia: Temple University Press, 1974.

Anderson, Bernhard W. "The Place of the Book of Esther in the Christian Bible." *JR* 30 (1950): 32-43.

Archer, Gleason L. Jr. *A Survey of Old Testament Introduction.* Chicago: Moody Press, 1974.

Baldwin, Joyce G. *Esther: An Introduction and Commentary.* Tyndale Old Testament Commentaries. Downers Grove, IL: InterVarsity, 1984.

Bashiri, Iraj. "Xerxes I." *The Ancient World*, vol. 1. Dictionary of World Biography. Edited by Frank N. Magill. Hackensack, NJ: Salem Press, 1999.

Beitzel, Barry J. "Exodus 3:14 and the Divine Name: A Case of Biblical Paranomasia." *Trinity Journal* 1 (1980): 5-20.

Berg, Sandra B. *The Book of Esther: Motifs, Themes and Structure.* SBLDS 44. Missoula, MT: Scholars Press, 1979.

Bergey, Ronald L. "Post-Exilic Hebrew Linguistic Developments in Esther: A Diachronic Approach." *JETS* 31 (1988): 161-168.

Bush, Frederic. *Ruth, Esther.* Word Biblical Commentary 9. Dallas: Word, 1996.

Clines, D.J. *Ezra, Nehemiah, Esther.* New Century Bible Commentary. Grand Rapids: Eerdmans, 1984.

_____. "In Quest of the Historical Mordecai." *VT* 41 (1991): 129-136.

Cohen, Abraham D. "'Hu Ha-Goral': The Religious Significance of Esther." *Judaism* 23 (1974): 87-94.

Craghan, John F. "Esther: A Fully Liberated Woman." *Bible Today* 24 (1986): 6-11.

Fox, Michael V. *Character and Ideology in the Book of Esther.* Columbia, SC: University of South Carolina Press, 1991.

Gehman, Henry S. "Notes on the Persian Words in the Book of Esther." *JBL* 43 (1924): 321-328.

Goldman, S. "Esther: Introduction and Commentary." In *The Five Megilloth*, pp. 192-243. Edited by A. Cohen. Soncino Books of the Bible. London: Soncino Press, 1961.

Goldman, Stan. "Narrative and Ethical Ironies in Esther." *JSOT* 47 (1990): 15-31.

Gordis, Robert. "Religion, Wisdom and History in the Book of Esther—A New Solution to an Ancient Crux." *JBL* 100 (1981): 359-388.

_____. "Studies in the Esther Narrative." *JBL* 95 (1976): 43-58.

Grasham, William W. "The Theology of the Book of Esther." *RQ* 16 (1973): 99-111.

Grossfeld, Bernard. *The Two Targums of Esther.* The Aramaic Bible. Vol.18. Collegeville, MN: The Liturgical Press, 1991.

Hallo, W.W. "The First Purim." *BA* 46 (1983): 19-29.

Hals, Ronald M. *The Theology of the Book of Ruth.* Philadelphia: Fortress Press, 1969.

Haupt, Paul. "Critical Notes on Esther." *AJSLL* 24 (1907–08): 97-186.

House, Paul R. *Old Testament Theology.* Downers Grove, IL: Inter-Varsity, 1998.

Howard, David M. Jr. *An Introduction to the Old Testament Historical Books.* Chicago: Moody Press, 1993.

Huey, F.B. Jr. "Esther." *The Expositor's Bible Commentary.* Vol. 4. Grand Rapids: Zondervan, 1988.

Humphreys, W. Lee. "A Lifestyle for Diaspora: A Study of the Tales of Esther and Daniel." *JBL* 92 (1973): 211-223.

Jobes, Karen H. *Esther*. The NIV Application Commentary. Grand Rapids: Zondervan, 1999.

Jones, Bruce W. "Two Misconceptions about the Book of Esther." *CBQ* 39 (1977): 171-181.

Keil, C.F. "The Book of Esther." *Commentary on the Old Testament*. Vol. 3. Grand Rapids: Eerdmans, 1980.

Lacocque, Andre. "Haman in the Book of Esther." *HAR* 11 (1987): 207-222.

Levenson, Jon D. "The Scroll of Esther in Ecumenical Perspective." *JES* 13 (1976): 440-451.

Livingston, G. Herbert. "Esther." In *Asbury Bible Commentary*, pp. 474-481. Edited by E.E. Carpenter and W. McCown. Grand Rapids: Zondervan, 1992.

Magonet, Jonathan. "The Liberal and the Lady: Esther Revisited." *Judaism* 29 (1980): 167-176.

McKane, W. "A Note on Esther IX and I Samuel XV." *JTS* 12 (1961): 260-261.

Metzger, Bruce M., ed. *The Oxford Annotated Apocrypha*. New York: Oxford University Press, 1977.

Millard, A.R. "The Persian Names in Esther and the Reliability of the Hebrew Text." *JBL* 96 (1977): 481-488.

Moore, Carey A. "Archaeology and the Book of Esther." *BA* 38 (1975): 62-79.

_____. *Esther: Introduction, Translation, and Notes*. The Anchor Bible. Garden City, NY: Doubleday, 1971.

_____. "On the Origins of the LXX Additions to the Book of Esther." *JBL* 92 (1973): 382-393.

_____. *Studies in the Book of Esther*. New York: KTAV Publishing House, 1982.

Morris, A.E. "The Purpose of the Book of Esther." *ExpTim* 42 (1930–31): 124-128.

Oppenheim, A. Leo. "On Royal Gardens in Mesopotamia." *JNES* 24 (1965): 328-333.

Paton, L.B. *A Critical and Exegetical Commentary on the Book of Esther.* ICC. Edinburgh: T. & T. Clark, 1908.

Pemberton, William E. "Herodotus." *The Ancient World*, vol. 1. Dictionary of World Biography. Edited by Frank N. Magill. Hackensack, NJ: Salem Press, 1999.

Pierce, Ronald W. "The Politics of Esther and Mordecai: Courage or Compromise?" *BBR* 2 (1992):75-89.

Pritchard, J.B. *Ancient Near Eastern Texts Relating to the Old Testament.* Princeton: Princeton University Press, 1969.

Radday, Yehuda T. "Chiasm in Joshua, Judges and Others." *LB* 27-28 (1973): 6-13.

_____. "Esther with Humour." In *On Humour and the Comic in the Hebrew Bible*, pp. 295-313. JSOTSupp. 92. Edited by Yehuda T. Radday and Athalya Brenner. Sheffield: Almond Press, 1990.

_____. "Humour in Names." In *On Humour and the Comic in the Hebrew Bible*, pp. 59-97. JSOTSupp. 92. Edited by Yehuda T. Radday and Athalya Brenner. Sheffield: Almond Press, 1990.

Roberts, Mark. *Mastering the Old Testament: Ezra, Nehemiah, Esther.* Dallas: Word, 1993.

Ryken, Leland. *Words of Delight.* 2nd ed. Grand Rapids: Baker, 1992.

Sélincourt, Aubrey de. *Herodotus: The Histories.* New York: Penguin Books, 1954.

Shea, William H. "Esther and History." *AUSS* 14 (1976): 227-246.

Talmon, S. "Wisdom in the Book of Esther." *VT* 13 (1963): 419-455.

Tawil, Hayim. "Two Notes on the Treaty Terminology of the Sefire Inscriptions." *CBQ* 42 (1980): 30-37.

Webb, Barry G. *Five Festal Garments: Christian Reflections on the Song of Songs, Ruth, Lamentations, Ecclesiastes, and Esther.* New Studies in Biblical Theology 10. Downers Grove, IL: InterVarsity, 2000.

Whitcomb, John C. *Esther: The Triumph of God's Sovereignty*. Chicago: Moody Press, 1979.

Wiebe, John M. "Esther 4:14: 'Will Relief and Deliverance Arise for the Jews from Another Place?'" *CBQ* 53 (1991): 409-415.

Wiersbe, Warren W. *Be Committed*. Wheaton, IL: Victor Books, 1993.

Wright, J. Stafford. "The Historicity of the Book of Esther." In *New Perspectives on the Old Testament*, pp. 37-47. Edited by J. Barton Payne. Waco, TX: Word, 1970.

Yahuda, A.S. "The Meaning of the Name Esther." *Journal of the Royal Asiatic Society* (1946): 174-178.

Yamauchi, Edwin M. "The Archaeological Background of Esther." *BSac* 137 (1980): 99-117.

_____. *Persia and the Bible*. Grand Rapids: Baker, 1990.

Young, E.J. *An Introduction to the Old Testament*. Grand Rapids: Eerdmans, 1977.

Zadok, Ran. "Notes on Esther." *ZAW* 98 (1986): 105-110.

ESTHER 1

I. OPENING AND BACKGROUND (1:1-22)

A. INTRODUCTION (1:1-9)

¹This is what happened during the time of Xerxes,ᵃ the Xerxes who ruled over 127 provinces stretching from India to Cushᵇ: ²At that time King Xerxes reigned from his royal throne in the citadel of Susa, ³and in the third year of his reign he gave a banquet for all his nobles and officials. The military leaders of Persia and Media, the princes, and the nobles of the provinces were present.

⁴For a full 180 days he displayed the vast wealth of his kingdom and the splendor and glory of his majesty. ⁵When these days were over, the king gave a banquet, lasting seven days, in the enclosed garden of the king's palace, for all the people from the least to the greatest, who were in the citadel of Susa. ⁶The garden had hangings of white and blue linen, fastened with cords of white linen and purple material to silver rings on marble pillars. There were couches of gold and silver on a mosaic pavement of porphyry, marble, mother-of-pearl and other costly stones. ⁷Wine was served in goblets of gold, each one different from the other, and the royal wine was abundant, in keeping with the king's liberality. ⁸By the king's command each guest was allowed to drink in his own way, for the king instructed all the wine stewards to serve each man what he wished.

⁹Queen Vashti also gave a banquet for the women in the royal palace of king Xerxes.

ᵃ*1* Hebrew *Ahasuerus*, a variant of Xerxes' Persian name; here and throughout Esther   ᵇ*1* That is, the upper Nile region

1:1 Xerxes I, in Hebrew Ahasuerus (אֲחַשְׁוֵרוֹשׁ, *'ăḥašwērôš*), son of

Darius I and Atossa, is the Persian king who reigned 485–465 B.C.[1] He consolidated the empire **from India to Cush**.[2] By **India** is meant the northwestern part of the Indus River, now modern day Pakistan, which Darius had conquered; **Cush** was the country south of Egypt, now part of the Northern Sudan. The primary divisions of the empire were the satrapies, of which the Persians never had more than thirty-one. Here, the empire is divided into **127 provinces** (Dan 6:1 speaks of 120 provinces), which could refer to the administrative subdivisions that were ruled by officials subordinate to the satraps (cf. 8:9).[3]

1:2 Having conducted successful campaigns against Egypt and Babylon in his first two years, Xerxes turned his attention to the governance of the realm, which he did from the **citadel of Susa** (where

---

[1]For a detailed presentation of the life of Xerxes, consult Edwin M. Yamauchi, *Persia and the Bible* (Grand Rapids: Baker, 1990), pp. 187-239. For a brief treatment of his life and accomplishment, see Iraj Bashiri, "Xerxes I," *The Ancient World*, Vol. 1, Dictionary of World Biography, ed. Frank N. Magill (Hackensack, NJ: Salem Press, 1999). For an excellent treatment of Xerxes' character in the Book of Esther, see Fox, *Character*, pp. 171-177, who suggests that Xerxes' most dangerous flaw is his failure to think. His princes (ch. 1), his servants (ch. 2), his vizier (ch. 3), and his queen (ch. 5–9) are able to bend him to their wills. He does not like to spend energy on thought. His indifference to Jewish life in chapter 3 is the capstone of his mental laziness.

[2]A foundation tablet from Persepolis parallels Esther 1:1: "I am Xerxes, the great king, the only king, the king of (all) countries (which speak) all kinds of languages, the king of this (entire) big and far (-reaching) earth,— the son of king Darius, the Achaemenian, a Persian, son of a Persian, an Aryan of Aryan descent. Thus speaks king Xerxes: These are the countries— in addition to Persia—over which I am king under the 'shadow' of Ahuramazda, over which I hold sway, which are bringing their tribute to me—whatever is commanded them by me, that they do and they abide by my law(s)—: Media, Elam, Arachosia, Urartu, Drangiana, Parthia, (H)aria, Bactria, Sogdia, Chorasmia, Babylonia, Assyria, Sattagydia, Sardis, Egypt, the Ionians who live on the salty sea and (those) who live beyond the salty sea, Maka, Arabia, Gandara, India, Cappodocia, Da'an, the Amyrgian Cimmerians, the Cimmerians (wearing) pointed caps, the Skudra, the Akupish, Libya, Banneshu (Carians) (and) Kush" (*ANET*, p. 316).

[3]Bush, *Ruth, Esther*, p. 345. C.F. Keil suggests that these "provinces" are a division of the kingdom into geographical regions, according to the races inhabiting the different provinces (*I & II Kings, I & II Chronicles, Ezra, Nehemiah, Esther*, Commentary on the Old Testament [Grand Rapids: Eerdmans, 1980], p. 321).

Darius built his palatial complex), one of the three capitals of Persian kings (the others being Ecbatana [Ezra 6:2] and Babylon). Daniel previously had a vision at Susa (Dan 8:2), and later Nehemiah served in Susa as cupbearer to Xerxes' son, Artaxerxes I (Neh 1:1).

1:3 In the third year of his reign (483 B.C.), Xerxes was ready to celebrate his early military successes. **He gave a banquet.** The Hebrew noun "banquet" (מִשְׁתֶּה, *mišteh*) is a derivative of the verb "to drink" (שָׁתָה, *šātāh*), implying that an ample supply of wine would be consumed.

Chronology in Esther

Reference	Year/Month/Day	Event
1:3	3/-/-	Banquet
2:16	7/10/-	Esther and Xerxes
3:7	12/1/-	Haman casts the lots
3:12	12/1/13	Haman's decree written
8:9	12/3/23	Mordecai's decree issued
9:1,15,18	12/12/13-15	Triumph of the Jews; Purim

Persia and Media is the usual sequence in Esther, the reverse of the order familiar from Daniel. Cyrus won the allegiance of both the Medes and Persians because his father was a Persian and his mother a Mede. He united these two great nations. From his time onward the consolidated empire he founded was referred to as the Persian-Median empire, showing the supremacy of the Persians within the joint empire.

1:4 This verse is probably parenthetical. The details of the banquet mentioned in verse 3 will be provided in verses 5-8. Accordingly, the banquet was a seven-day affair, not a full 180 days! Verse 4 simply says that the royal treasures were on display for a full six months preceding the banquet.

During this six-month period it is quite likely that Xerxes planned the Greek campaign. In Book 7 of *The Histories*, Herodotus writes: "After the conquest of Egypt, when he was on the point of taking in hand the expedition against Athens, Xerxes called a conference of the leading men of the country, to find out their attitude towards the war and explain to them his own wishes" (8). (According to Herodotus 7.20 four years would pass before Xerxes began his campaign against Greece. Once commenced Xerxes and the Persians would be eventually defeated by the Greeks at Salamis in 480 B.C. and in Plataea and Mycale in 479. This historical datum corroborates the statement of v. 3).[4]

"In this view," writes Keil, "'the riches of his kingdom,' etc., mentioned in ver. 4, must not be understood of the splendour and magnificence displayed in the entertainment of his guests, but referred to the greatness and resources of the realm, which Xerxes descanted on to his assembled magnates for the purpose of showing them the possibility of carrying into execution his contemplated campaign against Greece."[5]

1:5-7 After the 180 days of consultation were over, the banquet was held in the **garden of the king's palace**.[6] Verse 6 provides the impression of extravagant luxury. Couches of solid gold and silver were used for reclining on during the banquet. The variety of drinking goblets mentioned in verse 7 highlights the royal ostentation.

1:8-9 This verse begins literally, "And the drinking was according to the rule: let there be no restraining." This verse clearly depicts the king's liberality and the drinkers' excess. Even though there appears to have been no segregation of the sexes at Persian meals (cf. 5:4), according to verse 9, a banquet was being held for the women, presided over by Queen **Vashti**.

---

[4]Darius I had invaded Greece and been defeated at Marathon in 490. Xerxes felt compelled to avenge his father and to expand the empire at the same time. According to Herodotus, Xerxes reasoned, "I will bridge the Hellespont and march an army through Europe into Greece, and punish the Athenians for the outrage they committed upon my father and upon us. As you saw, Darius himself was making his preparations for war against these men; but death prevented him from carrying out his purpose. I therefore on his behalf, and for the benefit of all my subjects, will not rest until I have taken Athens and burnt it to the ground, in revenge for the injury which the Athenians without provocation once did to me and my father. . . . If we crush the Athenians and their neighbors in the Peloponnese, we shall so extend the empire of Persia that its boundaries will be God's own sky" (7.8).

[5]Keil, *Esther*, p. 325.

[6]A. Leo Oppenheim, "On Royal Gardens in Mesopotamia," *JNES* 24 (1965): 328-333.

According to Herodotus, the queen's name was Amestris (Herodotus 7.61). The name Vashti, which is unattested in extra-biblical sources, may be an honorific title meaning "the best" or "the beloved, the desired one."[7]

The king's power, wealth, majesty, and generosity are highlighted by the description of the banquets held in Susa, where the king is gathering support for his campaign against Greece. The original readers would have known that Xerxes returned from Greece four years later after a defeat that depleted his royal wealth. Karen Jobes observes, "Since the author of Esther was writing long after Xerxes' defeat, he could have introduced Xerxes as the Persian king who lost a famous battle to the Greeks at Hellespont. Instead, he chose to introduce Xerxes in the splendor and optimism of his glory days. The unstated reversal of the king's fortune, which would have been known to the author and original readers, sets the stage and foreshadows another reversal of destiny within the book."[8]

B. XERXES CALLS FOR QUEEN VASHTI (1:10-12)

[10]**On the seventh day, when King Xerxes was in high spirits from wine, he commanded the seven eunuchs who served him— Mehuman, Biztha, Harbona, Bigtha, Abagtha, Zethar and Carcas— [11]to bring before him Queen Vashti, wearing her royal crown, in order to display her beauty to the people and nobles, for she was lovely to look at. [12]But when the attendants delivered the king's command, Queen Vashti refused to come. Then the king became furious and burned with anger.**

1:10-12 After a week of indulgence, in which King Xerxes has "displayed the vast wealth of his kingdom," he is anxious to show his most precious possession, his beautiful wife. So he sends his **seven eunuchs** to summon **Queen Vashti**, to **display her beauty to the people and the nobles**. She refuses to appear, disobeying a formal command and humiliating the king before all the dignitaries of the realm. As a result, he burns with anger (cf. Prov 14:17).

---

[7]Moore, *Esther*, p. 8.

[8]Karen H. Jobes, *Esther*, The NIV Application Commentary (Grand Rapids: Zondervan, 1999), p. 62.

The Hebrew word סָרִיס (*sārîs*) here translated "eunuch" could mean merely "officer." The translation "eunuch" is appropriate here because these seven men had access to the royal harem. A king could trust a castrated man with the women of the palace.

The queen is to appear with the full escort of the king's attendants. Fox has captured their significance, writing, ". . . it is a phony ritual created for the nonce, to show that in this court, everything, even an invitation to the queen, is thick with pomp and circumstance."[9]

No reason is given for Vashti's refusal. Except for the crown on her head, was she required to appear naked?[10] (Herodotus relates a story of how the Lydian king Candaules arranged to display the naked beauty of his wife to his bodyguard Gyges [1.8-13]). Did she have a disfigurement which she was unwilling to reveal? Did she fear for her dignity before these inebriated guests? (In relating the events of a dinner party, Herodotus records that certain drunken Persians fondled female guests [5.18]). Was she pregnant?[11] Was there a conflict between the royal command and women's rights? Was there a conflict between the royal command and existing Persian law or custom?[12] (Josephus suggests that Vashti, "out of regard to the laws of

---

[9]Fox, *Character*, p. 20. "For the nonce" means "for the particular purpose."

[10]This viewpoint is reflected in *Targum Rishon*: "The king then ordered these seven princes to bring Queen Vashti in the nude. Because she used to make Israelite girls work in the nude and made them beat wool and flax on the Sabbath day, therefore it was decreed upon her to be brought (out) in the nude. However, the crown of royalty was on her head" (Bernard Grossfeld, *The Two Targums of Esther*, The Aramaic Bible, vol. 18 [Collegeville, MN: The Liturgical Press, 1991], p. 35). A Targum is an Aramaic translation of the Hebrew text replete with interpretive additions. Two targums exist for the Book of Esther.

[11]Amestris was the mother of Artaxerxes, who ruled from 464 to 425 B.C. Artaxerxes was born in 483 B.C., the year of the great banquet described in Esther 1. It is possible, then, that Amestris/Vashti was pregnant with her son at that time and unwilling to appear before the drunken men. For this view, see Warren W. Wiersbe, *Be Committed* (Wheaton, IL: Victor Books, 1993), p. 81.

[12]Bruce W. Jones has suggested that wives might attend banquets, but they left when the drinking began. At that point, only concubines and harem women would be present, and Vashti did not want to degrade herself to that level ("Two Misconceptions about the Book of Esther," *CBQ* 39 [1977]: 174). Fox also follows this line of interpretation: "By appearing before

the Persians, which forbid the wives to be seen by strangers, did not go to the king" [*Antiquities*, 11.6]). Was it merely a whim? Whatever the reason, "the king who rules the whole world cannot bend his own wife to his will!"[13] Jobes adds, "Because Xerxes was displaying his power and might in order to solidify his nobles as he went to war against Greece, the refusal of his own queen to obey his command must have been extremely embarrassing. No wonder Xerxes became furious and burned with anger. He needed his men to obey his commands as they went to war, but in his own palace he could not even get his own wife to obey!"[14]

"Although Vashti is no more disobedient here than Esther is later on in refusing to stay away at the king's command (see iv 11), they provoke a very different response: Vashti raises the king's anger while Esther stirs his mercy."[15]

The king's quick temper, according to Israel's wisdom literature, identifies him as a fool. "A fool shows his annoyance at once, but a prudent man overlooks an insult" (Prov 12:16). "A quick-tempered man does foolish things, and a crafty man is hated" (Prov 14:17). "A patient man has great understanding, but a quick-tempered man displays folly" (Prov 14:29).

C. CONSULTATION REGARDING VASHTI'S PUNISHMENT (1:13-15)

[13]Since it was customary for the king to consult experts in matters of law and justice, he spoke with the wise men who understood the times [14]and were closest to the king—Carshena, Shethar, Admatha, Tarshish, Meres, Marsena and Memucan, the seven nobles of Persia and Media who had special access to the king and were highest in the kingdom.

---

males, including commoners — especially when the king himself 'was light-headed with wine' — Vashti would be behaving like a mere concubine. The king's insistence that she wear the royal diadem heightens the degradation by calling attention to her true status, as does the repeated use of the title 'Queen'" (*Character*, pp. 168-169).

[13]Bush, *Ruth, Esther*, p. 354.
[14]Jobes, *Esther*, p. 68.
[15]Moore, *Esther*, p. 9.

¹⁵"According to law, what must be done to Queen Vashti?" he asked. "She has not obeyed the command of King Xerxes that the eunuchs have taken to her."

1:13-14 Royal advisers were a traditional institution (Herodotus 3.31,84,118). Here seven are named, as with Artaxerxes in Ezra 7:14. That these seven **had special access to the king** (lit., "saw the king's face") is mentioned by Herodotus: "any of the seven [may] enter the palace unannounced, except when the king was in bed with a woman" (3.84). Ordinarily the king was physically inaccessible to the people. These seven **were highest in the kingdom** (lit., "sat first in the kingdom," suggesting on ceremonial occasions that three sat on each side and one in front of the King).

1:15 With regard to Vashti's action (vv. 10-12), Xerxes consults with the wise men to determine the right course of action to follow (cf. 1 Chr 12:32). Since no legislation existed for queenly disobedience, the counsel of the wise men amounts to pragmatic advice.

D. THE ADVICE OF THE COUNSELORS (1:16-20)

¹⁶Then Memucan replied in the presence of the king and the nobles, "Queen Vashti has done wrong, not only against the king but also against all the nobles and the peoples of all the provinces of King Xerxes. ¹⁷For the queen's conduct will become known to all the women, and so they will despise their husbands and say, 'King Xerxes commanded Queen Vashti to be brought before him, but she would not come.' ¹⁸This very day the Persian and Median women of the nobility who have heard about the queen's conduct will respond to all the king's nobles in the same way. There will be no end of disrespect and discord.

¹⁹"Therefore, if it pleases the king, let him issue a royal decree and let it be written in the laws of Persia and Media, which cannot be repealed, that Vashti is never again to enter the presence of King Xerxes. Also let the king give her royal position to someone else who is better than she. ²⁰Then when the king's edict is proclaimed throughout all his vast realm, all the women will respect their husbands, from the least to the greatest."

1:16-17 Memucan, mentioned last in verse 14, but here spokesman for the seven nobles, sets the queen's disobedience against the king in a wider context: the queen has set a dangerous example for all the ladies of the realm, especially the ladies of nobility (v. 18). From India to Cush, wives will say, "The Queen did not obey, therefore we will not either." Memucan has thus turned a domestic squabble into a cause célèbre.

1:18 Disrespect or contempt of husbands and **discord** or wrath toward wives will result from Vashti's example.

1:19-20 If the king divorces the queen, then the example made of Vashti would intimidate any wife who defies her husband. The omission of the title "queen" in verse 19 (see also 2:1,4,17) is deliberate (contrast vv. 9,11,12,15,16,17,18).

The decree — **that Vashti is never again to enter the presence of King Xerxes** — is ironic: this was really her own decision (v. 12).

Memucan wants the decree irrevocable (cf. 8:8; Dan 6:8,12,15) so that he need not fear the wrath of a reinstated Vashti.

Better must mean more obedient.

"It is ironic," writes D.J. Clines, "that the news of Vashti's disobedience, which Memucan has conjectured will spread as rumor (v. 17), will necessarily be given official credibility by the decree designed to scotch its influence."[16]

E. THE ADVICE IS ACCEPTED (1:21-22)

[21]**The king and his nobles were pleased with this advice, so the king did as Memucan proposed.** [22]**He sent dispatches to all parts of the kingdom, to each province in its own script and to each people in its own language, proclaiming in each people's tongue that every man should be ruler over his own household.**

1:21-22 The content of these dispatches would seem to be ridiculous, for every husband was expected to rule already in his own home. The content of these dispatches, then, makes the king alone look incapable of ruling his own house!

---

[16]Clines, *Ezra, Nehemiah, Esther*, p. 282.

The book of Esther does not inform us what became of Vashti. She was not killed; this we know from Persian history (if she is indeed Amestris). She must have been demoted to a secondary role. Did she endure the same fate as Michal, the wife of David (2 Sam 6:23), banished to a life of lonely isolation?

Herodotus describes the Persian "pony express system" by which messages were delivered: "There is nothing in the world which travels faster than these Persian couriers. The whole idea is a Persian invention, and works like this: riders are stationed along the road, equal in number to the number of days the journey takes — a man and a horse for each day. Nothing stops these couriers from covering their allotted stage in the quickest possible time — neither snow, rain, heat nor darkness. The first, at the end of his stage, passes the dispatch to the second, the second to the third, and so on along the line, as in the Greek torch-race which is held in honor of Hephaestus" (8.98).

A more literal translation of the content of these dispatches would be: "Every man should be ruler over his own household and speak according to the tongue/language of his people." Apparently the rule of the husband was to be shown by the fact that only his language was to be used in the family (cf. Neh 13:23-24). "This emphasis on the husband's language (word) as an instrument of rule in the home mirrors its correlate that the king's language (word) in the form of a decree was the instrument of rule throughout the empire."[17]

By accepting Memucan's advice, Xerxes publicizes his embarrassing plight and assures what he fears. By ordering throughout the land what he could not accomplish in his own palace, namely, every man "should be ruler over his own household" (v. 22), the king goes public with his personal failure. Afraid that the women of the empire will hear of Vashti's disobedience, he ends up assuring what he fears by sending the dispatches to all parts of the kingdom.

The blindness of Memucan's advice is ironic humor. Is such humor out of place in a book that narrates the near genocide of God's people? Michael Fox has suggested that humor teaches us a valuable lesson. In his words, "Humor, especially the humor of ridicule, is a device for defusing fear. The author teaches us to make fun of the very forces that once threatened — and will threaten again

---

[17]Jobes, *Esther,* p. 83.

— our existence, and thereby makes us recognize their triviality as well as their power. 'If I laugh at any mortal thing,' said Byron, 't'is that I may not weep.' Jews have learned that kind of laughter. The book of Esther begins a tradition of Jewish humor."[18]

Since God laughs at the pretensions of earthly powers (Ps 2:4), we are allowed to assess the ultimate weaknesses (trivialities) of those powers. Psalm 37:12-13 speaks of God's laughter. "The wicked plot against the righteous and gnash their teeth at them; but the Lord laughs at the wicked, for he knows their day is coming." Likewise Psalm 59:8, "But you, O LORD, laugh at them; you scoff at all those nations." Wisdom laughs at its victory over folly; she laughs at the triumph of the righteous over the wicked (Prov 1:26-27).

In the context of human fear, divine laughter breaks the tension — it is the basis of our relief. God will prevail over the powers of any and every age! The book of Esther indeed reminds us that relief and deliverance do come from God (4:13). Laugh on!

---

[18]Fox, *Character*, p. 253.

ESTHER 2

II. THE KING'S FIRST DECREE (2:1–3:15)

A. THE PROPOSAL FOR FINDING A NEW WIFE (2:1-4)

[1]Later when the anger of King Xerxes had subsided, he remembered Vashti and what she had done and what he had decreed about her. [2]Then the king's personal attendants proposed, "Let a search be made for beautiful young virgins for the king. [3]Let the king appoint commissioners in every province of his realm to bring all these beautiful girls into the harem at the citadel of Susa. Let them be placed under the care of Hegai, the king's eunuch, who is in charge of the women; and let beauty treatments be given to them. [4]Then let the girl who pleases the king be queen instead of Vashti." This advice appealed to the king, and he followed it.

2:1-2 After an unidentified period of time (lit., "after these things"), uneasiness accompanies Xerxes' remembrance of the events detailed in chapter 1. Xerxes "realized that she [Vashti] had acted properly in refusing to display herself. His counselors might well fear the effects on themselves, if the king were allowed to brood on Vashti's fate; and so they hasten to suggest an alternative occupation for the king's thoughts, and one which would prove a pleasant diversion."[1]

2:3-4 These verses detail how the plan of the attendants is to be carried out. The noun **beauty treatments** is derived from the verb מָרַק (*māraq*) meaning "to rub, to polish," implying massage.

The word **harem** is literally "the house of the women" בֵּית הַנָּשִׁים

---

[1]S. Goldman, "Esther," in *The Five Megilloth*, ed. A. Cohen (London: Soncino Press, 1961), p. 202.

(*bêth hannāšîm*). Presumably none of these women pleased Xerxes enough to be considered a worthy replacement for Vashti.

B. INTRODUCTION OF MORDECAI AND ESTHER (2:5-7)

[5]Now there was in the citadel of Susa a Jew of the tribe of Benjamin, named Mordecai son of Jair, the son of Shimei, the son of Kish, [6]who had been carried into exile from Jerusalem by Nebuchadnezzar king of Babylon, among those taken captive with Jehoiachin[a] king of Judah. [7]Mordecai had a cousin named Hadassah, whom he had brought up because she had neither father nor mother. This girl, who was also known as Esther, was lovely in form and features, and Mordecai had taken her as his own daughter when her father and mother died.

[a]6 Hebrew *Jeconiah*, a variant of *Jehoiachin*

2:5 This brief paragraph interrupts the story of the king's search for a queen in order to introduce to the reader both **Mordecai** and **Esther**. In the Hebrew text of verse 5, the first two words are אִישׁ יְהוּדִי (*'îš yᵉhûdî*), "a Jewish man." Of first importance for the narrative that follows is the Jewishness of the hero and heroine. Mordecai is named in fifty verses in this book, and seven times he is identified as "a Jew" (2:5; 5:13; 6:10; 8:7; 9:29,31; 10:3).[2]

Bush has observed that this is the only time in the Old Testament where a native member of the community of Israel is named and identified by a gentilic (e.g., "the Hittite" or "a Philistine"). Only foreigners who are living in Israel as resident aliens are regularly identified only by their country or region of origin. "Thus, the use of this gentilic as the only identification of Mordecai signals a conscious

---

[2]A cuneiform tablet from Borsippa near Babylon identifies one Marduka as a civil servant in the early years of Xerxes. Some have identified this individual with Mordecai. Complicating this equation is the fact that more than thirty texts from Persepolis contain the name Marduka or Marduku, which may refer to up to four individuals (David J.A. Clines, "In Quest of the Historical Mordecai," *VT* 41 [1991]: 129-136; Carey A. Moore, "Archaeology and the Book of Esther," *BA* 38 (1975): 73-74; Yamauchi, *Persia*, pp. 234-236).

recognition of the foreign, the diaspora, status of both Mordecai and the Jewish community throughout the book."[3]

The names in Mordecai's genealogy may be from the family of King Saul: **Kish** was the father of Saul (1 Sam 9:1-2); **Shimei**, a man from the same clan as Saul's family, cursed David when he fled from the coup led by Absalom (2 Sam 16:5). Then again, these names may only coincidentally be linked with Saul.

2:6 The **who** of verse 6 is either linked to Mordecai or to Kish. If the former possibility is taken, and this is the most natural reading of the Hebrew, this would make Mordecai at least 120 years old at the time of our story, and Esther would have been only slightly younger, since **Jehoiachin** was deported to Babylon in 597 B.C. (cf. 2 Kgs 24:8-17). This is a rather improbable situation, "not least because Esther his cousin could hardly qualify as a good-looking girl."[4]

Keil points to a telescoping of the generations as a means of solving this difficulty. He writes, "For the relative clause: who had been carried away, need not be so strictly understood as to assert that Mordochai himself was carried away; but the object being to give merely his origin and lineage, and not his history, it involves only the notion that he belonged to those Jews who were carried to Babylon by Nebuchadnezzar with Jeconiah, so that he, though born in captivity, was carried to Babylon in the persons of his forefathers."[5]

If the **who** refers to Kish, the great-grandfather of Mordecai and not the Kish of the Book of Samuel, then the chronological improbability is addressed, but this is by no means the natural interpretation of the Hebrew syntax.[6]

---

[3]Bush, *Ruth, Esther,* p. 312.

[4]Clines, *Ezra, Nehemiah, Esther,* p. 287. If Mordecai had been carried into captivity as an infant, he would be 122-123 years of age when he became Prime Minister in the twelfth year of Xerxes' reign.

[5]Keil, *Esther,* p. 336. Compare Gen 46:27, where the sons of Joseph are spoken of as coming to Egypt with Jacob, although they were born in Egypt.

[6]J. Stafford Wright writes, "But if the relative pronoun applies to the last name in the genealogy (as in II Chr 22:9 and Ezra 2:61), it was Kish, Mordecai's great-grandfather, who was taken with Jehoiachin. In Esther 2:5, 6, there are three relative pronouns, and each refers to the name that immediately precedes" ("Historicity," p. 38).

The fact that Mordecai's family was taken into captivity with Jehoiachin implies that it belonged to the upper classes of Judahite society.

The Babylonian name Mordecai ("man of Marduk") honors Marduk, the chief god of the Babylon pantheon. If this man had a Hebrew name, we do not know. Daniel and his three friends had both Hebrew and Babylonian names.

2:7 Mordecai adopted his orphaned cousin Hadassah/Esther and brought her up. Her Hebrew name **Hadassah** means "myrtle." The Persian name Esther is either a form of the Babylonian goddess Ishtar, the goddess of love and war[7], or a derivative of the Persian stâra, "star."

If the names of Mordecai and Esther allude to their assimilation into Babylonian culture, "the outcome of the story suggests to the Babylonian pagans that Marduk and Ishtar are subservient to the purposes of the unnamed God of the Jews. The victory of the Jews in this story would then function as a polemic against the pagan deities."[8]

Esther is the only person in this story with two names. She is accordingly a woman forced to integrate two identities — her identity as a Jewess and her identity in the Persian court into which she was thrust.

C. ESTHER JOINS THE BEAUTY PAGEANT (2:8-11)

[8]**When the king's order and edict had been proclaimed, many girls were brought to the citadel of Susa and put under the care of Hegai. Esther also was taken to the king's palace and entrusted to Hegai, who had charge of the harem.** [9]**The girl pleased him and won his favor. Immediately he provided her with her beauty treatments and special food. He assigned to her seven maids selected**

---

[7]Xerxes makes Esther his queen — a "goddess" of love. It is Esther who asked that Haman's ten sons be hanged on gallows (9:13) — a "goddess" of war. Jobes suggests that it is thus easy to see how Hadassah may have been given this nickname (Esther) by her subjects after the Babylonian goddess of love and war (*Esther*, p. 97).

[8]Ibid., p. 97.

from the king's palace and moved her and her maids into the best place in the harem. [10]**Esther had not revealed her nationality and family background, because Mordecai had forbidden her to do so.** [11]**Every day he walked back and forth near the courtyard of the harem to find out how Esther was and what was happening to her.**

2:8 In verse 7 Esther is described as "lovely in form and features" (lit., "beautiful in form and lovely to look at"). This explains why she is included in the number of girls (according to Josephus the number is 400) **brought to the citadel of Susa**. In verse 8 nothing unpleasant is implied by the verb **taken**. This same verb is used in verses 7 and 15 to describe Mordecai's adoption of Esther.

2:9 Like Daniel in Daniel 1:9 Esther receives the special favor of a supervisor. When Hegai assigns seven maids to Esther and moves her and her entourage into the best place in the harem, he singles her out as the likely successor to Vashti. But unlike Daniel she does not protest eating the food of the Gentiles (Dan 1:8-15).

2:10 The noun "Mordecai" precedes the verb, thus emphasizing Esther's submission to Mordecai's authority. "He ruled his household!"[9]

Why Mordecai wanted Esther to conceal **her nationality and family background** is unknown. Perhaps he feared that Esther's chances of success with the king would be diminished, although the author gives no hint that Xerxes would have discriminated against a Jewess. Perhaps the reaction he received from Haman in chapter 3 bespeaks an anti-Semitism sentiment.

2:11 Since the access of outsiders to the women of the harem would not have been allowed, the reader is not informed how Mordecai learns of Esther's well-being. Perhaps the maids appointed to wait on her serve as the conduit of communication. Some have suggested that Mordecai himself could have been a eunuch in the palace and thus had access to Esther.

---

[9]Baldwin, *Esther,* p. 67.

D. THE GIRLS ARE PREPARED TO MEET THE KING (2:12-14)

[12]**Before a girl's turn came to go in to King Xerxes, she had to complete twelve months of beauty treatments prescribed for the women, six months with oil of myrrh and six with perfumes and cosmetics.** [13]**And this is how she would go to the king: Anything she wanted was given her to take with her from the harem to the king's palace.** [14]**In the evening she would go there and in the morning return to another part of the harem to the care of Shaashgaz, the king's eunuch who was in charge of the concubines. She would not return to the king unless he was pleased with her and summoned her by name.**

2:12-14 Joyce Baldwin reminds us that these verses highlight the inhumanity of polygamy. She writes, "The twelve months of beauty treatment provided 'marriage preparation,' but the sad part was that for the majority what awaited them was more like widowhood than marriage. Though each girl in turn moved from the house of Hegai to that of Shaashgaz once she had become a concubine, there was no guarantee that the king would remember her by name and call for her even once more. . . . The prestige of living in the royal palace was small compensation for the king's neglect, though girls with a passion for luxury could no doubt indulge it to the full."[10]

Anything she wanted undoubtedly refers to jewelry or clothing; anything that she thought would enhance her beauty. Whether she had to return these items after her visit to the king, we are not told. If she retained them, they were most likely viewed as a wedding gift. The use of the word **concubines** in verse 14 suggests that the marriage union was consummated. In verse 13 the translation **the king's palace** is incorrect; "the king's apartment" or "sleeping quarters" would be more appropriate.

W.F. Albright has suggested that the word translated in verse 12 as **with perfumes** should be rendered "with cosmetic burner." Evidently then the beauty program required the candidates to saturate their hair, skin, and pores with fumes from cosmetic burners.[11]

---

[10]Baldwin, *Esther,* pp. 67-68.

[11]W.F. Albright, "The Lachish Cosmetic Burner and Esther 2:12," in *A Light unto My Path: Old Testament Studies in Honor of Jacob M. Myers,* eds.

E. ESTHER IS CHOSEN AS QUEEN (2:15-18)

[15]When the turn came for Esther (the girl Mordecai had adopted, the daughter of his uncle Abihail) to go to the king, she asked for nothing other than what Hegai, the king's eunuch who was in charge of the harem, suggested. And Esther won the favor of everyone who saw her. [16]She was taken to King Xerxes in the royal residence in the tenth month, the month of Tebeth, in the seventh year of his reign.
[17]Now the king was attracted to Esther more than to any of the other women, and she won his favor and approval more than any of the other virgins. So he set a royal crown on her head and made her queen instead of Vashti. [18]And the king gave a great banquet, Esther's banquet, for all his nobles and officials. He proclaimed a holiday throughout the provinces and distributed gifts with royal liberality.

2:15 All the candidates remain nameless, save for Esther, the biological daughter of **Abihail** (meaning "[my] father is strength"). By trusting Hegai's knowledge of the king's preferences, Esther dresses according to the king's taste rather than her own, and thus distinguishes herself from the others who had gone before. If the special pieces of jewelry and/or articles of clothing became the possession of each female candidate, then Esther chooses not to enrich herself at the king's expense. Surely this would endear the king to her!

2:16-17 In verse 9 Esther won the "favor" (חֶסֶד, *ḥesed*) of Hegai. Now she wins the **favor** (חֵן, *ḥēn*) of all who look upon her beauty. These anticipate the **favor** (*ḥesed*) and **approval** (*ḥēn*) that she finds with the king in verse 17.

Esther's turn took place in December-January, mid-winter in Susa, of 479–478 B.C., four years after the dismissal of Vashti. Xerxes was away in Greece for two of these years.

2:18 The long contest ends when the king falls in love with Esther and makes her queen. Esther now wears the crown that Vashti forfeited (1:11). To honor his new bride the king declares a great feast and proclaims a holiday (lit., "a causing to rest"), which has been interpreted to mean a release from tribute, forced labor, prison, or military service. When the False Smerdis ascended the Persian throne, he proclaimed a three years' remission of taxes and military service (Herodotus 3.67).

F. MORDECAI FOILS A PLOT AGAINST THE KING'S LIFE
(2:19-23)

[19]**When the virgins were assembled a second time, Mordecai was sitting at the king's gate. [20]But Esther had kept secret her family background and nationality just as Mordecai had told her to do, for she continued to follow Mordecai's instructions as she had done when he was bringing her up.**

[21]**During the time Mordecai was sitting at the king's gate, Bigthana[a] and Teresh, two of the king's officers who guarded the doorway, became angry and conspired to assassinate King Xerxes. [22]But Mordecai found out about the plot and told Queen Esther, who in turn reported it to the king, giving credit to Mordecai. [23]And when the report was investigated and found to be true, the two officials were hanged on a gallows.[b] All this was recorded in the book of the annals in the presence of the king.**

[a]*21* Hebrew *Bigthan*, a variant of *Bigthana*   [b]*23* Or *were hung* (or *impaled*) *on poles*; similarly elsewhere in Esther

2:19-20 Even after the choice of Esther as queen, a second gathering of virgins actually took place. Polygamy knows no bounds!

Sitting at the king's gate (cf. 2:19,21; 3:2; 5:9,13; 6:10,12) suggests that Mordecai was or became some kind of palace official, as opposed to an idler, which gave him opportunity to learn of the planned assassination and access to Esther to report it. Perhaps Queen Esther had been instrumental in securing this governmental post for Mordecai.

The discovery of this gate at Susa took place in the archaeological expeditions of the 1970s. The gate was 131 by 92 feet. The gate was a large central room (69 feet square) and two rectangular side rooms. The large central room had four columns. The bases of two of these columns bore trilingual inscriptions of Xerxes,[12] which read:

---

[12]Yamauchi, *Persia*, pp. 298-300.

"Xerxes the King says, 'by the grace of Ahuramazda, this gate, Darius the King made it, he who was my father.'"

2:21-22 Quite possibly **Bigthana** and **Teresh** guarded the king's private apartment, and, thus, had easy access to the king's person. We are not told why Bigthana and Teresh became angry with Xerxes. Did they resent the demotion of Vashti, the promotion of Mordecai? They were probably impaled on wooden stakes. Xerxes died, according to Diodorus Siculus (II.69.1-2), as a result of such a conspiracy.

Midrashic tradition credited Mordecai with the mastery of seventy tongues. It is this accomplishment which, according to the Midrash, enabled Mordecai to understand the conversation of Bigthana and Teresh.[13]

2:23 Concerning the **book of the annals** see Ezra 4:15. According to Herodotus, at the battle of Salamis, "whenever he [Xerxes] saw one of his officers behaving with distinction, he would find out his name, and his secretaries wrote it down, together with his city and parentage" (8.90).

Some interpreters have faulted Mordecai for not protecting Esther from the events narrated in chapter two. Abraham Saba, a fifteenth-century Jewish commentator, writes, "Now when Mordecai heard the king's herald announcing that whoever had a daughter or a sister should bring her to the king to have intercourse with an uncircumcised heathen, why did he not risk his life to take her to some deserted place to hide until the danger would pass? Why did Mordecai not keep righteous Esther from idol worship? Why was he not more careful? Where was his righteousness, his piety, and his valor?"[14]

Ronald Pierce has recently contended that the author of Esther addresses the secular nature of the people of God in the ancient Diaspora. Mordecai is at best a secularized Jew. Pierce writes, "This came at a tragic time when many Jews (perhaps most) had forgotten their calling to separateness and had chosen to compromise their

---

[13]Talmon, "Wisdom," p. 437.

[14]Quoted in Barry D. Walfish, *Esther in Medieval Garb: Jewish Interpretation of the Book of Esther in the Middle Ages* (Albany, NY: SUNY Press, 1993), pp. 122-123.

socio-religious heritage for the sake of personal advancement under Persian domination."[15]

The biblical author neither reveals Mordecai's motives nor vindicates him by explaining extenuating circumstances or reporting that he had divine counsel to behave as he did.

And what about Esther herself? She finds herself in the sensual luxury of the Persian harem, being prepared for a sensual night with a Gentile to whom she is not married. And since she did whatever it took to please the king, she won the position of queen.

The text says nothing of how she felt about her situation. Maybe she hated her circumstances. Maybe she wondered how God could have let such a horrible set of circumstances envelop her. On the other hand, maybe she thought this was the best thing that ever happened to her. Perhaps she loved the attention of the most powerful man in the empire.

The author neither condemns nor exonerates Esther. Judgment would be close at hand. The Torah clearly prohibited intermarriage (Deut 7:3; cf. Exod 23:31-33; 34:12-16). The patriarchs did not want their sons to take brides from the Canaanites (Gen 24:3; 28:1). The Exile was brought about in part by the foreign marriages of kings of Israel and Judah (1 Kgs 11; 16:29-34; 2 Chr 21:4-7). Ezra condemns the Jews who returned to the Promised Land for marrying Gentiles and insists on their divorce (Ezra 9–10). The author never exonerates Esther's actions by inferring that her marriage, perhaps the lesser of two evils, led to the greater good for God's people. The author does not commend to us the actions of Esther as a case of "the end justifies the means."

But the author's silence makes it impossible to use Esther's behavior as a moral role model. Karen Jobes writes, "How would you use this episode from Esther's life to teach virtue to your teenage daughter as she stands on the threshold of womanhood? What message would she get? Make yourself as attractive as possible to powerful men? Use your body to advance God's kingdom? The end justifies the means?"[16]

---

[15]Ronald W. Pierce, "The Politics of Esther and Mordecai: Courage or Compromise?" *BBR* 2 (1992): 82.

[16]Jobes, *Esther,* p. 113.

Both Mordecai and Esther found themselves in what they may have considered morally ambiguous and complex situations. Esther may have looked back on this episode with shame and regret, or she may have looked back with a clear conscience. If the latter, then she acted as wisely as she knew how. "This episode from Esther's life offers great encouragement and comfort when we find ourselves in situations where every choice is an odd mix of right and wrong. Only God knows the end of our story from its beginning. We are responsible to him for living faithfully in obedience to his word in every situation as we best know how. Even if we make the 'wrong' decision, whether through innocent blunder or deliberate disobedience, our God is so gracious and omnipotent that he is able to use that weak link in a chain of events that will perfect his purposes in us and through us."[17]

---

[17]Ibid., p. 115.

ESTHER 3

G. MORDECAI WILL NOT BOW TO HAMAN (3:1-6)

[1]After these events, King Xerxes honored Haman son of Hammedatha, the Agagite, elevating him and giving him a seat of honor higher than that of all the other nobles. [2]All the royal officials at the king's gate knelt down and paid honor to Haman, for the king had commanded this concerning him. But Mordecai would not kneel down or pay him honor.

[3]Then the royal officials at the king's gate asked Mordecai, "Why do you disobey the king's command?" [4]Day after day they spoke to him but he refused to comply. Therefore they told Haman about it to see whether Mordecai's behavior would be tolerated, for he had told them he was a Jew.

[5]When Haman saw that Mordecai would not kneel down or pay him honor, he was enraged. [6]Yet having learned who Mordecai's people were, he scorned the idea of killing only Mordecai. Instead Haman looked for a way to destroy all Mordecai's people, the Jews, throughout the whole kingdom of Xerxes.

3:1 After Esther became Queen in the seventh year of Xerxes' reign (2:16), but before Xerxes' twelfth year (3:7), **Haman**[1] was exalted to a position second only to the king. Why Haman? In light of 2:19-23, why not Mordecai?

---

[1]Andre Lacocque, "Haman in the Book of Esther," *HAR* 11 (1987): 207-222. For an excellent summary of Haman's character in the Book of Esther, see Fox, *Character,* pp. 178-184, who suggests that Haman's primary motivation in all his actions is the need to confirm his power at every step, in short, control. "Haman is devoured by this obsession with control. Such an obsession is a single, ineradicable notion that dominates the thoughts and feelings in spite of one's own will. Mordecai's refusal to show fear, indeed

The Agagite takes the reader back to 1 Samuel 15, where Samuel, the prophet during Saul's reign, put Agag, king of the Amalekites, to death (cf. Num 24:7). If Mordecai was of the family of Saul (cf. 2:5), does this reference foreshadow the downfall of Haman?[2] According to Exodus 17:16, "The LORD will be at war against the Amalekites from generation to generation." According to Deuteronomy 25:17-19, God expected his people to be at war with the Amalekites. "Remember what the Amalekites did to you along the way when you came out of Egypt. When you were weary and worn out, they met you on your journey and cut off all who were lagging behind; they had no fear of God. When the LORD your God gives you rest from all the enemies around you in the land he is giving you to possess as an inheritance, you shall blot out the memory of Amalek from under heaven. Do not forget!"

Keil has suggested that the term **Agagite** is a *nomen dignitatis* of the kings of Amalek, as *Pharaoh* and *Abimelech* were of the kings of Egypt and Gerar.

Jobes has suggested that Haman need not have been genetically descended from the Amalekites to have earned the name *Agagite*. By using this term, the author is characterizing him as anti-Semitic, an enemy of the Jews.[3]

Everything about Haman is hateful. In fact, everything about Haman, God hated! "There are six things the LORD hates, seven that are detestable to him: haughty eyes, a lying tongue, hands that shed innocent blood, a heart that devises wicked schemes, feet that are quick to rush into evil, a false witness who pours out lies and a man who stirs up dissension among brothers" (Prov 6:16-19).[4] Keep these

---

his very presence in the King's Gate, proves to Haman that, whatever his might, he lacks control: he cannot govern the Jew's emotions; he cannot even prevent his current presence in the place of power. But ironically and appropriately, Haman's obsession with control in effect imposes Mordecai's presence upon all of his thoughts and gives Mordecai power over his mind, robbing him of all pleasure he might derive from the honor, wealth, and power in which he glories. Haman makes himself miserable" (p. 180).

[2]The founder of the Amalekites was a descendant of Esau (Gen 36:12), and Esau was an enemy of his brother Jacob.

[3]Jobes, *Esther*, p. 120.

[4]Wiersbe, *Be Committed*, pp. 94-95.

characteristics in mind as you read the book of Esther, for you will see them depicted in Haman.[5]

The name Haman appears forty-five times in this book, but only seven times with appellatives, such as we have here — **son of Hammedatha, the Agagite.**

   a. 3:10 Haman son of Hammedatha, the Agagite,
       the enemy of the Jews
     b. 8:1 Haman, the enemy of the Jews
       c. 8:3 Haman, the Agagite
       c'. 8:5 Haman son of Hammedatha, the Agagite
     b'. 9:10 Haman son of Hammedatha, the enemy of the Jews
   a'. 9:24 Haman son of Hammedatha, the Agagite,
       the enemy of all the Jews

3:2 Persians regularly bowed before high-ranking officials (Herodotus 1.134). For whatever reason, Mordecai refuses to bow before Haman. Mordecai's Jewishness does not preclude bowing before others, unless, of course, Haman claimed divine homage, a violation of the first and second commandments.[6] Bowing was customary in Israelite culture. According to Genesis 33:3, Jacob "bowed down to the ground seven times as he approached his brother" Esau (cf. Gen 23:7). According to 1 Samuel 24:8, David "bowed down and prostrated himself with his face to the ground" before King Saul (cf. 2 Sam 14:4; 1 Kgs 1:16). Perhaps national spirit and pride precludes Mordecai from bowing before an Agagite.

---

[5]The book of Proverbs recognizes the power of anger to cause harm. This is certainly true of Haman's anger. "A fool gives full vent to his anger, but a wise man keeps himself under control" (Prov 29:11). "An angry man stirs up dissension, and a hot-tempered one commits many sins" (Prov 29:22).

[6]From the apocryphal additions to the book of Esther, the following excerpt from the prayer of Mordecai is apropos here: "O Lord, Lord, King who rulest over all things, for the universe is in thy power and there is no one who can oppose thee if it is thy will to save Israel. . . . Thou knowest all things; thou knowest, O Lord, that it was not in insolence or pride or for any love of glory that I did this, and refused to bow down to this proud Haman. For I would have been willing to kiss the soles of his feet, to save Israel! But I did this, that I might not set the glory of man above the glory of God, and I will not bow down to any one but to thee, who art my Lord; and I will not do these things in pride" (13:9,12-14).

3:3 The royal officials see this incident as a test case: could Jews be exempted from certain Persian laws?

3:4-5 Apparently Haman did not notice Mordecai's behavior until it was pointed out to him. In verse 5 Haman makes a point of looking for the offense.

3:6 Haman's logic is a classic example of the stereotype. If Jewishness is the basis for Mordecai's opposition to the royal command, then all Jews are potential lawbreakers. Genocide would solve Haman's "Jewish problem." The verb שָׁמַד (šāmad, **to destroy**) appears five times in this book.

H. PLANS ARE MADE TO DESTROY THE JEWS (3:7-11)

[7]In the twelfth year of king Xerxes, in the first month, the month of Nisan, they cast the *pur* (that is, the lot) in the presence of Haman to select a day and month. And the lot fell on[a] the twelfth month, the month of Adar.

[8]Then Haman said to King Xerxes, "There is a certain people dispersed and scattered among the peoples in all the provinces of your kingdom whose customs are different from those of all other people and who do not obey the king's laws; it is not in the king's best interest to tolerate them. [9]If it pleases the king, let a decree be issued to destroy them, and I will put ten thousand talents[b] of silver into the royal treasury for the men who carry out this business."

[10]So the king took the signet ring from his finger and gave it to Haman son of Hammedatha, the Agagite, the enemy of the Jews. [11]"Keep the money," the king said to Haman, "and do with the people as you please."

[a]7 Septuagint; Hebrew does not have *And the lot fell on*   [b]9 That is, about 375 tons (about 345 metric tons)

3:7 Casting lots was a common practice in both the ancient East (cf. Herodotus 3.128) and in Israel (1 Sam 14:40-42; Josh 7:16-18). According to Proverbs 16:33 the lot was cast by the Israelite to discern the will of God. Haman casts the lot, however, to determine the "lucky day" to begin his reign of terror. **Nisan** (March-April) was, in Babylonian thought at least, the time of the year for determining destinies.[7] The date of the pogrom — **Adar** (February-March) — is almost a year in the future.

3:8-9 Haman suggests that Xerxes would profit from his plan. First, the king would be rid of a rebellious people — **they do not obey the king's laws** (cf. Ezra 4:12-16). Secondly, the king would reap a financial profit — **ten thousand talents of silver**. Haman knows that the Greek wars had impoverished the king's treasuries.

The amount of money promised by Haman expresses both the depth of his hatred for Mordecai and his fabulous wealth. It is possible that Haman figures to add to his wealth the property of the Jewish families he intends to destroy. The weight of a Babylonian standard talent in use at this time was 30.24 kg or 66.67 pounds.[8] Ten thousand talents, then, amounts to 333 tons of silver. That is impressive wealth! Ten thousand talents were equivalent to about two-thirds of the annual income of the entire Persian Empire (Herodotus 3.95).

3:10-11 Xerxes' response is literally, "The silver is given to you." This may mean that the king is returning Haman's bribe, or it may mean the money is Haman's to effectuate the planned atrocity. At 7:4 Esther says, "For I and my people have been sold as male and female slaves," suggesting the latter understanding (cf. 4:7).

The **signet ring** gave Haman executive power to carry out the pogrom against the Jews.

I. THE EDICT IS ISSUED (3:12-15)

[12]**Then on the thirteenth day of the first month the royal secretaries were summoned. They wrote out in the script of each province and in the language of each people all Haman's orders to the king's satraps, the governors of the various provinces and the nobles of the various peoples. These were written in the name of King Xerxes himself and sealed with his own ring. [13]Dispatches were sent by couriers to all the king's provinces with the order to destroy, kill and annihilate all the Jews—young and old, women**

---

[7]Clines, *Ezra, Nehemiah, Esther*, p. 295.
[8]Bush, *Ruth, Esther*, p. 381.

and little children—on a single day, the thirteenth day of the twelfth month, the month of Adar, and to plunder their goods. [14]A copy of the text of the edict was to be issued as law in every province and made known to the people of every nationality so they would be ready for that day.

[15]Spurred on by the king's command, the couriers went out, and the edict was issued in the citadel of Susa. The king and Haman sat down to drink, but the city of Susa was bewildered.

3:12 The **thirteenth day of the first month** was, according to Exodus 12:6, the day just before the slaying of the Passover lamb. The date then raises the question: Can God save his people now from this Persian pogrom as he saved his people from Egyptian oppression? The number 13 was unlucky among Babylonians and Persians.

Though Haman dictates the edict and the royal secretaries write down the words, it goes out in the king's name. **Sealed with his own ring** indicates the king's signature.

3:13-14 The royal letters were dispatched by post-riders. Eleven months would follow before the edict was carried out by force. What was the motive for such an interval? Keil answers the question with these words: "The motive seems to have been to cause many Jews to leave their property and escape to other lands, for the sake of preserving their lives. Thus Haman would attain his object. He would be relieved of the presence of the Jews, and be able to enrich himself by the appropriation of their possessions."[9]

The providence of God is unmistakably evident in the falling of the lot upon so distant a day. Again Keil writes, "It was only because there was so long an interval between the publication of the decree and the day appointed by lot for its execution, that it was possible for the Jews to take means for averting the destruction with which they were threatened."[10]

3:15 The callous indifference of the King and Haman regarding human life is evidenced by their drinking. Concerning the Persians,

---

[9]Keil, *Esther*, pp. 348-349. Clines adds, "Public knowledge of the planned pogrom over nearly a year can only intensify anti-Jewish feeling in order to be ready for that day" (*Ezra, Nehemiah, Esther*, p. 298).

[10]Keil, *Esther*, pp. 348-349.

Herodotus writes that "any decision they make when they are sober, is reconsidered afterwards when they are drunk" (1.133).

Xerxes' love for drink contradicts proverbial wisdom:

> "It is not for kings, O Lemuel—
> not for kings to drink wine,
> not for rulers to crave beer,
> lest they drink and forget what the law decrees,
> and deprive all the oppressed of their rights"
> (Prov 31:4-5).

In chapter 1 the disobedience of one woman, Queen Vashti, brings about an edict for all the women of the realm (1:22). Now in chapter 3, the disobedience of one man, Mordecai, brings an edict against all the Jews of the empire.

In both cases the word of the king had been disobeyed. Vashti refused to comply with the king's command to appear before his guests (1:11-12). Mordecai refused the king's order to bow before Haman (3:2).

The disobedience of one man, Adam, according to Paul, led to condemnation and death for all men. "Sin entered the world through one man, and death through sin, and in this way death came to all men. . . . the result of one trespass was condemnation for all men" (Rom 5:12,18).

If Haman's plot against all the Jews of the empire had been allowed to proceed, then the promises of God to the patriarchs and David would have been threatened. But thanks be to God — his love overcame the hatred of Haman.

Accordingly, Paul can write of another man, Jesus Christ.

> For if the many died by the trespass of the one man, how much more did God's grace and the gift that came by the grace of the one man, Jesus Christ, overflow to the many! . . . For if, by the trespass of the one man, death reigned through that one man, how much more will those who receive God's abundant provision of grace and of the gift of righteousness reign in life through the one man, Jesus Christ. . . . For just as through the disobedience of the one man the many were made sinners, so also through the obedience of the one man the many will be made righteous (Rom 5:15,17,19).

ESTHER 4

III. THE CLASH BETWEEN HAMAN AND MORDECAI (4:1–5:14)

A. THE JEWS MOURN BECAUSE OF THE EDICT (4:1-3)

[1]When Mordecai learned of all that had been done, he tore his clothes, put on sackcloth and ashes, and went out into the city, wailing loudly and bitterly. [2]But he went only as far as the king's gate, because no one clothed in sackcloth was allowed to enter it. [3]In every province to which the edict and order of the king came, there was great mourning among the Jews, with fasting, weeping and wailing. Many lay in sackcloth and ashes.

4:1 Learned of all that had been done implies the same secret sources of knowledge about affairs in the court by means of which Mordecai learned of the assassination plot in 2:19-23.[1]

Sackcloth, which refers to a garment of coarse cloth of goat or camel hair, and **ashes**, which were sprinkled on one's head, were conventional ways of expressing grief (Gen 37:29; Dan 9:3) and humiliation (2 Sam 13:19). Mordecai's bitter cry is not an expression of self-reproach, nor is it the cry of protest against the King by the unjustly treated, but a natural expression of grief over the fate of his people.

4:2 He went only as far as the king's gate because he wanted to get the attention of Esther. Verse 4 indicates he succeeded.

4:3 This verse mirrors the action of Mordecai with that of Jews throughout the empire. Communal mourning would prompt repentance and prayer before God, though the writer mentions neither.

---

[1]*Targum Rishon* suggests that Mordecai became aware of this matter "through Elijah the high priest."

B. ESTHER IS INFORMED OF THE EDICT (4:4-8)

[4]When Esther's maids and eunuchs came and told her about Mordecai, she was in great distress. She sent clothes for him to put on instead of his sackcloth, but he would not accept them. [5]Then Esther summoned Hathach, one of the king's eunuchs assigned to attend her, and ordered him to find out what was troubling Mordecai and why.

[6]So Hathach went out to Mordecai in the open square of the city in front of the king's gate. [7]Mordecai told him everything that had happened to him, including the exact amount of money Haman had promised to pay into the royal treasury for the destruction of the Jews. [8]He also gave him a copy of the text of the edict for their annihilation, which had been published in Susa, to show to Esther and explain it to her, and he told him to urge her to go into the king's presence to beg for mercy and plead with him for her people.

4:4a Esther's **great distress** is occasioned by Mordecai's actions and attire. Esther does not yet know of Haman's terrible decree. Does her ignorance bespeak an isolation from the general affairs of the empire?

4:4b-5 In order **to find out what was troubling Mordecai and why**, Esther first proposes a change of clothing. Since entry into the palace in sackcloth was forbidden, **she sent clothes for him**. When Mordecai refuses the change of attire, Esther sends **Hathach**, a trustworthy royal eunuch whose name means 'the good one,' to inquire of Mordecai.

Why does Mordecai refuse the offer of proper dress? Josephus's explanation that "the sad occasion that made him put it [the sackcloth] on had not yet ceased" seems right.

4:6-7 The fabulous size of the bribe would indicate to Esther the seriousness of the situation. "Now Haman's hatred had joined hands with the king's avarice."[2]

4:8 Mordecai gives Hathach documentary evidence: **He also**

---

[2]Moore, *Esther,* p. 48.

gave him a copy of the text of the edict for their annihilation, which had been published in Susa. Mordecai's last word orders her to use her influence with the king on behalf of **her people**.[3] This plea divulges to Hathach that Esther was a Jewess; nothing was to be gained now by secrecy. Could Hathach also have been a Jew?

C. ESTHER'S HESITATION (4:9-11)

[9]**Hathach went back and reported to Esther what Mordecai had said.** [10]**Then she instructed him to say to Mordecai,** [11]**"All the king's officials and the people of the royal provinces know that for any man or woman who approaches the king in the inner court without being summoned the king has but one law: that he be put to death. The only exception to this is for the king to extend his gold scepter to him and spare his life. But thirty days have passed since I was called to go to the king."**

4:9-11a In verse 11 Esther reminds Mordecai of what he already knows — that nobody can rush into the throne room and seek an immediate audience with the king, who needed to be protected from attempts on his life and from interruptions to his schedule. According to Herodotus, "Deioces introduced for the first time the ceremonial of royalty: admission to the king's presence was forbidden, and all communication had to be through messengers. Nobody was allowed to see the king, and it was an offence for anyone to laugh or spit in the royal presence. This solemn ceremonial was designed as a safeguard against his contemporaries, men as good as himself in birth and personal quality, with whom he had been brought up in earlier years. There was a risk that if they saw him habitually, it might lead to jealousy and resentment, and plots would follow; but if nobody saw him, the legend would grow that he was a being of a different order from mere men" (1.99; cf. 3.118,140).

---

[3]In the Greek versions, v. 8 adds: "Remembering your humble station when you were supported by my hand because Haman, who is second to the king, has sentenced us to death. Call upon the Lord, and speak to the king concerning us, and save us from death."

4:11b Esther then informs Mordecai of what he does not know – **But thirty days have passed since I was called to go to the king.** "These words clearly assert that Esther knows no way to obtain an audience with the king, except by waiting for a summons; and this she has no reason to expect, since she has not been called for a month."[4] If Esther has fallen out of favor with the king, then her situation is especially precarious.[5] If she were to appear unannounced, she would be taking her own life in her hands. Did Esther ever consider the safer course and formally request an audience with the king? Apparently not, and for the same reason, she is not in very good standing with the king.

Since Xerxes had a considerable collection of concubines in his harem, he did not necessarily need Esther to fulfill either his desire for companionship or his sensual cravings. Esther's initial hesitation may reflect her remembrance of what happened to the last queen who crossed Xerxes (ch. 1).

Jewish wisdom also counseled caution or hesitation before a king. "Do not exalt yourself in the king's presence, and do not claim a place among great men; it is better for him to say to you, 'Come up here,' than for him to humiliate you before a nobleman" (Prov 25:6-7).

D. MORDECAI ENCOURAGES ESTHER TO ACT (4:12-14)

[12]**When Esther's words were reported to Mordecai,** [13]**he sent back this answer: "Do not think that because you are in the king's house you alone of all the Jews will escape.** [14]**For if you remain silent at this time, relief and deliverance for the Jews will arise from another place, but you and your father's family will perish. And who knows but that you have come to royal position for such a time as this?"**

4:12-13 In response Mordecai reminds Esther of three facts.

---

[4]L.B. Paton, *The Book of Esther*, ICC (Edinburgh: T & T Clark, 1951), p. 221.

[5]Jobes writes, "Apparently five years into her marriage, the king's desire for her has cooled. Or given her mission, perhaps she does not wish to arouse the suspicions of the court by requesting an audience. Whatever her fears, it seems likely that the ruthless King Xerxes will not extend the golden scepter if the queen's death would be somehow expedient to his other interests" (*Esther*, p. 132).

First, the royal edict said, "all the Jews" (3:13), including those living "in the king's house."

4:14 Second, God will not be hindered by Esther's failure. To paraphrase Mordecai at this point, he is saying, "Esther, if you do not act, God has an infinite number of ways to accomplish his will. But you and your family will be the losers."[6] God's promise to Abram and his descendants in Genesis 12:3 — "I will bless those who bless you, and whoever curses you I will curse" — informs Mordecai's conviction of God's protection. Mordecai's threat concerning Esther and her father's family must be seen in light of divine punishment upon her for neglect of her opportunity.[7]

Your father's family is literally "the house of your father," which means none other than the house of Mordecai.

Many have seen in the word **place** (מָקוֹם, *māqôm*) an indirect reference to God. Both Targums of Esther and Josephus interpreted this word as such. In fact, the word "place" was often used in later Jewish literature as a surrogate for the name of God.[8]

Third, Esther "is at the moment when her life's purpose is at

---

[6]John M. Wiebe translates v. 14a as follows: "For if you certainly keep silent at this time, will relief and deliverance arise for the Jews from another place? Then you and the house of your father will be destroyed." With this rendering Mordecai is implying that Esther is the only possible source for relief and deliverance for the Jews. He has no reason to expect it from any other place. He is attempting to motivate her to act, not on the basis of a threat of divine judgment or Jewish retribution, but on the basis of her basic loyalty to her people and her family ("Esther 4:14; 'Will Relief and Deliverance Arise for the Jews from Another Place?" *CBQ* 53 [1991]: 413).

[7]Ronald Pierce sees Mordecai as actually threatening Esther's life in this passage. Mordecai "is threatening Esther with the proposition: 'If you do not help you will die, even if the rest of the Jewish people are delivered!' In short, it seems that he was prepared to take matters into his own hands if she refused to help. And, if it became necessary, he would make sure that she paid the price for her disloyalty to her people" ("Politics," p. 87).

[8]The adjective "another" is problematic. If "place" is a surrogate for God, then what does "another place" mean? Hence, the expression "another place" may refer to some other human source of deliverance, such as other Jews holding high offices in the realm, or a Jewish revolt, or even that Persians who were sympathetic to the Jewish plight would somehow intervene. Perhaps, "another place" is itself a substitute for the divine name.

[9]Baldwin, *Esther*, p. 80.

stake."[9] God raised up Joseph to a position of authority in Egypt "to accomplish what is now being done, the saving of many lives" (Gen 50:20). Speaking to his brothers, Joseph recognized his moment, "But God sent me ahead of you to preserve for you a remnant on earth and to save your lives by a great deliverance" (Gen 45:7). This is now Esther's moment of destiny.

Jewish wisdom also expresses this belief in providential calling. "The LORD made everything for a purpose, even the wicked for an evil day" (Prov 16:4, Jewish Publication Society). "In his heart a man plans his course, but the LORD determines his steps" (Prov 16:9).

E. ESTHER REQUESTS MORAL SUPPORT (4:15-17)

[15]**Then Esther sent this reply to Mordecai:** [16]**"Go, gather together all the Jews who are in Susa, and fast for me. Do not eat or drink for three days, night or day. I and my maids will fast as you do. When this is done, I will go to the king, even though it is against the law. And if I perish, I perish."**

[17]**So Mordecai went away and carried out all of Esther's instructions.**

4:15-16a In the Old Testament fasting is a preparation for concentrated prayer (Ezra 8:21,23; Neh 1:4; 9:1; Ps 35:13; Dan 9:3; Joel 1:14). Esther obviously seeks God's gracious assistance in the step she is about to take.

Fasting was usually for one day only and normally lasted from morning to night (1 Sam 14:24; 2 Sam 1:12). This three-day, twenty-four-hour fast indicates the seriousness of the moment.

The date of the drawing up and publication of the decree to annihilate the Jews, according to 3:12, was the day before Passover. Hence, Esther's fast would have abolished that celebration, the most important festival of the Jewish liturgical year, despite Exodus 12.

4:16b And if I perish, I perish are words of perfect submission to the providence of God (cf. Gen 43:14; Dan 3:16-19) or, more likely, courageous determination.

4:17 Esther 4:15-16 marks a turning point in the development of the character of Esther. When she *commands* Mordecai to convene an assembly, she is assuming the role of a leader; she has taken control. John Craghan has written, "She is a woman for all seasons because she is a woman for others."[10] At 4:8 Mordecai commanded Esther, now she commands him, and he obeys (4:17). Heretofore Mordecai has been Esther's counselor/advisor (2:10; 4:13-14), now he will take his cues from her.

Esther's defining moment comes when she is faced with taking responsibility for the life God has given her by identifying herself with the people of God. Jobes writes, "After her decision to identify herself with God's people, Esther becomes the active agent, commanding Mordecai, planning a strategy to save her people, and even confronting Haman to his face. Her decision energizes her, gives her purpose, and emboldens her to face a threatening and uncertain future."[11]

The New Testament instructs us to define our lives according to belief in God's Son, Jesus Christ. "For God so loved the world that he gave his one and only Son, that whoever believes in him shall not perish but have eternal life. For God did not send his Son into the world to condemn the world, but to save the world through him. Whoever believes in him is not condemned, but whoever does not believe stands condemned already because he has not believed in the name of God's one and only Son" (John 3:16-18).

Our identification with God's Son makes us responsible for the new life God has given us by identifying with the people of God. According to the New Testament we identify with God's people through worship and sharing within the body our spiritual gifts.

Community within the body of Christ is evident when we worship. Paul writes, "Let the peace of Christ rule in your hearts, since as *members of one body* you were called to peace. And be thankful. Let the word of Christ dwell in you richly as you *teach and admonish one another with all wisdom, and as you sing psalms, hymns and spiritual*

---

[10]John F. Craghan, "Esther: A Fully Liberated Woman," *The Bible Today* 24 (1986): 11. For an excellent treatment of Esther's character, see Fox, who traces her development from passivity to activity to authority (*Character*, pp. 196-211).

[11]Jobes, *Esther*, p. 139-140.

songs with gratitude in your hearts to God" (Col 3:15-16, emphasis mine; cf. Heb 10:24-25).

Our identity with the people of God compels us to share our spiritual gifts. Each and every Christian possesses a gift of the Spirit, "a manifestation of the Spirit," *for the common good* (1 Cor 12:7). "We have different gifts, according to the grace given us. If a man's gift is prophesying, let him use it in proportion to his faith. If it is serving, let him serve; if it is teaching, let him teach; if it is encouraging, let him encourage; if it is contributing to the needs of others, let him give generously; if it is leadership, let him govern diligently; if it is showing mercy, let him do it cheerfully" (Rom 12:6-8). "Each one should use whatever gift he has received to serve others, faithfully administering God's grace in its various forms. If anyone speaks, he should do it as one speaking the very words of God. If anyone serves, he should do it with the strength God provides, so that in all things God may be praised through Jesus Christ" (1 Pet 4:10-11).

Esther's defining moment comes when she identifies herself with the people of God. The Gospel confronts us to identify ourselves with God's Son, Jesus, and God's people, the church. "The decision to be identified with Christ energizes our lives. It gives us a purpose bigger than our own concerns and problems and a hope that goes beyond our own death. It transforms us into people moved by the Holy Spirit, human agents of God's grace and love in the world."[12]

---

[12]Jobes, *Esther,* p. 141.

ESTHER 5

F. ESTHER APPROACHES THE KING (5:1-2)

¹On the third day Esther put on her royal robes and stood in the inner court of the palace, in front of the king's hall. The king was sitting on his royal throne in the hall, facing the entrance. ²When he saw Queen Esther standing in the court, he was pleased with her and held out to her the gold scepter that was in his hand. So Esther approached and touched the tip of the scepter.

5:1-2 On the third day of her fast, Esther comes before the king, who is sitting in the throne room able to see who is waiting in the forecourt. When he caught sight of Queen Esther, Xerxes **was pleased with her**, which is literally, "she lifted up/carried favor in his eyes" (see 2:9,15, and 17 for the same idiom). Was her beauty the cause? Was a divine impulse the cause? (cf. Prov 21:1)[1]

Two nearly identical bas-reliefs about 20 feet in length were discovered in Persepolis in 1936. The reliefs show a king sitting on a throne holding a staff in his right hand. Standing behind the king is

---

[1]The Septuagint (and Latin Vulgate) adds the following explanation: "When she had gone through all the doors, she stood before the king. He was seated on his royal throne, clothed in the full array of his majesty, all covered with gold and precious stones. And he was most terrifying. Lifting his face, flushed with splendor, he looked at her in fierce anger. And the queen faltered, and turned pale and faint, and collapsed upon the head of the maid who went before her. Then God changed the spirit of the king to gentleness, and in alarm he sprang from his throne and took her in his arms until she came to herself. And he comforted her with soothing words, and said to her, 'What is it, Esther? I am your brother. Take courage; you shall not die, for our law applies only to the people. Come near'" (15:7-10).

a weapon bearer in Median dress who carries the royal axe.[2] The threat of death was certainly present as Esther approached the king!

G. ESTHER PREPARES A BANQUET (5:3-8)

[3]Then the king asked, "What is it, Queen Esther? What is your request? Even up to half the kingdom, it will be given you."

[4]"If it pleases the king," replied Esther, "let the king, together with Haman, come today to a banquet I have prepared for him."

[5]"Bring Haman at once," the king said, "so that we may do what Esther asks."

So the king and Haman went to the banquet Esther had prepared. [6]As they were drinking wine, the king again asked Esther, "Now what is your petition? It will be given you. And what is your request? Even up to half the kingdom, it will be granted."

[7]Esther replied, "My petition and my request is this: [8]If the king regards me with favor and if it pleases the king to grant my petition and fulfill my request, let the king and Haman come tomorrow to the banquet I will prepare for them. Then I will answer the king's question."

5:3 When Esther appeared before the king unannounced, Xerxes must have assumed that the queen's request was an urgent one. His offer — **up to half the kingdom** — was pure hyperbole, a conventional phrase (cf. Herodotus 9.109-111; Mark 6:22-23).

5:4 The queen's request then seems anticlimactic. Instead of asking for the life of her people, she says, "**Let the king, together with Haman, come today to a banquet I have prepared for him.**" Why did Esther not make her request known the moment the king indicated that he was willing to grant it? Perhaps the polite requirements of Persian protocol (**If it pleases the king**) compel Esther to invite the king to a banquet. Fox's perception is quite right: "Vashti's fate showed that the king may react badly to strong-willed women who do not temper their strength with subtlety. What would a direct and

---

[2]For a description and photo of these reliefs see Yamauchi, *Persia*, pp. 360-362.

bold demand have achieved, besides giving Esther a self-satisfied feeling of moral virtue as she was deposed in turn?"[3]

5:5-6 At this banquet she still refuses to announce her petition. "Postponing her real request another time was a most questionable gamble," writes Moore, "any number of things could go wrong in the interval between the two dinners: the king's benevolent mood could change, for example, or Haman could learn of Esther's true feelings toward him or of her relationship to Mordecai."[4]

5:7 Here Esther starts to tell the king what is in her mind — **My petition and my request?** (contra NIV) — then breaks off, resolving to put the matter off to another day.

5:8 Why does Esther delay a second time? She is again attentive to courtesies, using the doubly polite phrase: **If the king regards me with favor and if it pleases the king**. More importantly, she is pursuing a well-designed plan, unfolding a premeditated strategy.[5] "With Esther's subtle restatement of the invitation, the king's future compliance (which he can hardly now refuse) has become virtually a public pledge to grant her unstated request."[6]

Esther's well-designed plan requires patience, as is suggested in Proverbs 25:15, "Through *patience* a ruler can be persuaded, and a gentle tongue can break a bone." Her plan also requires exact timing, as is suggested in Ecclesiastes 8:4-6, "Since a king's word is supreme, who can say to him, 'What are you doing?' Whoever obeys his command will come to no harm, and the wise heart will know the proper time and procedure. *For there is a proper time and procedure for every matter*, though a man's misery weighs heavily upon him."

---

[3]Fox, *Character,* p. 201.
[4]Moore, *Esther,* pp. 57-58.
[5]Once we grant that Esther is unfolding a strategy, we are justified in scrutinizing her words for signs of this plan. "Such a scrutiny shows her building up to the accusation with great care," writes Fox, "piquing the king's suspense, eliciting a near-promise to fulfill her wish, withholding information that could put the king on the defensive (by making him face his own culpability), delaying other information (the identity of the offender) until she has given full momentum to the king's anger, softening her speech with deferential courtesies and demurrals that play to his ego, cracking out her accusation like a whip, then allowing matters to take their course once she has set Haman careening toward destruction" (*Character,* p. 201).
[6]Bush, *Ruth, Esther,* p. 407.

Then I will answer the king's question is literally, "I will do according to the king's word." Making her request known is seen then as doing what the king has said. "By the end of her speech Esther has been able to represent what she wants as what the king has said; it has all been a delicate play of bargaining, while the object of the play has remained undisclosed."[7]

Why does Esther invite Haman to the banquets? Esther wishes to expose Haman in the king's presence so that he might not have an opportunity to prepare excuses or persuade the king against relenting.[8]

An acronym is formed when the initial letter of each of the successive words in a series is extracted to form a separate word. This is beautifully illustrated in 5:4.[9] Esther's initial response includes the words יָבוֹא הַמֶּלֶךְ וְהָמָן הַיּוֹם (*yābô' hammelek wᵉhāmān hayyôm*), "let the king and Haman come today." The first letters of these four words, *yhwh*, spell God's personal name, the LORD. The divine name may be explicitly absent from the narrative, but *he* is not. In this critical passage, the LORD is present. "It is easy to imagine," writes David Howard, "that the author is whispering here, by his very choice of words, that God is indeed present (although silently) at this time of crisis."[10]

H. HAMAN EXULTS IN HIS HONORS
BUT HATES MORDECAI EVEN MORE (5:9-14)

The narrator creates suspense for the reader by breaking off the plot line at this point. He turns again to the relationship between Haman and Mordecai.

Esther 5:9-14 is marked by an inclusio — a passage of Scripture in which the opening phrase or idea is repeated, paraphrased, or otherwise returned to at the close. At the beginning, "Haman went out that day happy and in high spirits" (verse 9). At the end, "Then go with the king to the dinner and be happy" (vs. 14).

---

[7]Clines, *Ezra, Nehemiah, Esther,* p. 305.

[8]Goldman, "Esther," p. 220.

[9]Barry J. Beitzel, "Exodus 3:14 and the Divine Name: A Case of Biblical Paranomasia," *Trinity Journal* 1 (1980), pp. 7-8; Paton, *Esther,* p. 8.

[10]David M. Howard, Jr., *An Introduction to the Old Testament Historical Books* (Chicago: Moody Press, 1993), p. 325.

⁹Haman went out that day happy and in high spirits. But when he saw Mordecai at the king's gate and observed that he neither rose nor showed fear in his presence, he was filled with rage against Mordecai. ¹⁰Nevertheless, Haman restrained himself and went home.

Calling together his friends and Zeresh, his wife, ¹¹Haman boasted to them about his vast wealth, his many sons, and all the ways the king had honored him and how he had elevated him above the other nobles and officials. ¹²"And that's not all," Haman added. "I'm the only person Queen Esther invited to accompany the king to the banquet she gave. And she has invited me along with the king tomorrow. ¹³But all this gives me no satisfaction as long as I see that Jew Mordecai sitting at the king's gate."

¹⁴His wife Zeresh and all his friends said to him, "Have a gallows built, seventy-five feetª high, and ask the king in the morning to have Mordecai hanged on it. Then go with the king to the dinner and be happy." This suggestion delighted Haman, and he had the gallows built.

ª14 Hebrew *fifty cubits* (about 23 meters)

5:9-10a Leaving the palace Haman encounters Mordecai, who **neither rose nor showed fear in his presence**. Like Xerxes in 1:12, now Haman is angry.

5:10b-13 After Haman has returned home from the banquet, he calls together his friends and wife and boasts of his greatness. **"I'm the only person Queen Esther invited to accompany the king to the banquet she gave. And she has invited me along with the king tomorrow."** But he confesses that he can find no satisfaction (literally, "is not sufficient for me") as long as Mordecai remains alive. Haman's "hatred of the Jews in general and Mordecai in particular had so poisoned his system that he couldn't even enjoy talking about his greatness."¹¹

5:14 His confession is in reality a plea for counsel, an invitation for advice. Accordingly, Zeresh, his wife, and all his friends instruct him to **have a gallows built, seventy-five feet high, and ask the king**

---

¹¹Wiersbe, *Be Committed,* p. 124.

in the morning to have Mordecai hanged on it. These gallows are probably a stake on which a human body is impaled.

Haman's haste to follow the evil advice of both his wife and friends contrasts with the king's order at 1:22. "By commanding respect through the brute exercise of power, the king and Haman may be able to save face, but reality laughs behind their backs."[12]

"The king still does not know Mordecai saved his life; and now a gallows has been set up for Mordecai. Never have things looked worse!"[13] According to the advice, the death must be arranged **in the morning**, so that Haman can **go with the king to the dinner and be happy**. If the death is indeed arranged in the morning, then it will be too late to expect any intervention by Esther at the evening banquet!

The **gallows** (עֵץ, ʿēṣ, literally "wood, pole") were fifty cubits high, that is **seventy-five feet high**. This extravagant height is intended as a public humiliation of Mordecai, in that the body would be visible throughout all of Susa. A cubit was the length of the forearm from elbow to fingertip, approximately 18 inches.

Absolute power held by flawed leaders, such as Xerxes and Haman, is a terrifying scenario. Ancient history and today's newspaper headlines chronicle horrific reigns of terror. The spirit of Xerxes and Haman's dictatorial power either lived on or lives on in the leaders listed in this brief roll call of the nations: the Perons in Argentina, Milosevic in the Balkans, Gen. Than Shwe in Burma, Pol Pot in Cambodia, Pinochet in Chile, Chairman Mao and Deng Xiaoping in China, Castro in Cuba, Hitler in Germany, the Duvaliers in Haiti, Suharto in Indonesia, Khomeini in Iran, Hussein in Iraq, Mussolini in Italy, Qaddafi in Libya, Noriega in Panama, Marcos in the Philippines, Ceausescu in Romania, Stalin in Russia, Idi Amin in Uganda, and Mobutu in Zaire.

As we have all seen, horrific violence against humankind is not the exclusive domain of world leaders. George F. Will has written an article entitled "July 10, 1941, in Jedwabne" (*Newsweek*, July 9, 2001, p. 68). The opening sentences frame his comments. "Sixty years ago, on July 10, 1941, half the Polish town of Jedwabne murdered the

---

[12]Jobes, *Esther*, p. 146.
[13]Moore, *Esther*, p. 61.

other half. Of 1,600 Jews, about a dozen survived. Why did the murderers do it?"

Will concludes his essay by rephrasing the question and then answering it. "So, again: Why in Jedwabne did neighbors murder their neighbors? Because it was permitted. Because they could." Will's essay is a sickening reminder of the human condition severed from social restraints.

Genesis 6:5 explains the actions of Xerxes, Haman, and the neighbors at Jedwabne. "The LORD saw how great man's wickedness on the earth had become, and that every inclination of the thoughts of his heart was only evil all the time."

Haman is also characterized by pride, which he parades before his wife and friends in verses 11-12. He brags about his wealth, his position, and his family. Among the Persians, says Herodotus, "After prowess in fighting, the chief proof of manliness is to be the father of a large family of boys" (1.136). Haman has ten sons (9:7-10).

The book of Proverbs warns that pride foreshadows destruction. "The LORD detests all the proud of heart. Be sure of this: They will not go unpunished" (16:5). "Pride goes before destruction, a haughty spirit before a fall" (16:18).

ESTHER 6

IV. 'ON THAT NIGHT, THE KING COULD NOT SLEEP' (6:1)

[1]That night the king could not sleep; so he ordered the book of the chronicles, the record of his reign, to be brought in and read to him.

Of the forty-six occurrences of the Hebrew word מִשְׁתֶּה (mišteh) in the Hebrew Bible, translated in the NIV of Esther as "banquet" (1:3,5,9; 2:18 [twice]; 5:4,5,8,12; 6:14; 7:8), "feasting" (e.g., 8:17; 9:17,18,19,22), "drinking" (5:6; 7:2,7 [wine]), or "dinner" (5:14), twenty are in Esther. This fact suggests the importance of this concept for the book.

Eight banquets are celebrated throughout the book. The banquets are all paired, as the following diagram demonstrates.

A[1] Xerxes' banquet for the nobility of the empire (1:3,5-8)
A[2] Vashti's banquet for the women (1:9)

B[1] Esther's coronation banquet (2:18)
C[1] Esther's first banquet for the king and Haman (5:4-8)
C[2] Esther's second banquet for the king and Haman (7:1-9)
B[2] The Jews' feasting in celebration of Mordecai's promotion (8:17)

D[1] The first feast of Purim (9:17,19)
D[2] The second feast of Purim (9:18)

The first two feasts (A[1] and A[2]), which were hosted by royalty — Xerxes and Vashti, correspond to the final two (D[1] and D[2]), which celebrate the Jews' victory over the royal decree of Xerxes and Haman.

B[1] and B[2] celebrate the exaltation of Esther and Mordecai, the former to Queen, the latter to Prime Minister. These two feasts are separated in the text by C[1] and C[2]. The "C" feasts mark the climax of the story — the downfall of Haman.

Haman's downfall begins between the first and second of Esther's banquets (C[1] and C[2]) when the king has a sleepless night (6:1)!

The three pairs of feasts which are closely knit (A[1]/A[2], C[1]/C[2], and D[1]/D[2]) mark the beginning, the climax and conclusion of Esther's story.

The scene of highest narrative tension in the story of Esther comes during Esther's second banquet, when the Queen confronts Haman to his face. Notice, however, that the pivot point in the overall structure of the book — the king's insomnia — is not found in the scene of narrative climax. Jobes has noted the significance of this observation:

> By making the pivot point of the peripety an insignificant event rather than the point of highest dramatic tension, the author is taking the focus away from human action. Had the pivot point of the peripety been at the scene where Esther approaches the king uninvited or where Esther confronts Haman, the king and/or Esther would have been spotlighted as the actual cause of the reversal. By separating the pivot point of the peripety in Esther from the point of highest dramatic tension, the characters of the story are not spotlighted as the cause of the reversal. This reinforces the message that no one in the story, not even the most powerful person in the empire, is in control of what is about to happen. An unseen power is controlling the reversal of destiny.[1]

---

[1]Jobes, *Esther*, p. 158. Peripety is a sudden turn of events that reverses the expected or intended outcome. If the reader is familiar with the C.S. Lewis series *The Chronicles of Narnia*, then s/he knows how the plot in *The Horse and His Boy* is controlled by an unseen power — Aslan. Aslan, the lion, says to Shasta, the *boy* in the book's title, "I was the lion who forced you to join with Aravis. I was the cat who comforted you among the houses of the dead. I was the lion who drove out the jackals from you while you slept. I was the lion who gave the Horses the new strength of fear for the last mile so that you should reach King Lune in time. And I was the lion you do not remember who pushed the boat in which you lay, a child near death, so that it came to shore where a man sat, wakeful at midnight, to receive you" ([Harper Trophy, 1982], pp. 175-176).

6:1 What will become of Mordecai? His life is hanging in the balance. There appears to be no time for human initiatives to save Mordecai. Everything must be providential. The king's sleeplessness (v. 1), the finding of the passage about Mordecai's loyalty (v. 2), the fact that he had not already been rewarded (v. 3), and the arrival of Haman to give his advice (v. 4) all testify to God's providence.

Why does Xerxes have trouble sleeping? Did he eat too much at the queen's banquet? Was he preoccupied with the queen's request? Was it the cares of state? Or is this the hand of God? (cf. Dan 6:18). The Septuagint at 6:1 reads, "But the Lord removed sleep from the king that night."

Why does Xerxes decide to have a book read to him to deal with his insomnia? Could he not have called for a woman from his harem? Could he not have called for the court musicians?

Why does Xerxes ask for **the book of the chronicles, the record of his reign**? Did he not have other books at his disposal? And why was the volume that contained the record of Mordecai's service selected? This was five years ago. Certainly volumes of more recent events were available.

V. MORDECAI'S TRIUMPH OVER HAMAN (6:2–7:10)

A. THE KING IS REMINDED OF MORDECAI'S LOYALTY (6:2-4)

[2]**It was found recorded there that Mordecai had exposed Bigthana and Teresh, two of the king's officers who guarded the doorway, who had conspired to assassinate King Xerxes.**

[3]**"What honor and recognition has Mordecai received for this?" the king asked.**

"Nothing has been done for him," his attendants answered.

[4]**The king said, "Who is in the court?" Now Haman had just entered the outer court of the palace to speak to the king about hanging Mordecai on the gallows he had erected for him.**

6:2-3 Since Persian kings were known for their eagerness to reward well-wishers (Herodotus 3.138,140; 5.11; 8.85; 9.107), why was Mordecai's good deed written down but forgotten? "Did an office memo go astray? We don't know; but this we do know, that God was in charge and already had the day selected for Mordecai to be honored."[2]

6:4 The king wants to consult with any statesman he can find at this very early hour. And it just happens to be Haman! Haman has not slept all night either, seeing to the erection of the gallows. He has come to the palace to make sure he secures the first appointment with the king.

B. HAMAN IS FORCED TO HONOR MORDECAI (6:5-10)

[5]**His attendants answered, "Haman is standing in the court."**
"Bring him in," the king ordered.
[6]**When Haman entered, the king asked him, "What should be done for the man the king delights to honor?"**
Now Haman thought to himself, "Who is there that the king would rather honor than me?" [7]**So he answered the king, "For the man the king delights to honor,** [8]**have them bring a royal robe the king has worn and a horse the king has ridden, one with a royal crest placed on its head.** [9]**Then let the robe and horse be entrusted to one of the king's most noble princes. Let them robe the man the king delights to honor, and lead him on the horse through the city streets, proclaiming before him, 'This is what is done for the man the king delights to honor!'"**

[10]**"Go at once," the king commanded Haman. "Get the robe and the horse and do just as you have suggested for Mordecai the Jew, who sits at the king's gate. Do not neglect anything you have recommended."**

6:5-6a As usual the king must seek advice before he acts. So he asks Haman, **"What should be done for the man the king delights to honor?"**

6:6b-9 Since Esther, the queen, had honored Haman by inviting him to two very private dinner-parties, Haman presumes that now Xerxes, the king who had recently promoted him (3:1), seeks a way

---

[2]Wiersbe, *Be Committed,* p. 130.

to honor him.[3] So Haman asked for the very best! What he describes here sounds like a coronation. Perhaps Haman wanted to leave the impression that Xerxes had chosen him to be his successor.

What will become of such pride? If the book of Proverbs is considered, then Haman will surely be brought low. "When pride comes, then comes disgrace, but with humility comes wisdom" (11:2). "The LORD detests all the proud of heart. Be sure of this: They will not go unpunished" (16:5). "Pride goes before destruction, a haughty spirit before a fall" (16:18). "Before his downfall a man's heart is proud, but humility comes before honor" (18:12). "A man's pride brings him low, but a man of lowly spirit gains honor" (29:23).

6:10 Accordingly, what Haman intends to be a supreme honor for himself turns out to be his total humiliation! "The bitter irony of the complete reversal of Haman's fortunes is indicated by the way that the narrator now has the king for the first time designate Mordecai as 'Mordecai the Jew.'"[4]

Since the king does not know the identity of the people destined for destruction (3:8-11), there is no difficulty with the king seeking a way to honor Mordecai, **the Jew.**

C. HAMAN'S EMBARRASSMENT (6:11-14)

[11]**So Haman got the robe and the horse. He robed Mordecai, and led him on horseback through the city streets, proclaiming before him, "This is what is done for the man the king delights to honor!"**

[12]**Afterward Mordecai returned to the king's gate. But Haman rushed home, with his head covered in grief,** [13]**and told Zeresh his wife and all his friends everything that had happened to him.**

His advisers and his wife Zeresh said to him, "Since Mordecai, before whom your downfall has started, is of Jewish origin, you

---

[3]In verses 7-9 notice the absence of the formula 'if it please the king.' This absence speaks of Haman's preoccupation with his future honor. Haman is so eager to answer the king that he begins with what is foremost in his thoughts, "the man whom the king wishes to honor." Then he begins again to describe the honor he wishes to have.

[4]Bush, *Ruth, Esther*, p. 420.

**cannot stand against him—you will surely come to ruin!" [14]While
they were still talking with him, the king's eunuchs arrived and
hurried Haman away to the banquet Esther had prepared.**

6:11 What delicious irony! The thing that Mordecai would not
do for Haman — bow down — Haman had to tell others to do for
Mordecai. God's wisdom again sheds light on this episode: "Evil
men will bow down in the presence of the good, and the wicked at
the gates of the righteous" (Prov 14:19).

6:12 When the pageantry is over, Mordecai returns to his position: **afterward Mordecai returned to the king's gate.** But Haman
returns home, his head covered as if he were grieving for the dead.
This had been the way Mordecai had responded to the king's edict
concerning the Jews (4:1-2). Again, notice the irony! "Haman adopts
Mordecai's garb while Mordecai is clothed in the garment Haman
had coveted for himself."[5]

6:13-14 Haman's advisers and his wife see in the events of the
day a foreshadowing of Haman's further failure, for they say, **"Since
Mordecai, before whom your downfall has started, is of Jewish origin, you cannot stand against him—you will surely come to ruin!"**
(cf. Exod 17:16; Num 24:20; Deut 25:17-19; 1 Sam 15:2; 2 Sam
1:8,13-16).

Haman had wanted to go to the queen's banquet in high spirits.
But now he leaves for the banquet humiliated and uncertain.

In the book of Exodus we encounter the miraculous and visible
power of the LORD. He appeared before Moses as flames of fire
from within a bush, and yet the bush was not consumed. Through a
series of devastating plagues, He overpowered Egypt's pantheon
and pharaoh. He parted the waters of the sea, and the Israelites
went through on dry ground. He providentially provided water and
food for an entire generation wandering through an inhospitable
wasteland.

But in the book of Esther God works without miracles through
seemingly insignificant events and through the decisions of flawed
people. "God delivered an entire race of people in Persia because

---

[5]Clines, *Ezra, Nehemiah, Esther,* p. 309.

the king had a sleepless night, because a man would not bow to his superior, because a woman found herself taken to the bedroom of a ruthless man for a night of pleasure. How inscrutable are the ways of the Lord!"[6]

---

[6]Jobes, *Esther,* p. 160. Fox adds, "Esther becomes a sort of judge (of the type we see in the book of Judges) without benefit of the Spirit of the Lord. She is a leader whose charisma comes not in a sudden divine imposition of spirit but as the result of a difficult process of inner development and self-realization. . . . In Esther, not miracles, but inner resources — intellectual as well as spiritual — even of people not naturally leaders, are to be relied upon in crisis" (*Character,* p. 205).

ESTHER 7

D. ESTHER PLEADS FOR THE LIFE OF HER PEOPLE AND HERSELF (7:1-4)

[1]So the king and Haman went to dine with Queen Esther, [2]and as they were drinking wine on that second day, the king again asked, "Queen Esther, what is your petition? It will be given you. What is your request? Even up to half the kingdom, it will be granted."

[3]Then Queen Esther answered, "If I have found favor with you, O king, and if it pleases your majesty, grant me my life—this is my petition. And spare my people—this is my request. [4]For I and my people have been sold for destruction and slaughter and annihilation. If we had merely been sold as male and female slaves, I would have kept quiet, because no such distress would justify disturbing the king.[a]"

[a]4 Or *quiet, but the compensation our adversary offers cannot be compared with the loss the king would suffer*

7:1-2 When the wine is served, the king broaches the subject of Esther's petition. In verse 2 the king uses the same language he used at 5:6, with the exception that now he adds **Queen Esther**, perhaps expressing respect and goodwill towards her.

7:3 She begins politely, **"If I have found favor with you, O king, and if it pleases your majesty . . . ."** She then focuses her petition on the danger she and her people are in and how the king must do something about it. "Paradoxically, in the moment when she pleads for her own safety she puts herself in greater danger by revealing her Jewishness."[1] If Xerxes loves his queen, he would not want any harm to befall her. A loving husband would surely intercede to save his wife.

---

[1]Clines, *Ezra, Nehemiah, Esther,* p. 311.

7:4 Esther emphasizes the murderous intention of the plot by suggesting that if she and her people had merely been sold into slavery, that would have occasioned no protest. Slavery is one thing, but genocide is entirely different.

E. HAMAN'S TREACHERY EXPOSED (7:5-10)

⁵King Xerxes asked Queen Esther, "Who is he? Where is the man who has dared to do such a thing?"

⁶Esther said, "The adversary and enemy is this vile Haman."

Then Haman was terrified before the king and queen. ⁷The king got up in a rage, left his wine and went out into the palace garden. But Haman, realizing that the king had already decided his fate, stayed behind to beg Queen Esther for his life. ⁸Just as the king returned from the palace garden to the banquet hall, Haman was falling on the couch where Esther was reclining.

The king exclaimed, "Will he even molest the queen while she is with me in the house?"

As soon as the word left the king's mouth, they covered Haman's face. ⁹Then Harbona, one of the eunuchs attending the king, said, "A gallows seventy-five feetª high stands by Haman's house. He had it made for Mordecai, who spoke up to help the king."

The king said, "Hang him on it!" ¹⁰So they hanged Haman on the gallows he had prepared for Mordecai. Then the king's fury subsided.

ª9 Hebrew *fifty cubits* (about 23 meters)

7:5-6a In verse 4 Esther revealed that she had "been sold for destruction and slaughter and annihilation." Now in verse 5 the king asks, **"Where is the man who has dared to do such a thing?"** In reality, it is the king himself who has sold Esther and her people; Haman simply bought them. The threat against Esther and her people has two perpetrators, Haman and the king. Esther must expose the guilt of Haman, while never appearing to bring any charge against the king. So, she says, **"The adversary and enemy is this vile Haman."**

"The plot on the life of the king was foiled by one Jew, Mordecai; the plot on the life of the queen by another Jew, Esther."[2]

7:6b-7a When Haman is unmasked, the king is enraged. A king's anger is not a good thing. Just ask Vashti! "A king's wrath is a messenger of death, but a wise man will appease it" (Prov 16:14). "A king's wrath is like the roar of a lion; he who angers him forfeits his life" (Prov 20:2).

7:7b Since Haman knows the king well enough to interpret his expressions and his moods, he senses that the king had already decided his fate. What the NIV translates as **realizing that the king had already decided his fate** is literally, "for he saw that evil was determined for him." When the Hebrew letters for this are observed, an interesting pattern develops. The letters are: כי ראה כי כלתה אליו הרעה (*ky r'h ky klth 'lyw hr'h*). The final letters of each word yield *YH YHWH*, the divine names Yah, Yahweh (LORD). "The acrostic is like a great shout of triumph because the enemy is now doomed."[3]

Why does the king withdraw to the garden? Does he go to calm his rage? Does he withdraw to find the courtiers whose advice he has always depended upon (1:13-15; 2:2-4; 6:3-6)? Does he depart because he is at a loss to know what to do?

The text does not explain the king's behavior. But his absence will allow Haman to add insult to injury — securing his final defeat!

7:8 What options were available to Haman? Should he follow the king? The king's anger makes that option seem unlikely. Should he flee the room? Flight would leave the impression of guilt. Should he stay with Esther? Protocol dictated that no one but the king could be left alone with a woman of the harem. Haman was trapped. Hindsight suggests he should have left Esther's presence!

Sensing that his only hope now is the mercy of the queen, Haman falls at the feet of Esther.[4]

---

[2]Clines, *Ezra, Nehemiah, Esther*, pp. 311-312.

[3]G. Herbert Livingston, "Esther," in *Asbury Bible Commentary*, ed. Eugene E. Carpenter (Grand Rapids: Zondervan, 1992), p. 479. Paton notes that in three Hebrew manuscripts these final letters are written larger than the other letters, as we have done here (*Esther*, p. 8).

[4]Haman's malice against the Jews is triggered by Mordecai's refusal to bow before him (3:5). Ironically, it is now Haman who must bow on his

Here is Haman who that morning expected to slay the Jew who had not bowed before him, fallen on the ground before the Jewess to beg for his life. Here is Esther, one moment pleading for her own life, the next importuned by Haman for his. Here is Esther who recognizes that her fate is identical with that of her people, and Haman, whose professed anxiety for the security of the empire (3:8) has been completely eclipsed by his own personal danger.[5]

In approaching Esther while she reclines, Haman violates court etiquette, which dictates that a man should not approach a woman of the king's harem closer than seven steps.[6] **Falling on the couch where Esther was reclining** surely sealed his execution, and allows the king to save face. Could the king punish Haman for a plot to which he gave full concurrence? Could the king punish Haman for an edict that went out in his name? Hardly! When the king returns to find Haman falling on the couch, providence resolves the king's dilemma.

It simply strains credulity to believe that he actually thought that Haman under these circumstances was really attempting to assault the queen. Rather, he chooses so to interpret Haman's action, thereby providing a charge with which to condemn him that relieves the king from raising publicly the true reason for the condemnation, the plot against the Jews. Thus, in keeping with the irresponsibility that has consistently marked Ahasuerus' character, he can leave hidden and unexamined his own complicity in the matter.[7]

7:9 Harbona suggests an appropriate way to execute Haman, **"A gallows seventy-five feet high stands by Haman's house."** Harbona's words have the effect of introducing a second accusation against Haman — he had intended to kill a benefactor of the king, namely

---

knees before a Jew — Esther. For an informative study of irony in Esther, consult, Stan Goldman, "Narrative and Ethical Ironies in Esther," *JSOT* 47 (1990): 15-31. Edwin M. Good, (*Irony in the Old Testament* [Sheffield: Almond Press, 1981]) deals with irony in Jonah, 1 Samuel, Genesis, Isaiah, Ecclesiastes, and Job.

[5]Clines, *Ezra, Nehemiah, Esther,* p. 312.
[6]Yamauchi, *Persia,* p. 262.
[7]Bush, *Ruth, Esther,* p. 433.

Mordecai (**who spoke up to help the king**). "The last hanging on gallows, or rather, impalement on a stake, in the story was the fate of the conspirators against the king; the story neatly folds back upon itself by making this impalement that of the man who plots both against the queen and against the man who saved the king from the earlier conspiracy."[8]

The shame foreseen in 6:12-13 is complete, as now **they covered Haman's face**.

7:10 Haman is executed on the gallows he had intended for Mordecai. This is irony! Haman is executed for a crime he did not commit. This is irony upon irony!

The death of Haman is in keeping with the proverbial principle that the evil will be punished by the work of their own hands. Proverbs 26:27 states: "If a man digs a pit, he will fall into it; if a man rolls a stone, it will roll back on him." Likewise, Proverbs 21:7 reads: "The violence of the wicked will drag them away, for they refuse to do what is right." The prophet Obadiah adds: "As you have done, it will be done to you; your deeds will return upon your own head" (15b).

Josephus also sees this point. "And from hence I cannot forbear to admire God, and to learn hence his wisdom and justice, not only in punishing the wickedness of Haman, but in so disposing it, that he should undergo the very same punishment which he had contrived for another; as also, because thereby he teaches others this lesson, *that which mischiefs any one prepares against another, he without knowing of it, first contrives it against himself.*"[9]

Even though Haman was executed for crimes he did not actually commit (he was not molesting the queen), do not feel any sympathy for Haman. The author does not invite us to feel for this fallen villain. Haman did get what he deserved.

In this chapter Esther is in such control of the situation that she never had to explicitly mention that she is a Jew! Throughout both banquets her confident display of wisdom shows her the superior of both the king and her people's archenemy.

---

[8]Clines, *Ezra, Nehemiah, Esther*, p. 313.

[9]Josephus, *Antiquities of the Jews*, trans. W. Whiston (Grand Rapids: Kregel, 1960), p. 241.

Writing of the importance of irony in the book of Esther, John Walton opines, "It demonstrates that there is always more going on than meets the eye, and more possibilities available than any single person understands or is aware of. God's control cannot be calculated, God's solution cannot be anticipated, and God's plan cannot be thwarted, because no one has all the necessary information."[10]

God's control cannot be calculated. Paul teaches that in all things God works for the good of those who love him (Rom 8:28). This divine working is a manifestation of his love for us. God's control in all situations (Ps 135:6) is certainly beyond human calculations because we are unable to plumb the depths of God's love for his own. Paul himself struggles to find words adequate to express the measure of God's love for us. "For I am convinced that neither death nor life, neither angels nor demons, neither the present nor the future, nor any powers, neither height nor depth, nor anything else in all creation, will be able to separate us from the love of God that is in Christ Jesus our Lord" (Rom 8:38-39).

The psalmists also struggled to define the extent of God's love for his own. "For as high as the heavens are above the earth, so great is his love for those who fear him; as far as the east is from the west, so far has he removed our transgressions from us" (Ps 103:11-12). "Many, O LORD my God, are the wonders you have done. The things you planned for us no one can recount to you; were I to speak and tell of them, they would be too many to declare" (Ps 40:5).

God's solution cannot be anticipated. Because of God's love for his covenant people, we knew that somehow Haman would be defeated. And because God governs the universe justly, we knew that Haman would be condemned. But how?

David says at Psalm 21:8,11-12, "Your hand will lay hold on all your enemies; your right hand will seize your foes. . . . Though they plot evil against you and devise wicked schemes, they cannot succeed; for you will make them turn their backs when you aim at them with drawn bow." But how would God lay hold of Haman?

At the close of chapter 5, Haman "was on top of the world, with

---

[10]Andrew E. Hill and John H. Walton, *A Survey of the Old Testament* (Grand Rapids: Zondervan, 1991), p. 242.

[11]Jobes, *Esther,* p. 171.

all the wealth and power that attends high political rank."[11] The next day, he is executed in disgrace. How did God do it?

God's plan cannot be thwarted. Haman was delighted with the suggestion to hang Mordecai on a tree (gallows). Satan was elated that the Son of God was crucified on a tree (cross). Would evil overpower good? Would God lose to the Evil One? Would the plan and promise of salvation be aborted? No! In time Haman was hanged on the gallows he had prepared for Mordecai. On the third day after the crucifixion, Jesus was raised to life, overcoming the power of both death (1 Cor 15:54-57) and Satan (Gen 3:15). God's plan cannot be thwarted!

ESTHER 8

VI. THE KING'S SECOND DECREE (8:1-9:32)

A. MORDECAI IS HONORED (8:1-2)

¹That same day King Xerxes gave Queen Esther the estate of Haman, the enemy of the Jews. And Mordecai came into the presence of the king, for Esther had told how he was related to her. ²The king took off his signet ring, which he had reclaimed from Haman, and presented it to Mordecai. And Esther appointed him over Haman's estate.

8:1-2 The property of Haman reverts to the crown (cf. Herodotus 3.128-129; *Antiquities* 11.17). Xerxes then gives the estate to Esther, as a way of compensation for her suffering, who, in turn, appoints Mordecai to manage it. ("A good man leaves an inheritance for his children's children, but a sinner's wealth is stored up for the righteous" [Prov 13:22].) The king also promotes Mordecai to prime minister, the position that Haman once had. The fall of Haman, both personally and officially, has now been totally balanced by the rise of Mordecai ("Humble yourselves, therefore, under God's mighty hand, that he may lift you up in due time" [1 Pet 5:6]). Mordecai now has wealth commensurate with his new position. **Came into the king's presence** means that Mordecai now has the status of those who had access to the king without being explicitly summoned (cf. 1:14; 6:4). With Haman the **signet ring** had the power of death (3:10-11); would the same ring on the hand of Mordecai have the power of life?

B. THE PLOT TO DESTROY THE JEWS IS STILL IN FORCE (8:3-8)

[3]Esther again pleaded with the king, falling at his feet and weeping. She begged him to put an end to the evil plan of Haman the Agagite, which he had devised against the Jews. [4]Then the king extended the gold scepter to Esther and she arose and stood before him.

[5]"If it pleases the king," she said, "and if he regards me with favor and thinks it the right thing to do, and if he is pleased with me, let an order be written overruling the dispatches that Haman son of Hammedatha, the Agagite, devised and wrote to destroy the Jews in all the king's provinces. [6]For how can I bear to see disaster fall on my people? How can I bear to see the destruction of my family?"

[7]King Xerxes replied to Queen Esther and to Mordecai the Jew, "Because Haman attacked the Jews, I have given his estate to Esther, and they have hanged him on the gallows. [8]Now write another decree in the king's name in behalf of the Jews as seems best to you, and seal it with the king's signet ring—for no document written in the king's name and sealed with his ring can be revoked."

8:3-4 Haman may be dead, but his murderous edict still threatens to destroy the Jews. Esther and Mordecai face a seemingly impossible task — find a way to revoke an irrevocable decree.

8:5-6 Since no one, not even the king himself, has the power to reverse the unalterable laws of Persia and Media, a second decree has to be issued which in effect would override the first one. This was Esther's request. **"Let an order be written overruling the dispatches that Haman son of Hammedatha, the Agagite, devised and wrote to destroy the Jews in all the king's provinces."**

8:7-8a Citing what he has already done for the Jews — **"Because Haman attacked the Jews, I have given his estate to Esther, and they have hanged him on the gallows"** — showing he is kindly disposed towards them, Xerxes adds, **"Now write another decree in the king's name in behalf of the Jews as seems best to you."** The king clearly and emphatically empowers queen and prime minister together to draft their own decree, to render the edict of Haman harmless. Xerxes has done what he can; the rest is now up to Esther and Mordecai.

Again notice how careful Esther is in crafting her request. First, she multiplies the phrases of courtly politeness: **If it pleases the king, if he regards me with favor, and thinks it the right thing to do**, and **if he is pleased with me**. Second, she focuses the blame upon Haman for the planned pogrom against the Jews — **the dispatches that Haman . . . devised and wrote to destroy the Jews**.

In the end Esther makes it an issue of whether the king will spare her suffering or not. **"How can I bear to see disaster fall on my people?"**

In verse 7 the NIV has translated, **Because Haman** *attacked* **the Jews**. A better translation is "For scheming against the Jews."[1]

C. A COUNTEREDICT IS ISSUED (8:9-14)

[9]**At once the royal secretaries were summoned—on the twenty-third day of the third month, the month of Sivan. They wrote out all Mordecai's orders to the Jews, and to the satraps, governors and nobles of the 127 provinces stretching from India to Cush.**[a] **These orders were written in the script of each province and the language of each people and also to the Jews in their own script and language.** [10]**Mordecai wrote in the name of King Xerxes, sealed the dispatches with the king's signet ring, and sent them by mounted couriers, who rode fast horses especially bred for the king.**

[11]**The king's edict granted the Jews in every city the right to assemble and protect themselves; to destroy, kill and annihilate any armed force of any nationality or province that might attack them and their women and children; and to plunder the property of their enemies.** [12]**The day appointed for the Jews to do this in all the provinces of King Xerxes was the thirteenth day of the twelfth**

---

[1]Hayim Tawil, "Two Notes on the Treaty Terminology of the Sefire Inscriptions," *CBQ* 42 (1980): 36. The NRSV reads, "because he plotted to lay hands on the Jews."

month, the month of Adar. [13]A copy of the text of the edict was to
be issued as law in every province and made known to the people
of every nationality so that the Jews would be ready on that day to
avenge themselves on their enemies.

[14]The couriers, riding the royal horses, raced out, spurred on
by the king's command. And the edict was also issued in the
citadel of Susa.

[a]9 That is, the uppoer Nile region

The report of Mordecai's counterdecree in verses 9-16 is virtually identical with the report of Haman's decree in 3:12-15. This is evident from a verse-by-verse comparison of the two accounts. The *plus-
es* in 8:9-16 are marked by italicized type.

3:12 Then were the king's scribes called in the first month, on the thirteenth day thereof,	8:9 Then were the king's scribes called *at that time*, in the third month, which is *the month Sivan*, on the twenty-third day thereof;
and there was written, according to all that Haman commanded, unto the king's satraps, and to the governors that were over every province, and to the princes of every people;	and there was written, according to all that Mordecai commanded, *unto the Jews*, even to the satraps, and the governors and princes of the provinces *which are from India unto Ethiopia, one hundred twenty-seven provinces*
to every province according to the writing thereof, and to every people after their language;	to every province according to the writing thereof, and to every people after their language, *and to the Jews according to their writing, and according to their language.*
in the name of king Ahasuerus was it written, and it was sealed with the king's ring.	10 And it was written in the name of king Ahasuerus, and it was sealed with the king's ring,
13 And letters were sent by couriers into all the king's provinces,	and sent letters by couriers on horseback, riding on swift steeds that were used in the king's service, bred of the stud; 11 *that the king had granted the Jews that were in every city to gather themselves together, and to stand for their life,*
to destroy, to slay, and to cause to perish,	to destroy, and to slay, and to cause to perish,

all Jews, both young and old, little children and women [included],	all the forces of the people and province that would assault them, little children and women [included]; and to take the spoil of them for a prey
in one day, even upon the thirteenth day of the twelfth month, which is the month Adar,	12 in one day *in all the provinces of king Ahasuerus*, namely, upon the thirteenth day of the twelfth month, which is the month Adar.
and to take the spoil of them for a prey. 14 The copy of the writing, to be given out for a decree in every province, was to be published unto all the peoples, that they should be ready for this day.	13 The copy of the writing, to be given out for a decree in every province, was to be published unto all the peoples, and that the Jews should be ready for this day *to avenge themselves on their enemies.*
15 The couriers went forth in haste by the king's commandment, and the decree was given out in the citadel of Susa;	14 So the couriers *that rode upon swift steeds that were used in the king's service* went out, *being hastened and pressed on by the king's commandment; and the decree was given out in the citadel of Susa.
and the king and Haman sat down to drink; but the city of Susa was perplexed.	15 And Mordecai went forth from the presence of the king in royal apparel of blue and white, and with a great crown of gold, and with a robe of fine linen and purple; and the city of Susa shouted and was glad. 16 *The Jews had light and gladness, and joy and honor.*

8:9 The first people now addressed is the Jews. They now stand before **the satraps, governors and nobles**, suggesting that they rank before these three administrative officials. Equally important is the last clause of the verse. Here the Jews are given equal status with **each province** and **each people**.

8:10 Mordecai takes responsibility for drawing up the edict that the royal secretaries translate into all the languages of the realm, including Hebrew. This new edict was then delivered by royal mail. Mordecai's letter goes out two months and ten days after Haman's

(3:12). "The seventy days between the threatened annihilation of the Jews and their release from danger will have struck a chord with every attentive post-exilic reader of the book: the seventy days are (are they not?) the seventy years of exile."[2] The seventy days become a signal that a reversal of their circumstances was as certain as the earlier return from exile.

In Haman's edict couriers went forth with the threatening news. Now the couriers are riding swift and royal mounts, emphasizing "both the speed and authority with which the edict in favor of the Jews is disseminated."[3]

8:11-13 This new edict grants the Jews first, **the right to assemble**, presumably to make plans and preparations, and second, to **protect themselves**.

The edict allows the Jews the specific right to defend themselves against those **that might attack them**. It is in this sense that we must understand the Jews taking **vengeance on their enemies** (v. 13).

Finally, while the king and Haman sat down to drink (3:15), Mordecai "put on sackcloth and ashes, and went out into the city, wailing loudly and bitterly" (4:1). In 8:15 Mordecai leaves the presence of the king wearing royal garments. Chapter 8 began with Esther "weeping," but ends with the Jews enjoying a time of "happiness and joy, gladness and honor" (v. 16).

"All of this," writes Bush, "powerfully and expressively portrays the utter reversal of Haman's edict by skillfully capturing the radically changed position of power and authority that Mordecai's edict has accorded the Jews throughout the empire of Ahasuerus."[4]

The mention of **women and children** in verse 11 has engendered a lively discussion. Does this verse give the Jews the right to **destroy, kill and annihilate** the women and children of their enemies? This view is seen in the NRSV translation: "to destroy, to kill, and to annihilate any armed force of any people or province that might attack them, with their children and women." In other words, the Jews were given exactly the same terms of destruction that had been pronounced against them, their women and their children (cf. 1 Sam

---

[2]Clines, *Ezra, Nehemiah, Esther,* p. 316.
[3]Bush, *Ruth, Esther,* p. 453.
[4]Ibid.

15:2-3). Or are the women and children objects of the participle "attacking"? The NIV translation has adopted this second possibility: "**to destroy, kill and annihilate any armed force of any nationality or province that might attack them** [Jewish adult males] **and their women and children.**"[5]

Many will object to the former possibility on ethical grounds. The debate is moot, however, since the ensuing text expressly says that the Jews only put to death men (9:6,12,15). There is no mention of the annihilation of women and children.

If the decree indeed gave the Jews permission to kill the women and children of their enemies, but it was not carried out, we are still left with the deaths of Persian men. Are not their deaths morally offensive? It must be remembered that the decree empowered the Jews to defend themselves against attackers. In other words, the Jews were defending themselves.

D. THE SALVATION OF THE JEWS
BRINGS JOY TO THE NATION (8:15-17)

[15]**Mordecai left the king's presence wearing royal garments of blue and white, a large crown of gold and a purple robe of fine linen. And the city of Susa held a joyous celebration.** [16]**For the Jews it was a time of happiness and joy, gladness and honor.** [17]**In every province and in every city, wherever the edict of the king went, there was joy and gladness among the Jews, with feasting and celebrating. And many people of other nationalities became Jews because fear of the Jews had seized them.**

8:15-16 The Jews responded to Haman's edict with mourning, fasting, weeping, and wailing (4:3). Now the Jews respond with **hap-**

---

[5]Robert Gordis has argued for the following translation: "By these letters the king permitted the Jews in every city to gather and defend themselves, to destroy, kill, and wipe out every armed force of a people or a province attacking 'them, their children and their wives, with their goods as booty.'" In this translation the last five words in the Hebrew text of 8:11 are not a paraphrase of 3:13, giving the Jews permission to retaliate in precisely the manner planned by Haman, but a citation of Haman's original edict, against which his intended victims may now protect themselves. See "Studies in the Esther Narrative," *JBL* 95 (1976): 49-53.

piness and joy, gladness and honor. "Happiness" is literally "light," a metaphor for prosperity and well-being (Ps 36:9; 97:11). "Joy" and "gladness" describe the consequent emotional state. "Honor" describes the esteem in which they are now held.

The Gentile populace of Susa reacted to Haman's edict with bewilderment. Now the city responds with a "joyous celebration." Proverbs 11:10 promises: "When the righteous prosper, the city rejoices; when the wicked perish, there are shouts of joy."

8:17 The verb **became Jews** occurs only here in the Old Testament. Does the verb mean that Gentiles adopted Jewish beliefs, customs, and practices? (The Greek version claims they were circumcised.) Or does it imply nothing more than that the Gentiles were favorably disposed toward the Jews? How ironic that those Haman sought to set against the Jews now actually join them!

The reason for the change is stated as **fear of the Jews**. What is the nature of this fear? Is it a dread of the political and military power now wielded by Mordecai and the Jewish community?[6] Does the author, who has steered clear of direct reference to deity, really mean a religious awe of the God of the Jews, parallel with Joshua 2:9; Exodus 15:16; Psalm 105:38?

The unmasking of Haman as the villain in chapter 7 is at the same time the unmasking of Esther. There "she accepts her Jewish identity before the king, her husband. Having risen to the occasion with heroic courage, Esther masterfully controls the destiny of her nation in the concluding phases of the story."[7]

Here in chapter 8 Esther again appears (uninvited) before the king. She pleads with the king "to put an end to the evil plan of Haman." As the story unfolds, the only solution is to write another decree to counteract Haman's decree. And so she and Mordecai do so.

---

[6]Bush writes, "The enemies of the Jews might have been aware of an unnamed power ranged on the side of the Jews, but in the context it can hardly be some sense of the numinous that prompts the non-Jewish peoples to profess to be Jews, let alone a religious awe of the God of the Jews. It is surely, rather, the dread of the superior political and military power now wielded by Mordecai and the Jewish community that prompts their profession" (*Ruth, Esther*, p. 449).

[7]Leland Ryken, *Words of Delight*, 2nd. ed. (Grand Rapids: Baker, 1992), p. 119.

Since Mordecai is now the prime minister, this chapter focuses on his role in drafting this new edict. In fact, the name of Esther is absent from 8:8 to 9:11.

"Esther masterfully controls the destiny of her nation." "This chapter," chapter 8, "focuses on his [Mordecai's] role in drafting this new edict." But what about the main character in the drama? Where is God?

Mordecai's decree permitted the Jews the right to defend themselves against attackers. Chapter 9 reveals that God did defend his people from the attackers. And if the attackers do lose their lives, as chapter 9 will make clear, their deaths are evidence of God's judgment upon sin and evil. Even in the action that follows the scene of highest narrative tension (ch. 7), God is ever present!

ESTHER 9

E. THE JEWS TRIUMPH OVER THEIR ENEMIES (9:1-5)

¹On the thirteenth day of the twelfth month, the month of Adar, the edict commanded by the king was to be carried out. On this day the enemies of the Jews had hoped to overpower them, but now the tables were turned and the Jews got the upper hand over those who hated them. ²The Jews assembled in their cities in all the provinces of King Xerxes to attack those seeking their destruction. No one could stand against them, because the people of all the other nationalities were afraid of them. ³And all the nobles of the provinces, the satraps, the governors and the king's administrators helped the Jews, because fear of Mordecai had seized them. ⁴Mordecai was prominent in the palace; his reputation spread throughout the provinces, and he became more and more powerful.

⁵The Jews struck down all their enemies with the sword, killing and destroying them, and they did what they pleased to those who hated them.

9:1 Mordecai's counterdecree had gone forth in late-May, early-June, 474 B.C., and so the Jews had nine months to prepare for this historic day in early March, 473 B.C. On this day the Jews, instead of being the victims, became the victors. **The tables were turned** is literally "it was changed." Changed by whom? The author again declines a reference to deity's providence (cf. 4:3,14,16; 6:1). *Targum Rishon* adds, "It was reversed from Heaven for the sake of the merit of their ancestors."

9:2-3 The king, to say nothing of Mordecai, his Prime Minister, now favors the Jews. The highest authorities also **helped the Jews**. It is in their best interests to ingratiate themselves with Mordecai if they are to remain in office. To have attacked the Jews would have brought wrath upon them sooner or later. Verse 3 mentions that the **king's administrators** also side with the Jews. These are the very officials who deposited Haman's bribe in the king's treasury (3:9)!

9:4 A supernatural influence can be the only explanation for the increasing popularity of Mordecai.

9:5 The decree of Haman called for the enemies of the Jews "to destroy, kill and annihilate" (וּלְאַבֵּד לַהֲרֹג לְהַשְׁמִיד, *l°hašmîd lahărōg ûl°ʾabbēd*). Instead **the Jews struck all their enemies with sword-blow, slaughter, and destruction** (וְאַבְדָן וְהֶרֶג מַכַּת־חֶרֶב, *makkath-ḥereb w°hereg w°ʾab°don*). In Hebrew the noun "slaughter" is related to the verb "to kill." Likewise, the noun "destruction" is related to the verb "to annihilate." The tables were indeed turned!

To be able to do as one pleases is a sign of imperial favor in 1:8.

F. THE JEWS' ENEMIES IN SUSA ARE DESTROYED (9:6-10)

⁶**In the citadel of Susa, the Jews killed and destroyed five hundred men. ⁷They also killed Parshandatha, Dalphon, Aspatha, ⁸Poratha, Adalia, Aridatha, ⁹Parmashta, Arisai, Aridai and Vaizatha, ¹⁰the ten sons of Haman son of Hammedatha, the enemy of the Jews. But they did not lay their hands on the plunder.**

9:6-10a Verse 5 spoke in general terms: "The Jews struck down all their enemies." Verses 6-10 speak specifically about what transpired in Susa, namely the Jews killed **five hundred men** and the **ten sons of Haman.**

Presumably the sons of Haman perpetuated their father's hostility, all the more so since they had lost their inheritance (8:1)!

9:10b The Jews **did not lay their hands on the plunder.** This note is repeated at verses 15 and 16, perhaps suggesting that the slaughter was self-preservation and not self-aggrandisement. "The deliberate decision not to enrich themselves at the expense of their enemies would not go unnoticed in a culture where victors were expected to take the spoil. The very novelty of such self-denial would be remarked upon and remembered, and taken as proof of the upright motives of the Jewish communities."[1]

When Saul and his army plundered Agag and the Amalekites, the LORD rejected him as king over Israel. Here the curse upon Saul is reversed, for the Jews do not plunder the Persians, though they had been given permission to do so (8:11).[2] Mordecai's decree included the permission to plunder because he was reversing the exact terms of Haman's decree. "However, unlike the Agagite's intent, the Jews understood the execution of Mordecai's decree as governed by the ancient command of holy war against the Amalekites."[3] There was to be no personal profit in holy war (Josh 7:11-12; 1 Sam 15:18-19). God's people were acting not for personal gain but as agents of God's wrath.

In Hebrew manuscripts of Esther, the names of Haman's sons are written in one column on the right-hand side of the page and the word "and" plus the sign of the definite direct object in a second column on the left-hand side of the page, thus:

וְאֵת	פַּרְשַׁנְדָּתָא
וְאֵת	דַּלְפוֹן
וְאֵת	אַסְפָּתָא
וְאֵת	. . .

This may be derived from the tradition that the ten sons were hanged on a tall gallows, one above the other. Additionally, the empty space between the two columns reminds the reader that there is no resurrection for the sons of Haman.[4] It is a Jewish custom, to this very day, that when the Scroll of Esther is recited in the synagogue, the names of the ten Hamanides must be read in a single breath, suggesting utter contempt.[5]

Yamauchi has suggested that the names of Haman's sons can be analyzed as *daiva* names. The word *daiva*, which meant god in early

---

[1]Baldwin, *Esther*, p. 105.

[2]W. McKane, "A Note on Esther IX and I Samuel XV," *JTS* 12 (1961): 260-261.

[3]Jobes, *Esther*, p. 196.

[4]Moore, *Esther*, p. 87; Goldman, "Esther," p. 236.

[5]Yehuda T. Radday, "Humour in Names," in *On Humour and the Comic in the Hebrew Bible*, eds. Yehuda T. Radday and Athalya Brenner (Sheffield: Almond Press, 1990), p. 72.

Iranian and Hindu texts, came to mean demon in Zoroastrian texts.[6] Do these names reflect Haman's allegiance to the demonic powers of evil?

G. FURTHER DEFENSE NECESSARY IN SUSA (9:11-15)

[11]**The number of those slain in the citadel of Susa was reported to the king that same day. [12]The king said to Queen Esther, "The Jews have killed and destroyed five hundred men and the ten sons of Haman in the citadel of Susa. What have they done in the rest of the king's provinces? Now what is your petition? It will be given you. What is your request? It will also be granted."**

[13]**"If it pleases the king," Esther answered, "give the Jews in Susa permission to carry out this day's edict tomorrow also, and let Haman's ten sons be hanged on gallows."**

[14]**So the king commanded that this be done. An edict was issued in Susa, and they hanged the ten sons of Haman. [15]The Jews in Susa came together on the fourteenth day of the month of Adar, and they put to death in Susa three hundred men, but they did not lay their hands on the plunder.**

9:11-12 What is the exact force of the king's question, "**What have they done in the rest of the king's provinces?**" Perhaps it is astonishment, prompted by his calculation of the extent of the slaughter throughout the whole empire. Perhaps it is admiration. The king seems impressed by the death toll.

9:13 Esther proved to be a careful strategist. She sought the king's permission for a second day of self-defense. She petitioned the king to allow the Jews to do on a second day only what was allowed by his previous decree (**give the Jews in Susa permission to carry out this day's edict tomorrow also**). **If it pleases the king** recalls 5:4 "and serves as an inclusio for the whole series of episodes hinging on the king's good will."[7]

---

[6]Yamauchi, *Persia*, pp. 237-238.
[7]Moore, *Esther*, p. 88.

9:14 According to 9:10 the sons of Haman had already been killed. The purpose of hanging their dead bodies on the gallows was "to warn the enemies of the Jews of the utter futility of attacking a people whose providential protection was already proverbial in Persia (cf. 6:13). At least from the time of Moses it was Israelite custom to hang the dead bodies of criminals to warn against similar crimes (Deut 21:22-23; cf. Num 25:4; 2 Sam 21:6)."[8]

9:15 Presumably Haman's strongest support was in the capital city where people had benefited from his favors. Since these supporters had the most to lose politically, they pressed the attack against the Jews to a second day. And for a second day the Jews defended themselves. This time **three hundred men** died.

H. A FESTIVAL OF JOY ESTABLISHED (9:16-19)

[16]**Meanwhile, the remainder of the Jews who were in the king's provinces also assembled to protect themselves and get relief from their enemies. They killed seventy-five thousand of them but did not lay their hands on the plunder.** [17]**This happened on the thirteenth day of the month of Adar, and on the fourteenth they rested and made it a day of feasting and joy.**

[18]**The Jews in Susa, however, had assembled on the thirteenth and fourteenth, and then on the fifteenth they rested and made it a day of feasting and joy.**

[19]**That is why rural Jews—those living in villages—observe the fourteenth of the month of Adar as a day of joy and feasting, a day for giving presents to each other.**

9:16-19 Beyond the capital city the **rural Jews**[9] defend themselves, needing just a single day, by killing **seventy-five thousand** attackers. These Jews spend the next day – the fourteenth – celebrating. Of course the Jews in Susa must wait until the fifteenth to celebrate. "The narrative takes for granted the solidarity of the

---

[8]John C. Whitcomb, *Esther: The Triumph of God's Sovereignty* (Chicago: Moody Press, 1979), p. 117.

[9]That is, Jews living outside of the territory belonging to the jurisdiction of the capital city of Susa.

Jewish communities; scattered though they were over the empire, they kept their identity and rejoiced together in their common experience of deliverance. Thus a plot intended to destroy them resulted in a festival which helped to unite and sustain them as a people."[10]

I. MORDECAI MAKES THE CELEBRATION OFFICIAL (9:20-22)

[20]Mordecai recorded these events, and he sent letters to all the Jews throughout the provinces of King Xerxes, near and far, [21]to have them celebrate annually the fourteenth and fifteenth days of the month of Adar [22]as the time when the Jews got relief from their enemies, and as the month when their sorrow was turned into joy and their mourning into a day of celebration. He wrote them to observe the days as days of feasting and joy and giving presents of food to one another and gifts to the poor.

9:20-21 Mordecai now issues a decree that there should no longer be two holidays (the fourteenth in the provinces and the fifteenth in Susa), but that both days should together constitute one celebration. Adar roughly corresponds to March.

9:22 Mordecai specifies that the celebration include **giving presents of food to one another and gifts to the poor**. The giving of gifts to the poor is also characteristic of true fasting, as Isaiah says, "Is not this the kind of fasting I have chosen: to loose the chains of injustice and untie the cords of the yoke, to set the oppressed free and break every yoke? Is it not to share your food with the hungry and to provide the poor wanderer with shelter—when you see the naked, to clothe him, and not to turn away from your own flesh and blood?" (58:6-7).

Interpreters differ over whether **these events** refer to what has preceded or to what follows. Some argue that the phrase refers to the contents of Mordecai's letter, which appears either in verses 21-22 or, more likely, 24-25.

---

[10]Baldwin, *Esther*, p. 107.

J. PURIM TO BE CELEBRATED BY THE JEWS
IN PERPETUITY (9:23-28)

[23]So the Jews agreed to continue the celebration they had begun, doing what Mordecai had written to them. [24]For Haman son of Hammedatha, the Agagite, the enemy of all the Jews, had plotted against the Jews to destroy them and had cast the *pur* (that is, the lot) for their ruin and destruction. [25]But when the plot came to the king's attention,[a] he issued written orders that the evil scheme Haman had devised against the Jews should come back onto his own head, and that he and his sons should be hanged on the gallows. [26](Therefore these days were called Purim, from the word *pur*.) Because of everything written in this letter and because of what they had seen and what had happened to them, [27]the Jews took it upon themselves to establish the custom that they and their descendants and all who join them should without fail observe these two days every year, in the way prescribed and at the time appointed. [28]These days should be remembered and observed in every generation by every family, and in every province and in every city. And these days of Purim should never cease to be celebrated by the Jews, nor should the memory of them die out among their descendants.

[a]*25 Or when Esther came before the king*

9:23-25 In verses 24-25 the author telescopes all the major events of this remarkable story. This is obviously so, since Xerxes' decree did not deal specifically with Haman or his sons, and Haman and his sons are executed nine months apart.

In verse 24 Haman is for the first time **the enemy of *all* the Jews**. All the Jews (vv. 20 and 30) will celebrate deliverance from his plot. There may be a play on the assonance between **Haman** (הָמָן, *hāmān*) and **for their ruin** (הֻמָּם, *hummām*).

9:26 In 3:7 the *pur* (that is, the lot) was cast. Why, then, is this festival called Purim, "lots"? It may be because the festival occupies two days. Clines has offered another possibility. "It is hard to resist the possibility that the name *Purim* is intended by the author to signify the *double* chance that created the story and the festival in celebration of it: the chance that determined disaster for the Jews and the 'chance' that provided for their deliverance, a 'chance' which was in reality a divine providence."[11]

David had earlier recognized that he and Israel were secure because the Lord determines the lot of his people. "LORD, you have assigned me my portion and my cup; you have made my *lot* secure. The boundary lines have fallen for me in pleasant places; surely I have a delightful inheritance" (Ps 16:5-6).

The Yale Babylonian Collection, one of the world's great repositories of cuneiform inscriptions, possesses an ancient lot (*pur*), a simple little cube, a die, inscribed on four sides. The cube measures $27 \times 27 \times 28$ millimeters, or little more than an inch. This cube was the "lot of Iahali," a high official of Shalmaneser III, King of Assyria from 858 to 824 B.C. In translation this cube reads: "Oh Assur, the great lord, oh Adad the great lord, the lot of Iahali the grand vizier of Salmaneser king of Assyria, governor of the land for the city of Kibshuni in the land of Qumeni, the land of Mehrani, Uqu and the Cedar Mountain, and minister of trade — in his year assigned to him by lot may the harvest of the land of Assyria prosper and thrive, in front of the gods Assur and Adad may his lot fall."[12]

9:27 All who join them is the same as **and many . . . became Jews** in 8:17.

9:28 Like the laws of the Medes and Persians, the **days of Purim** shall be irrevocable. Does this emphasis give legitimacy to a celebration not authorized in the Mosaic Law? The great feasts prescribed in the Torah were imposed on the people from above as God's commands. Purim, however, began as a spontaneous celebration by God's people of God's faithfulness to the covenant promises.

---

[11]Clines, *Ezra, Nehemiah, Esther,* p. 328.
[12]W.H. Hallo, "The First Purim," *BA* 46 (1983): 19-29.

EXCURSUS
PURIM[13]

By the second century A.D. a whole tractate of the Mishnah was devoted to the details of Purim, especially to the rules governing the reading of the scroll of Esther. The Book of Esther is read both at night and during the day. The four verses of "redemption" — 2:5; 8:15-16; 10:3 — are read in louder voice than the other verses. Children make a loud noise with rattles whenever the name of Haman is read, in order to blot out the "memory of Amalek." The reader recites the names of the ten sons of Haman in one breath to show that they were executed simultaneously.

Special Purim foods include boiled beans and peas, a reminder of the cereals Daniel ate in lieu of the king's rich food, and three-cornered pies known as *hamantashen* ("Haman's ears").

According to the Babylonian teacher Rava, a man is obliged to drink so much wine on Purim that he become incapable of knowing (*ad de-lo yada*) whether he is cursing Haman or blessing Mordecai.

In the development of Judaism, Psalm 7 was traditionally associated with the feast of Purim. Read the psalm and note how appropriate the association is.

> ¹O LORD my God, I take refuge in you;
> save and deliver me from all who pursue me
> ²or they will tear me like a lion
> and rip me to pieces with no one to rescue me.
>
> ³O LORD my God, if I have done this
> and there is guilt on my hands—
> ⁴if I have done evil to him who is at peace with me
> or without cause have robbed my foe—
> ⁵then let my enemy pursue and overtake me;
> let him trample my life to the ground
> and make me sleep in the dust.

---

[13]For a summary of the details of Purim celebration, see *Encyclopedia Judaica*.

[6]Arise, O LORD, in your anger;
    rise up against the rage of my enemies.
    Awake, my God; decree justice.
[7]Let the assembled peoples gather around you.
    Rule over them from on high;
[8]   let the LORD judge the peoples.
Judge me, O LORD, according to my righteousness,
    according to my integrity, O Most High.
[9]O righteous God,
    who searches minds and hearts,
bring to an end the violence of the wicked
    and make the righteous secure.

[10]My shield is God Most High,
    who saves the upright in heart.
[11]God is a righteous judge,
    a God who expresses his wrath every day.
[12]If he does not relent,
    he will sharpen his sword;
    he will bend and string his bow.
[13]He has prepared his deadly weapons;
    he makes ready his flaming arrows.

[14]He who is pregnant with evil
    and conceives trouble gives birth to disillusionment.
[15]He who digs a hole and scoops it out
    falls into the pit he has made.
[16]The trouble he causes recoils on himself;
    his violence comes down on his own head.

[17]I will give thanks to the LORD because of his righteousness
    and will sing praise to the name of the LORD Most High.

K. THE DECREE OF PURIM RECORDED (9:29-32)

This paragraph reports a second official letter, written by Esther and cosigned by Mordecai, to deal with continued resistance to the idea of celebrating both days.

[29]**So Queen Esther, daughter of Abihail, along with Mordecai the Jew, wrote with full authority to confirm this second letter concerning Purim.** [30]**And Mordecai sent letters to all the Jews in the 127 provinces of the kingdom of Xerxes—words of goodwill and assurance—** [31]**to establish these days of Purim at their designated times, as Mordecai the Jew and Queen Esther had decreed for them, and as they had established for themselves and their descendants in regard to their times of fasting and lamentation.** [32]**Esther's decree confirmed these regulations about Purim, and it was written down in the records.**

9:29-30 Esther's authority is stressed. She is **Queen** Esther. She writes **with full authority**. The NIV reading **words of good will and assurance** may be read "kindly but authoritative."

9:31 "Esther is urging the Jewish community voluntarily to take upon themselves the Purim festival just as they have done with the fasts that they have imposed upon themselves on various occasions of national danger and disaster in the past, including the very recent occasions related in 4:3; 4:16."[14]

9:32 The word **decree** (מַאֲמַר, *ma'ămar*) occurs in the Old Testament only in Esther (1:15; 2:20). "The command of King Xerxes" in 1:15 is contrasted with **Esther's decree** here. In 1:15 Vashti's disobedience to the king's command brought about her expulsion. What is the implication here?

"No other woman among God's people wrote with authority to confirm and establish a religious practice that still stands today. The importance of most biblical women, such as Sarah and Hannah, lies in their motherhood. Esther's importance to the covenant people is not as a mother, but as a queen."[15]

---

[14]Bush, *Ruth, Esther,* p. 486.
[15]Jobes, *Esther,* p. 224.

Esther 2:5 identified Mordecai as a descendant of Kish from the tribe of Benjamin. This would make him a descendant of the family of Saul. Esther 3:1 identified Haman as a member of the Agag family and, therefore, an Amalekite, the prototypical enemy of the Israelites. They were the first to attack the Israelites after they left Egypt (Exod 17:8). Saul's failure to kill Agag was one cause of his demise (1 Sam 15:7-9,26).

In the story of Esther would a descendant of Saul's family also come to his demise at the hands of a descendant of Agag? Or would Mordecai vanquish the vile enemy Haman?

These questions intertwine two men — Mordecai vs. Haman. In point of fact, these questions intertwine two families — Mordecai and Esther against Haman and his sons (9:7-10) — and two nations — Jews against Persians (9:6,15,16).

As the Esther story unfolds, Mordecai, Esther, and the Jews are condemned to death. But through a series of reversals the Jews get the upper hand over those who hate them. Against all expectation Haman loses his power and is destroyed whereas Mordecai is saved and then empowered through high rank.

The reversal of fortune in the Esther story is analogous to the story of redemptive history. We, too, once stood condemned to death. Paul reminds us that "the wages of sin is death." But we have seen the ultimate reversal of expected ends. God took upon himself our sentence — he died! And more wondrously, that death — his death — is the gateway to glorious triumph — eternal life! Jobes has said it well. "Because of the death and resurrection of Jesus Christ, our destiny has been reversed from death to life against all expectation. The cross of Jesus Christ is the pivot point of the great reversal of history, where our sorrow has been turned to joy."[16]

---

[16]Ibid., p. 161.

ESTHER 10

VII. EPILOGUE (10:1-3)

The book ends as it began, with the focus on the prosperity and power of King Xerxes. But here, the mention of the king's greatness is intended to increase the stature of Mordecai, the king's Prime Minister.

¹King Xerxes imposed tribute throughout the empire, to its distant shores. ²And all his acts of power and might, together with a full account of the greatness of Mordecai to which the king had raised him, are they not written in the book of the annals of the kings of Media and Persia? ³Mordecai the Jew was second in rank to King Xerxes, preeminent among the Jews, and held in high esteem by his many fellow Jews, because he worked for the good of his people and spoke up for the welfare of all the Jews.

10:1 The mention of an empire-wide taxation at this point may show how Xerxes prospers from the counsel of Mordecai.

10:2 The author cites his source of information — **the book of the annals of the kings of Media and Persia** — and invites his readers to check out the veracity of the recorded account (compare with 1 Kgs 14:29; 15:7,23,31; 22:45; 2 Kgs 15:36; 1 Chr 27:24; 2 Chr 12:15; 13:22). This **book** may not be identical with the royal diary mentioned in 2:23 and 6:1.

Media and Persia refers to the two kingdoms in their chronological order.

10:3 Like Joseph long before him, Mordecai rose to **second in rank** (Gen 41:43). Mordecai did not use his position to promote his advantage but the **welfare** of the Jewish community.

The book of Lamentations grieves over the destruction of Jerusalem and the deportation of its populace into Babylonian captivity in
587 B.C. Theologically this tragedy was God's judgment upon the sin
of his people. "The LORD has brought her grief because of her many
sins. Her children have gone into exile, captive before the foe" (1:5bc).

The book ends with the haunting possibility that God has rejected his people forever.

> Restore us to yourself, O LORD, that we may return;
>   renew our days as of old
> unless you have utterly rejected us
>   and are angry with us beyond measure (5:21-22).

The book of Esther sets aside the fear expressed in Lamentations
5:21-22. Even though Israel's sin led to the forfeiture of the promised land, and even though Israel had been driven into exile, the
LORD still protects and sustains his people. In short, he is still interested in their well-being. In fact, his people may find themselves in
perilous circumstances throughout their exilic history, but he has
already provided a means of release.

Purim, like Passover, is a celebrative reminder that God's deliverance never ends. Paul House adds,

> The inclusion of Esther in the canon highlights the necessity of
> Israel's survival. This survival is as certain as it is sacred, for the
> Lord must keep all promises that require Jewish participants.
> All nations must still be blessed through Abraham. David must
> still be given an eternal kingdom. The promised land must
> receive Israel back, and the new covenant must still be initiat-
> ed. Therefore, . . . Israel must survive for the whole program
> of biblical theology to be completed.[1]

The apostle Paul said it this way. "But as surely as God is faith-
ful, our message to you is not 'Yes' and 'No.' For the Son of God,
Jesus Christ, who was preached among you by me and Silas and
Timothy, was not 'Yes' and 'No,' but in him it has always been 'Yes.'
For no matter how many promises God has made, they are 'Yes' in
Christ. And so through him the 'Amen' is spoken by us to the glory
of God" (2 Cor 1:18-20).

---

[1]Paul R. House, *Old Testament Theology* (Downers Grove, IL: InterVarsity,
1998), p. 496.

THE BOOK OF
DANIEL

INTRODUCTION

In the Hebrew Bible (the Old Testament) the book of Daniel is found in the collection known as "The Writings."[1] This location surprises most readers, who think that the book belongs obviously to "The Prophets." The book of Daniel, however, differs from the prophetic books in two obvious ways. First, it does not contain the typical prophetic introduction "Thus says/declares the LORD." Additionally, since Daniel must be regarded primarily as a statesman, he did not occupy the office of a prophet. E.J. Young has suggested that Daniel did possess the prophetic gift (*donum propheticum*) but not the prophetic office (*munus propheticum*).[2] Second, it is not "historical in the sense that the books of Kings are historical, though it begins from a point in history and is clearly concerned with history."[3] The books of Kings present a theological assessment of a very specific period of time, namely 971–562 B.C. The book of Daniel provides a philosophy of history, mapping history's course from the Neo-Babylonian Empire to the *eschaton*, the end of days.

AUTHORSHIP AND DATE

The Book of Daniel was written by Daniel himself. This conclusion is based on both internal and external evidence. First, the internal evidence. If Daniel is named as the one who received the revelations contained in chapters 7 (v. 2), 8 (v. 1), 9 (v. 22), 10–12 (10:2;

---

[1]The Old Testament consists of the Law (Gen–Deut), Prophets (Josh, Judg, 1–2 Sam, 1–2 Kgs, Isa, Jer, Ezek, and the twelve minor prophets), and Writings (the rest).

[2]Edward J. Young, *The Prophecy of Daniel: A Commentary* (Grand Rapids: Eerdmans, 1978), p. 20.

[3]Joyce G. Baldwin, *Daniel*, Tyndale Old Testament Commentaries (Downers Grove, IL: InterVarsity Press, 1978), p. 13.

12:5), and if Daniel is commanded to preserve the words of the scroll (12:4), then Danielic authorship is an easy inference.

The external evidence is simple, yet profoundly important. Jesus speaks of Daniel as having foretold the abomination of desolation (Dan 9:27; 11:31; 12:11). In Matthew 24:15-16 we read, "So when you see standing in the holy place 'the abomination that causes desolation,' spoken through the prophet Daniel — let the reader understand — then let those who are in Judea flee to the mountains" (cf. Mark 13:14). If Jesus attributes this specific prophecy to Daniel, then, again, Danielic authorship is an easy inference.

According to the text of Daniel, Daniel was deported into Babylonian captivity in 605 B.C. (Dan 1:1-2,6). He completed his civil service in the first year of King Cyrus (539; Dan 1:21) and his prophetic ministry in the same king's third year (10:1).

Living in the third century A.D., Porphyry wrote a 15-volume work entitled *Against the Christians*. In this work, he concluded that the book of Daniel must be history, not prophecy, since predictive prophecy is impossible. In light then of this assumption, and given that the author of Daniel possessed an extensive knowledge of the reign of Antiochus IV Epiphanes (175–163 B.C.), Porphyry argued for an anonymous author living in the second century B.C. Following Porphyry's lead the majority of commentators date the book of Daniel to the period of the Maccabees, that is, the second century B.C. One example will suffice. E.W. Heaton writes, "The immediate occasion which called forth the Book of Daniel was the persecution of the Jews by the Seleucid king Antiochus Epiphanes, who reigned from 175 to 163 B.C. The writer, a pious scribe living in the middle of the persecution, is addressing his contemporaries through the medium of an ancient sage, about whom he recounts stories and to whom he ascribes visions."[4]

Proponents of this viewpoint argue that every accurate prediction in Daniel was written after it had already been fulfilled (a *vaticinium ex eventu*), a "prophecy after the fact." Towner's commentary reflects this assumption. He writes,

We need to assume that the vision as a whole is a prophecy after the fact. Why? Because human beings are unable accu-

---

[4]E.W. Heaton, *The Book of Daniel*, Torch Bible Commentaries (London: SCM Press, 1956), p. 17.

rately to predict future events centuries in advance and to say that Daniel could do so, even on the basis of a symbolic revelation vouchsafed to him by God and interpreted by an angel, is to fly in the face of the certainties of human nature. So what we have here is in fact not a road map of the future laid down in the sixth century B.C. but an interpretation of the events of the author's own time, 167–164 B.C.[5]

Towner is correct when he asserts that "human beings are unable accurately to predict future events centuries in advance." But God can and does (Amos 3:7; Isa 43:8-10,14-21; 44:6-8; 44:24–45:1; 45:21; 48:3-5,14-16). A sixth-century date for the book of Daniel safeguards the belief in the revelatory nature of Scripture. The second-century date reduces Scripture to mere historical reflection.[6]

PURPOSE

The culmination of Babylonian presence in Judea was the ransacking of Jerusalem, the burning of the temple, and the deporting of the populace (587 B.C.).

The Babylonians had vanquished Israel, the people of God. But had they vanquished God? In the sixth century Israel had a history, but would she have a future? If she had a future, would it be detoured as the present had been? The Book of Daniel answers all of these questions.

Had Babylon vanquished God? Hardly. In spite of present circumstances, God had always been in control. God had merely used the Babylonians to manifest his righteousness. Daniel's prayer in chapter 9 gives the proper perspective on the recent course of events. "Just as it is written in the Law of Moses, all this disaster has come upon us, yet we have not sought the favor of the LORD our God by turning from our sins and giving attention to your truth. The LORD did not hesitate to bring the disaster upon us, for the LORD our God is righteous in everything he does; yet we have not obeyed him" (Dan 9:13-14).

---

[5]W. Sibley Towner, *Daniel*, Interpretation (Atlanta: John Knox Press, 1984), p. 115.

[6]See Gordon J. Wenham, "Daniel: The Basic Issues," *Themelios* 2 (1977): 49-52.

In a relatively short period of time, God would vanquish Babylon. The fall of arrogant Babylon is narrated in Daniel 5, with a warning to that effect in chapter 4.

But is the fall of Babylon merely a function of historical exigencies? Again, the answer is the same. Hardly! The dreams and interpretations found in the Book of Daniel reveal God's sovereign control of human history.

> He does as he pleases
> with the powers of heaven
> and the peoples of the earth.
> No one can hold back his hand
> or say to him: "What have you done?" (Dan 4:35).

The God of Israel willed the rise and fall of Babylon. After Babylon, he willed the rise and fall of Medo-Persia, Greece, Rome, and the entire context of human history.

Had God been vanquished? Hardly! Nebuchadnezzar said,

> His dominion is an eternal dominion;
> his kingdom endures from generation to generation
> (4:34).

King Darius would add,

> He is the living God
> and he endures forever;
> his kingdom will not be destroyed,
> his dominion will never end (6:26).

And Israel, would she have a future? If so, what could she expect? Just as God had delivered Shadrach, Meshach, and Abednego from the fiery furnace (Dan 3) and Daniel from the lions' den (Dan 6), Israel would be delivered from her captivity (9:24-27). God "rescues and he saves" (6:27).

Israel is promised a future in order to fulfill God's sovereign plan for the cosmos. "Seventy sevens are decreed for your people and your holy city to finish transgression, to put an end to sin, to atone for wickedness, to bring in everlasting righteousness, to seal up vision and prophecy and to anoint the most holy" (9:24).

But what detours would this future take? Israel is warned that she will endure a grievous persecution under the reign of Antiochus Epiphanes (8:10,24; 11:33). In fact, the people of God can expect persecution throughout the remaining course of history (7:8,25). But just as God vindicated the faith of Daniel and his three friends in chapter 1, so he will vindicate all those who endure. "As I watched, this horn was waging war against the saints and defeating them, until the Ancient of Days came and pronounced judgment in favor of the saints of the Most High" (7:21-22).

The saints of the Most High will receive God's eternal kingdom and "will possess it forever—yes, for ever and ever" (7:18). But how can the mortal, and often persecuted, possess this kingdom for ever and ever? Daniel 12:2 promises a resurrection to "everlasting life."

TEXT

The Septuagint (LXX) inserted a lengthy apocryphal passage after Daniel 3:23, known as the *Song of the Three Young Men*. The apocryphal *Susanna* appeared in the LXX as a thirteenth chapter and the twin narratives *Bel* and *The Dragon* as a fourteenth chapter.

CANONICITY

In the Hebrew Bible the Book of Daniel is found among the Writings not the Prophets. Some have suggested that this is so because the book was composed after the canon of the prophets had been completed. If Malachi is dated to the second half of the fifth century B.C., the prophetic canon would have stood complete by approximately 400 B.C. The composition of Daniel would perhaps then be Maccabean in origin.

Since Daniel served as a statesman in a royal court, and since the Book of Daniel differs from the prophetic books (as was argued in the introduction), placement in the "Writings" is the only choice (Daniel could not have been placed in the "Law" with Genesis through Deuteronomy!). Position in the canon of Scripture is not necessarily an indication of the date of composition.[7]

---

[7]It is clear, however, that the residents at Qumran considered Daniel a prophet. In 4Q174 2:3 we read "which is written in the book of Daniel the prophet." Christ referred to Daniel as a prophet in Matt 24:15.

The discovery of several fragments of the Book of Daniel in Qumran Cave 1 testifies to the special esteem in which Daniel was held by this famous Dead Sea community.[8] New Testament quotation of and allusion to the book of Daniel also bears witness to its authority.

GENRE (DANIEL 1–6)

The events narrated in Daniel 1–6 are typically called Court Tales. The tales are of two types: conflict or contest. Daniel 3 and 6 are the "Tales of Court Conflict." When the faith of Daniel's three friends conflicts with Nebuchadnezzar's edict to "fall down and worship the image of gold" (3:5), they are thrown into the fiery furnace. When Daniel's commitment to "the law of his God" (6:5) conflicts with the "laws of the Medes and Persians" (6:8), he is thrown into the lions' den.

Daniel 1, 2, 4, and 5 are "Tales of Court Contest." When Daniel and his three friends "win" the diet contest, they are found "ten times better than all the magicians and enchanters in [the] whole kingdom" (1:20). In Daniel 2, 4, and 5, Daniel alone is either able to interpret a king's dream (2:27-28; 4:7-8) or read the mysterious writing on the wall (5:15,17). On two occasions after Daniel wins a "contest," the king rewards him (2:48; 4:16).

GENRE (DANIEL 7–12)

Between 200 B.C. and A.D. 100 a number of literary pieces were composed in the style of what is commonly termed *apocalyptic* – a style or genre for which it is exceedingly difficult to arrive at a satisfactory definition.[9] In fact, many scholars despair of defining the term and resort rather to listing characteristics of the genre. D.S. Russell has offered this explanation: "The apocalyptic literature is essentially a literature of people who saw no hope for their nation simply in terms of politics or on the plain of history. The battle they

---

[8]William H. Brownlee, *The Meaning of the Qumran Scrolls for the Bible* (New York: Oxford University Press, 1964), pp. 35-42, 47-48.
[9]See Margaret Barker, "Slippery Words III. Apocalyptic," *ExpTim* 89 (1977–78): 324-329.

were fighting was on a spiritual level, against 'spiritual powers of wickedness in high places.' And so they were compelled to look beyond history to the dramatic and miraculous intervention of God who would set to rights the injustices done to his people."[10]

The New Testament book of Revelation is an apocalypse. In Revelation 1:1 the word translated as "revelation" is the Greek word from which we get such words as *apocalypse* and *apocalyptic*. Most scholars of the Bible categorize or associate the book of Daniel with the Revelation of John. These two books contain horrific images of evil; both rely heavily on symbolism and numbers; but both comfort oppressed readers with the vision of the time when God will intervene and bring all evil to an end once and for all.[11]

If Daniel 7–12 is truly apocalyptic, and if this genre was popular during the second century B.C., then another reason is commonly adduced for seeing the Book of Daniel as a product of the era of the Maccabees. But this line of reasoning is not sound.

Apocalyptic features are not necessarily evidences for a late date for Daniel. Many of these features are also found in such works as Isaiah 24–27, Ezekiel, and Zechariah — books that predate the popularity of the apocalyptic genre by many centuries.

Since the origins of biblical apocalyptic are within the prophetic tradition,[12] one is hard-pressed to disassociate the book of Daniel from its prophetic predecessors. Youngblood has shown that the major apocalyptic themes of Isaiah 24–27 are paralleled elsewhere — not only in apocalyptic sections of other prophetic books but also in nonapocalyptic sections.[13] Similar comparisons can also be adduced for the other apocalyptic passages in the Old Testament. Accordingly, it is a misstep to date the book of Daniel based on what are

---

[10]D.S. Russell, *Divine Disclosure* (Minneapolis: Fortress Press, 1992), p. 14.

[11]For an in-depth analysis of the characteristics of the apocalyptic genre, consult: Leon Morris, *Apocalyptic* (Grand Rapids: Eerdmans, 1972); and John J. Collins, "Apocalypse: The Morphology of a Genre," *Semeia* 14 (1979).

[12]R.F. Youngblood, "A Holistic Typology of Prophecy and Apocalyptic," in *Israel's Apostasy and Restoration*, ed. Avraham Gileadi (Grand Rapids: Baker, 1988), p. 214. In the words of Youngblood, "Virtually all students of the subject agree on at least two features of Hebrew apocalyptic: it contains a strongly futuristic and/or eschatological dimension, and its ultimate wellspring is Israelite prophecy."

[13]Youngblood, "Holistic Typology," p. 218.

perceived to be apocalyptic features. (See also the section "Apocalyptic" later in this Introduction.)

HISTORICITY

A number of historical issues are raised by the text of Daniel.

THE YEAR OF NEBUCHADNEZZAR'S INVASION

Daniel 1:1 states, "In the third year of the reign of Jehoiakim king of Judah, Nebuchadnezzar king of Babylon came to Jerusalem and besieged it." Jeremiah 25:1,9, however, date this same event to the "fourth year of Jehoiakim" (cf. Jer 46:2). This slight chronological difference confirms that the author of Daniel wrote from a Babylonian perspective. How so?

In Judah the calendar year in which a new king came to the throne was reckoned as that king's first year of reign (nonaccession-year method). In Babylon, however, the year when the new king came to power would simply be called his accession year (accession-year method). The first year of his reign did not begin until the beginning of the next calendar year. This slight difference can best be seen in the following chart.

Judah	Babylon
First Year	The year of the accession to the kingdom
Second Year	First Year
Third Year	Second year
Fourth Year	Third Year

The difference is easily understood. Jeremiah writes from the chronological perspective of Judah, while Daniel from that of Babylon.

NEBUCHADNEZZAR'S ILLNESS (DAN 4)

Daniel 4 recounts how the great Nebuchadnezzar was stricken with boanthropy, a rare form of mental imbalance in which a man imagines himself to be a cow or bull.

Not surprisingly Babylonian records do not mention this illness. However, a Babylonian priest named Berossus preserved a tradition that Nebuchadnezzar took ill suddenly towards the end of his reign. Harrison conjectures that this tradition "comprised a discreet way of referring to some embarrassing ailment that polite persons refrained from mentioning."[14]

The "Prayer of Nabonidus," a fragmentary text found in Qumran Cave 4, bears some resemblance to Daniel 4. Accordingly, some scholars have asserted that this text was an earlier form of the "legend" of Nebuchadnezzar's illness and that the author of Daniel transferred the illness from Nabonidus to Nebuchadnezzar. In other words, Daniel diagnosed the wrong patient! Brownlee, who represents this position, writes, "Many scholars have seen a distorted reminiscence of Nabonidus in the story of Nebuchadnezzar's madness. . . . It is therefore a doublet, and an historically inferior one at that, to the Nabonidus story at Qumran."[15]

This opinion confers greater historical confidence to a fragmentary text from Qumran than to the text of Scripture. Instead of viewing this piece from Qumran as a source for Daniel 4 (notice that this opinion also assumes a late date for the book of Daniel), a far more objective view is that at present there is no known connection between the two pieces. In fact, two different ailments are represented in the two pieces. In Daniel 4 Nebuchadnezzar suffers from boanthropy; at Qumran Nabonidus suffers "with a severe inflammation."[16]

BELSHAZZAR

According to Daniel 5, 7, and 8, Belshazzar was the final king of the Neo-Babylonian Empire, whereas in extrabiblical Greek sources and in the Babylonian king-lists Nabonidus was ruler in Babylon when it fell to the Persians in 539.

---

[14]R.K. Harrison, *Introduction to the Old Testament* (Grand Rapids: Eerdmans, 1969), p. 1115.

[15]Brownlee, *Meaning*, p. 39.

[16]For a translation of the "Prayer of Nabonidus," see Michael Wise, Martin Abegg, Jr., and Edward Cook, *The Dead Sea Scrolls: A New Translation* (New York: HarperSanFrancisco, 1996), p. 266.

Archaeological finds have resolved this difficulty. The picture that emerges from these finds again suggests that the writer of Daniel was historically accurate. The picture has developed as follows. While Nabonidus was in Teima (in the Arabian Desert), his son, Belshazzar, was co-regent, exercising rule in Babylon. In fact, Nabonidus had entrusted the kingship to his son. But as long as Nabonidus lived, Belshazzar could not bear the title "king" in the official records. Belshazzar's promise recorded in Daniel 5:7 and 16 — "he will be made the third highest ruler in the kingdom" — indicates that the author knew that Belshazzar was second to his father (cf. 5:29).

In Daniel 5:2,11 (thrice), and 18, Nebuchadnezzar is identified as the **father** of Belshazzar. But since this word can be used metaphorically for one's predecessor, the author of Daniel is not mistaken. And if Nebuchadnezzar was the (grand)father of Belshazzar, then the author is literally accurate.[17]

DARIUS THE MEDE (5:31)

Daniel 5:30-31 reads, "That very night Belshazzar, king of the Babylonians, was slain, and Darius the Mede took over the kingdom, at the age of sixty-two." The problem is that history tells us that the Neo-Babylonian Empire was followed by the Persian Empire headed by Cyrus. Who, then, is this Darius the Mede?

Some have suggested that the Darius of Daniel is pure fiction or that the author of Daniel was so confused that he thought Darius I Hystaspes (522–486) preceded Cyrus (539–530). This explanation will hardly do. Baldwin warns, "To assume that Darius did not exist, and so to dismiss the evidence provided by the book, is high-handed and unwise, especially in the light of its vindication in connection with Belshazzar, who at one time was reckoned to be a fictional character."[18]

J.C. Whitcomb has opined that Darius was an alternate name for Gubaru, who is frequently mentioned in cuneiform texts as governor of Babylon during the period of transition to Persian rule in

---

[17]The Hebrew word for father (*ab*) was also used to refer to a grandfather (Gen 28:13; 32:9), a great-grandfather (1 Kgs 15:10-13), or even a great-great-grandfather (1 Kgs 15:11,24). If the mother of Belshazzar was a daughter of Nebuchadnezzar, then the text is literally true.

[18]Baldwin, *Daniel,* p. 24.

Babylonia.[19] D.J. Wiseman identifies Darius the Mede as Cyrus the Persian. This identification requires that 6:28 be translated, "So Daniel prospered during the reign of Darius, that is, the reign of Cyrus the Persian."[20] Wiseman's suggested translation of the conjunction ("and") as "that is" is certainly acceptable and in keeping with other examples found in the book of Daniel (cf. 1:3; 6:9; 7:1).

In 11:1 the Septuagint (LXX) has Cyrus instead of Darius. "This suggests that the Greek translator knew of the double name, and preferred to use the one that was better known to avoid confusing his readers."[21]

In short, plausible suggestions exist for the identity of the enigmatic Darius the Mede. Accordingly one does not have to accuse the author of being either imaginative or historically inept.

CHALDEANS

In Daniel 3:8; 5:30; and 9:1 the author uses the term "Chaldean" in an ethnic sense, referring to a Semitic people who had formerly settled around the Persian Gulf from at least the tenth century B.C. Nebuchadnezzar was a Chaldean. In 2:2,4,5,10; 4:7; 5:7,11 the same term refers to a class of astrologers. This secondary usage, unknown in Babylonian sources, is commonly assumed to be an inaccuracy. Against this assumption, Harrison has noted that this secondary usage was known by the fifth-century B.C. historian Herodotus (1.181).[22]

FOREIGN VOCABULARY IN DANIEL

The presence of foreign vocabulary has often been used as proof for the late date of composition. S.R. Driver, for example, remarked, "The verdict of the language of Daniel is thus clear. The Persian words presuppose a period after the Persian empire had been well

[19]J.C. Whitcomb, *Darius the Mede* (Grand Rapids: Eerdmans, 1959), p. 24.
[20]D.J. Wiseman, "The Last Days of Babylon," *Christianity Today* (November 25, 1957): 7-10. See also David W. Baker, "Further Examples of the *Waw Explicativum*," *VT* 30 (1980): 129-136.
[21]Baldwin, *Daniel*, p. 27.
[22]Harrison, *Introduction*, p. 1113.

established; the Greek words *demand*, the Hebrew *supports*, and the Aramaic *permits*, a date *after the conquest of Palestine by Alexander the Great*."[23]

The Persian words (largely referring to government and administration) found in the text of Daniel indicate that Daniel lived under Persian rule. The three Greek words — denoting musical instruments — merely show cultural contact between the Aegean and Mesopotamia. These contacts can be traced from the dawn of history.[24] In fact, the argument based on Greek words ultimately betrays the late-date hypothesis. By the time of Antiochus Epiphanes a Greek-speaking government had been in place in Palestine for a century and a half. Why then have no Greek political or administrative terms found their way into the text of Daniel? The Aramaic of Daniel constitutes a strong argument for a sixth-century period of composition.[25]

Kitchen concludes the matter with these words: "One would—on the Greek and Persian evidence—prefer to put the Aramaic of Daniel in the late sixth, the fifth, or the fourth centuries B.C., not the third or the second. The latter is not ruled out, but is much less realistic and not so favored by the facts as was once imagined."[26]

THEOLOGY

The Book of Daniel possesses a rich theology. The "God of heaven" (2:18,28,37,44), the "Most High" (4:17,25,32,34), the "King of Heaven" (4:37), the "Lord of heaven" (5:23), does as he pleases "with the powers of heaven and the peoples of the earth" (4:35). "He performs signs and wonders in the heavens and on the earth" (6:27). His sovereign sway over all matters of history and the peoples of the earth is a major theme of the author. "He sets up kings and deposes

---

[23]S.R. Driver, *An Introduction to the Literature of the Old Testament* (Cleveland: World Publishing, 1963), p. 508.

[24]Edwin M. Yamauchi, *Greece and Babylon* (Grand Rapids: Baker, 1967).

[25]Gleason L. Archer Jr., "The Aramaic of the 'Genesis Apocryphon' Compared with the Aramaic of Daniel," in *New Perspectives on the Old Testament*, ed. J. Barton Payne (Waco, TX: Word, 1970), pp. 160-169.

[26]K.A. Kitchen, "The Aramaic of Daniel," in *Notes on Some Problems in the Book of Daniel*, ed. D.J. Wiseman et al. (London: Tyndale Press, 1965), p. 50.

them" (2:21). He "is sovereign over the kingdoms of men and gives them to anyone he wishes and sets over them the lowliest of men" (4:17; cf. 2:37-38; 5:21).

The God of heaven is living (6:20,26), righteous (4:37; 9:7,14,16), great and awesome (9:4), merciful and forgiving (2:18; 9:9,18). He possesses wisdom and power (2:20). He is the "God of gods and the Lord of kings" (2:47).

Even though God is transcendent, He is also personal and present. He is called "God of my fathers" (2:23), "their own God" (3:28), "your God" (6:20), "our God" (9:9,14), and "my God" (6:22). He "keeps His covenant of love with all who love him and obey his commands" (9:4). Men trust (3:28), serve (3:17; 6:20), and worship (2:23; 4:34,37; 7:27) him. Angels attend to him and stand before him (7:10).

He caused the official of chapter 1 to show favor to Daniel (1:9). He gave "knowledge and understanding" to the four young men of chapter 1 (1:17). He "gives wisdom to the wise and knowledge to the discerning" (2:21). He "reveals deep and hidden things" (2:22; cf. 2:23,28,47). He saves (3:17,28; 6:20,22,27).

Since he is righteous and just (7:9), he judges the sin of his people (1:2; 9:14,16,18) and that of the world (4:25,32; 5:23,26; 7:10,21-22). "And those who walk in pride he is able to humble" (4:37).

Since God is great and awesome (9:4), "No one can hold back his hand or say to him: 'What have you done?'" (4:35). He will "set up a kingdom that will never be destroyed" (2:44). "His kingdom is an eternal kingdom; his dominion endures from generation to generation" (4:3; cf. 4:34). "For he is the living God and he endures forever; his kingdom will not be destroyed, his dominion will never end" (6:26).

The people of God will possess this kingdom (7:22). In fact, the "sovereignty, power and greatness of the kingdoms under the whole heaven will be handed over to the saints, the people of the Most High" (7:27).

THE FIVE KINGDOMS

In Daniel 2, 7, and 8 five kingdoms are symbolically presented. The obvious parallels suggest that these chapters are unified. For example, the second beast of chapter 7 "was raised up on one of its sides," suggesting prominence for that side. In chapter 8 a ram with two horns appears; one of the horns was longer than the other. This extra length also suggests prominence or importance.

Given these parallels, the textual identification of four of the five kingdoms is easily understood and is obviously authoritative. The fourth kingdom is not specifically named by the text. But following the great empires of Babylon, Persia, and Greece, the fourth kingdom in all likelihood is Rome.

Chapter 2	Chapter 7	Chapter 8	Identification
The head of the statue was made of pure gold (32)	The first was like a lion, and it had the wings of an eagle (4)		Babylon (2:38)
Its chest and arms of silver (32)	And there before me was a second beast, which looked like a bear (5)	A ram with two horns (3)	Medo-Persia (8:20)
Its belly and thighs of bronze (32)	And there was another beast, one that looked like a leopard. And on its back it had four wings like those of a bird (6)	A goat with a prominent horn between his eyes came from the west, crossing the whole earth without touching the ground (5)	Greece (8:21)
Its legs of iron, its feet partly of iron and partly of baked clay (33)	And there was a fourth beast—terrifying and frightening and very powerful. It had large iron teeth (7)		(Rome)
The rock that struck the statue became a huge mountain and filled the whole earth (35)	Heavenly Court: Ancient of Days (9-10) One like a son of man (13-14)		God's Kingdom (2:44-45)

Earliest Jewish interpreters and the Church fathers favor the view that Rome was the fourth kingdom.[27] Present-day liberal scholarship

---

[27]H.H. Rowley, *Darius the Mede and the Four World Empires in the Book of Daniel* (Cardiff: University of Wales, 1958); John H. Walton, "The Four Kingdoms of Daniel," *JETS* 29 (March 1986): 26-27.

and a very small corner of evangelicalism, however, favor the position that the fourth kingdom is the Hellenistic Empire.[28]

This modern position suggests that either Babylon or Assyria is the first kingdom, Media the second, and Persia the third. The view is doomed from the outset given that Media did not rule over a territory comparable to the other empires, and that the biblical writer associates Media with Persia (Dan 8:20). Additionally, since the fourth beast of chapter 7 is nondescript, that is, it is not likened to any known animal, and the he-goat of chapter 8 is identified as Greece (8:21), then logically the last beast of chapter 7 does not represent Greece.

The proponents of a late date for Daniel, who also typically dismiss the predictive possibility of the text, tend to identify the second, third, and fourth kingdoms with Media, Persia, and Greece. This approach is improper for the simple reason that it does not let the text of Daniel speak for itself. The text has spoken — we must listen.

DANIEL 11

The historical clarity of Daniel 11 is positive proof for the divine origin of the revelation received by Daniel. No man living in the sixth century B.C. could predict with such absolute precision events that would unfold two to four centuries later. Consult the commentary for the details associated with these kings of the south and of the north.

The King of the South	The King of the North
Ptolemy I Soter (322–285) [5a]	Seleucus I Nicator (312–280) [5b]
Ptolemy II Philadelphus (285–246) [6]	Antiochus I Soter (280–261)
	Antiochus II Theos (261–246) [6]
Ptolemy III Euergetes (246–221) [7-9]	Seleucus II Callinicus (246–226) [7-9]
Ptolemy IV Philopator (221–203) [10-12]	Seleucus III Soter Ceraunus (226–223) [10]
	Antiochus III Magnus (223–187) [10-19]
Ptolemy V Epiphanes (203–181) [14-17]	
Ptolemy VI Philometor (181–146) [25-28]	Seleucus IV Philopator (187–175) [20]
	Antiochus IV Epiphanes (175–163) [21-45]

---

[28]Robert Gurney ["The Four Kingdoms of Daniel 2 and 7," *Themelios* 2 (1977): 39-45] and Walton ["The Four Kingdoms," pp. 25-36] are two evangelicals who defend this viewpoint.

STRUCTURE

The book of Daniel was composed in two languages — Hebrew and Aramaic.[29] The book commences in Hebrew (1:1–2:4a), continues in Aramaic (2:4b–7:28), and concludes in Hebrew (8:1–12:13). This ABA pattern is deliberate. The Aramaic section (B) is addressed to the kings of the earth and therefore written in the international language, the *lingua franca*. The remaining chapters are written in Hebrew because they are addressed to Jews.

The six chapters within the Aramaic section are organized chiastically (ABCCBA). This arrangement was first noted by A. Lenglet.[30]

   A. Nebuchadnezzar's vision of four kingdoms (2)
     B. God delivers his servants from a fiery furnace (3)
       C. God's judgment upon the pride of Nebuchadnezzar (4)
       C′. God's judgment upon the pride of Belshazzar (5)
     B′. God delivers his servant from a den of lions (6)
   A′. Daniel's vision of four kingdoms (7)

The first Hebrew section (A) introduces the reader to Daniel and his friends, *dramatis personae* significant to the Aramaic section. The second Hebrew section (A) details what the visions of chapters 2 and 7 will mean for the city of Jerusalem and God's people.

The chiastic arrangement of chapters 2–7 cuts across the genre distinction noted above. This is just one of the many proofs for the unity of this book.

David W. Gooding has proposed that the author of Daniel arranged his material to stand in two groups with five items in each.[31]

---

[29]B.T. Arnold, "The Use of Aramaic in the Hebrew Bible: Another Look at Bilingualism in Ezra and Daniel," *Journal of Northwest Semitic Languages* 22/2 (1996): 1-16.

[30]A. Lenglet, "La structure litteraire de Daniel 2-7," *Biblica* 53 (1972): 169-190.

[31]David W. Gooding, "The Literary Structure of the Book of Daniel and Its Implications," *TynBul* 32 (1981): 58-59.

GROUP 1	GROUP 2
Ch. 1 — Nebuchadnezzar reverently places God's vessels in his idol's temple. Daniel and others refuse to indulge in pagan impurities. Court officials sympathetic. Daniel and his colleagues' physical and mental powers vindicated. They are promoted to high office.	Ch. 6 — Darius bans prayer to God for thirty days. Daniel refuses to cease practicing the Jewish religion. Court officials intrigue against him. Daniel's political loyalty to the king vindicated. He is restored to high office.
Ch. 2 — A survey of the whole course of Gentile imperial power. Four empires in the form of a man. The fatal weakness: an incoherent mixture of iron and clay in the feet. The whole Man destroyed by the stone cut out by divine power. The universal Messianic kingdom set up.	Ch. 7 — A survey of the whole course of Gentile imperial power. Four empires in the form of wild beasts. The hideous strength: a frightening mixture of animal destructiveness with human intelligence. The final beast destroyed and universal domination given to the Son of Man.
Ch. 3 — Nebuchadnezzar thinks that 'no god can deliver (the Jews) out of his hand.' He commands them to worship his god. The Jews defy him. They are preserved in the furnace. God's ability to deliver is thereby demonstrated.	Ch. 8 — The little horn: 'none can deliver out of his hand.' He stops the Jews' worship of their God, and defies God himself. God's sanctuary and truth are finally vindicated.
Ch. 4 — The glory of Babylon. Nebuchadnezzar is warned that he deserves discipline. He persists in pride, is chastised, and his chastisement lasts for 7 times. He is then restored.	Ch. 9 — The desolations of Jerusalem: Israel's sins have brought on them the curse warned of in the OT. Jerusalem will be restored, but Israel's persistence in sin will bring on further desolations lasting to the end of 70×7 years. Then Jerusalem will be finally restored.
Ch. 5 — Belshazzar makes a god of his pleasures, but still recognizes the gods of stone etc. The writing on the wall. The end of Belshazzar and the end of the Babylonian empire.	Ch. 10–12 — The king exalts himself above every god, and regards no god. The Writing of Truth. The series of apparent 'ends' leading up to 'the time of the end' and eventually to The End itself.

DISPENSATIONALISM

In terms of the flow of biblical history, dispensationalists recognize seven different time periods: innocency or freedom, conscience, civil government, promise, Mosaic law, grace, and the millennium.[32]

The first dispensation terminated at the time Adam and Eve lapsed into sin, losing their freedom (Gen 1:28–3:6). The next period, which is described in Genesis 4:1–8:14, ended when God brought judgment upon the evil consciences of mankind through the flood. During the third dispensation God gave mankind the

---

[32]The Bible of Dispensationalism is the *Scofield Reference Bible*, first published in 1909.

right to develop human government. Mankind turned this right into rebellion against God by building the Tower of Babel (Gen 8:15–11:9). The fourth interval covers the patriarchs — Abraham, Isaac, and Jacob — and Israel's sojourn in Egyptian slavery (Gen 11:10–Exod 18:27). God's promise to Abraham of family, land, and blessing forms the basis for this dispensation. The fifth interval lasted from the time of Moses until the death of Christ (Exod 19:1–Acts 1:26). During the interval of grace man's responsibility is to accept God's gift of righteousness. This age will end with man's rejection of God's gracious gift, resulting in the tribulation (Acts 2:1–Rev 19:21). The final interval of time is dominated by the personal, visible, and millennial rule of Christ. At the end of this interval a final rebellion will break out and result in the final judgment (Rev 20).

Daniel 2:44 is an important verse in dispensational interpretation. This verse reads as follows: "In the time of those kings, the God of heaven will set up a kingdom that will never be destroyed, nor will it be left to another people. It will crush all those kingdoms and bring them to an end, but it will itself endure forever."

The view of this commentary is that the victorious kingdom foretold in this passage was set up two millennia ago during the time of the Roman Caesars by Jesus and his apostles, and has been growing and spreading ever since. The reference to "those [vanquished] kingdoms" is best understood as a reference to the kingdoms of Babylon, Medo-Persia, Greece, and Rome, the quintessential representatives of Gentile world dominion. The "kingdom of God," which Jesus proclaimed as present in his ministry, is an irresistible spiritual might that has not passed and will not pass to another people.

The dispensational interpretation is quite different, insisting that its fulfillment is wholly future. Dispensationalists identify "those kings" with the ten horns of the fourth beast of Daniel 7, which they regard as ten kingdoms which will arise out of a restored (hence future) Roman Empire. "Those kings" will be destroyed during the final dispensation, during Christ's millennial kingdom.

The difference between the view of this commentary and that of dispensationalists is obvious: in this work this prophecy is fixed to the First Advent of Jesus, while the dispensationalists would fix it to his Second.

Leon Wood's Daniel commentary fixes this prophecy to Jesus'

Second Advent. Wood suggests that the fifth kingdom of Daniel 2, which he considers to be the earthly and millennial reign of Christ, will be earthly, physical, and temporal (1000 years) in character. Such a conclusion ignores the contrast drawn between the physical and temporal kingdoms of human government and the divine (and hence, by nature, spiritual) and eternal ("the God of heaven will set up a kingdom that will never be destroyed") kingdom of God. His view also ignores the simple words of Jesus to Pilate: "My kingdom is not of this world. If it were, my servants would fight to prevent my arrest by the Jews. But now my kingdom is from another place" (John 18:36).

Wood also suggests that Christ's spiritual kingdom, inaugurated at his first coming, has never filled all the earth. But according to Daniel 2:35 this kingdom is to fill the whole earth. Wood writes, "In fact, today people continue to be born faster than they are being won to Christ. Ground actually is being lost, rather than gained. But Christ's millennial kingdom will indeed come to fill all the earth. The capital will be established in Jerusalem; Israel will be the special kingdom in the world community; and all the world will be under the supreme rule of the perfect King."[33] Wood has apparently overlooked the first-century pronouncement of Paul in Colossians 1:6. "All over the world this gospel is bearing fruit and growing, just as it has been doing among you since the day you heard it and understood God's grace in all its truth."

Dispensationalists also see the consummation of Daniel 9:24 ("Seventy sevens [weeks] are decreed for your people and your holy city to finish transgression, to put an end to sin, to atone for wickedness, to bring in everlasting righteousness, to seal up vision and prophecy and to anoint the most holy.") as still pending. Accordingly, they assert that the seventieth week does not follow immediately upon the sixty-ninth week. Rather, a long parenthesis, that is, an indefinite interval of time, interrupts these two weeks. The prophetic clock stopped ticking with the death of Jesus on the cross (end of the 69th week) and will commence again when the Antichrist leads a great army against the people of God.

---

[33]Leon Wood, *A Commentary on Daniel* (Grand Rapids: Zondervan, 1973), p. 73.

This gap of now well over 1900 years appears to destroy the natural reading of the weeks as consecutive. More importantly, this view ignores NT passages that support the contention that the First Advent of Jesus easily fulfills the six purpose statements of Daniel 9:24. With regard to the first three—"to finish transgression, to put an end to sin, to atone for wickedness"—Jesus himself said, "This is my blood of the covenant, which is poured out for many for the forgiveness of sins" (Matt 26:28). Apropos of the fourth purpose — "to bring in everlasting righteousness" — the Apostle Paul writes,

> But now a righteousness from God, apart from law, has been made known, to which the Law and the Prophets testify. This righteousness from God comes through faith in Jesus Christ to all who believe. There is no difference, for all have sinned and fall short of the glory of God, and are justified freely by his grace through the redemption that came by Jesus Christ. God presented him as a sacrifice of atonement, through faith in his blood (Rom 3:21-25a).[34]

The fifth purpose — "to seal up vision and prophecy" — is reflected in the words of Paul found in 2 Corinthians 1:20: "For no matter how many promises God has made, they are 'Yes' in Christ. And so through him the 'Amen' is spoken by us to the glory of God."

Finally, dispensationalists understand the sixth purpose statement — "to anoint the most holy" — as a reference to a restored millennial temple.[35] At 9:24 in the commentary evidence will be presented for a personal and messianic understanding of "the most holy." Let it suffice here simply to state that we have no indication whatever that Israel's temples were anointed — whether the first one or the second one. But at his baptism Jesus clearly was. When Jesus came up out of the waters, he saw the Spirit of God descending like a dove and lighting on him (Matt 4:16), fulfilling Isaiah 61:1. "The Spirit of the Sovereign LORD is on me, because the LORD has anointed me to preach good news to the poor" (cf. Isa 11:2).

---

[34]J. Barton Payne, "The Goal of Daniel's Seventy Weeks," *JETS* 21 (June 1978): 97-115.

[35]Robert C. Newman, "Daniel's Seventy Weeks and the Old Testament Sabbath-Year Cycle," *JETS* 16 (Fall 1973): 229-234.

MAJOR MILLENNIAL VIEWS[36]

MILLENNIALISM OR PREMILLENNIALISM

According to this view, at the Second Coming of Jesus, Satan will be bound so that he may not deceive the nations (Rev 20:1-3). Christ will then reign with his resurrected saints for a millennium, a thousand years (Rev 20:4), over the earth. The unbelieving nations that are still on the earth at this time are ruled over by Christ with a rod of iron. Sin and death still exist, but evil is greatly restrained.

Near the end of the millennium Satan will be loosed. He will gather the rebellious nations together for one final assault upon God's people. Fire from heaven will consume these nations and Satan will be cast into the lake of fire.

After the millennium has ended, there follows the resurrection of unbelievers who have died, the great judgment, and then the final states of heaven and hell are ushered in.

A literal reading of Revelation 20:4 is precarious for two reasons. First, a literal reading of apocalyptic material, as the Book of Revelation surely is, is a methodological misstep. Secondly, and more importantly, the belief in a millennial reign of Christ upon the earth conflicts with 2 Peter 3:10-13. Peter states quite clearly that the Second Coming of Christ will be followed at once by the dissolution of the old earth and the creation of the new earth.

> But the day of the Lord will come like a thief. The heavens will disappear with a roar; the elements will be destroyed by fire, and the earth and everything in it will be laid bare.
>
> Since everything will be destroyed in this way, what kind of people ought you to be? You ought to live holy and godly lives as you look forward to the day of God and speed its coming. That day will bring about the destruction of the heavens by fire, and the elements will melt in the heat. But in keeping with his promise we are looking forward to a new heaven and a new earth, the home of righteousness.

---

[36]Excellent discussions of the millennium may be found in: Anthony A. Hoekema, *The Bible and the Future* (Grand Rapids: Eerdmans, 1979), pp. 173-193; and Robert C. Clouse, ed., *The Meaning of the Millennium: Four Views* (Downers Grove, IL: InterVarsity, 1980).

149

DISPENSATIONAL PREMILLENNIALISM

Proponents of this view suggest that Christ's return will occur in two stages. The first stage is the so-called rapture. At the time of the rapture, resurrected believers (exclusive of Old Testament saints) and glorified believers are caught up in the clouds to meet the descending Lord in the air. This body of believers then ascends with the Lord to heaven to celebrate for seven years the marriage supper of the Lamb.

Dispensationalists assert that this seven-year period is Daniel's seventieth week (Dan 9:24-27). During this seven-year period, a number of events will unfold here on earth: (1) the tribulation predicted in Daniel 9:27 will begin; (2) the antichrist will begin his cruel reign; (3) terrible judgments will fall upon the earth; (4) the 144,000 Israelites of Revelation 7:3-8 will turn to Jesus as Messiah; (5) this believing remnant will preach a twofold message: the coming Davidic Kingdom and the message of the cross; (6) through this Jewish witness an innumerable multitude of Gentiles will be brought to salvation; and (7) the armies of the beast and the false prophet will gather to attack the people of God in the Battle of Armageddon.

At the end of this seven-year period, Christ will come all the way down to earth and destroy his enemies thus ending the Battle of Armageddon. The majority of Israelites then living will turn to Christ and be saved. The devil will be bound, cast into the abyss, and sealed there for a literal thousand years. Now follows the judgment of living Gentiles (Matt 25:31-46) and of Israel. Those Gentiles and Israelites who have turned to the Lord will enter the millennial reign and enjoy its blessings. Those who have failed the test will be cast into everlasting fire.

The saints who died during the seven-year tribulation and the Old Testament saints are now raised from the dead and join the risen and translated saints who constitute the raptured church in heaven.

Christ then begins his millennial reign. At the beginning of this reign no unregenerate people are living on the earth. This is truly a golden age. Worship in the millennium will center around a rebuilt temple in Jerusalem. Animal sacrifices will be offered in this temple, in remembrance of Christ's death for us.

The resurrected saints mentioned earlier will be living in the new, heavenly Jerusalem, which will be in the air above the earth.

Many of the children born during the millennium will them-selves become believers. Those children that turn out to be rebel-lious against the Lord will be held in check by Jesus. At the end of the millennium, after Satan has been loosed from his prison, he will gather together an army for a final attack upon the saints of God. This rebellion will be smashed, and Satan will be cast into the lake of fire. All believers who died during the millennium will be raised.

After the millennium has ended, all the unbelieving dead will be raised, judged, and cast into the lake of fire. This is known as the second death.

The heavenly Jerusalem, the dwelling place of the resurrected saints, will then descend to a new earth, where God and his people will dwell together for eternity.

AMILLENNIALISM

This view teaches that the thousand years of Revelation 20:4-6 symbolize the present reign of the souls of deceased believers with Christ in heaven. This reign of Christ is not exclusively future but is now in process of realization. At the end of this millennial reign, the Second Coming of Christ will immediately usher in the consumma-tion, final judgment, and the new heavens and earth.

POSTMILLENNIALISM

Like amillennialism, postmillennialism posits that the millennial reign of Christ does not involve a visible reign of Christ from an earthly throne. His reign is not literally a thousand years in duration. The present age will merge into the millennial age when the world becomes Christianized through the preaching of the gospel. The Christianizing of society is a prerequisite to the Second Coming of Jesus, which, in turn, will be followed by the general resurrection, the general judgment, and the introduction of heaven and hell in their fullness.

Speaking of this "golden age" of Christianity, Loraine Boettner writes, "This does not mean that there ever will be a time on this earth when every person will be a Christian, or that all sin will be abolished. But it does mean that evil in all its many forms eventually will be reduced to negligible proportions, that Christian principles will be the rule, not the exception, and that Christ will return to a truly Christianized world."[37]

APOCALYPTIC LITERATURE

Paul Hanson defines *apocalyptic* writing as follows: "A group of writings concerned with the renewal of faith and the reordering of life on the basis of a vision of a prototypical heavenly order revealed to a religious community through a seer. The author tends to relativize the significance of existing realities by depicting how they are about to be superseded by God's universal reign in an eschatological event that can neither be hastened nor thwarted by human efforts, but which will unfold, true to an eternal plan, as the result of divine action."[38]

In short, apocalyptic writing is a crisis literature intended to offer comfort and hope to the afflicted. This hope is conveyed through two powerful messages: the whole of history is in God's control, and the goal of history is the Kingdom of God.[39]

For the apocalyptist, the present age is evil and oppression is commonplace, but ultimate power lies in the hands of God and in the end he will prevail. Kings and kingdoms inevitably arise, but only by the permissive will of God. Their rise is known in advance by God and their fall is a predetermined function of his righteous judgment. Russell writes, "There is a moral factor at work in history and a judgment upon history that is inevitable and decisive. It is a judgment that falls on individuals and institutions alike as inevitably and as decisively as night follows day."[40]

For the apocalyptic visionary, only a short step is needed to come to the conclusion that the goal of history is the Kingdom of God. Russell writes, "They were able to interpret the happenings of his-

---

[37]Loraine Boettner, *The Millennium* (Grand Rapids: Baker, 1958), p. 14.
[38]Paul D. Hanson, *Old Testament Apocalyptic* (Nashville: Abingdon Press, 1987), pp. 27-28.
[39]Russell, *Divine*, p. 135.
[40]Ibid., p. 136.

tory in the light of eternity. They saw meaning and judgment in history because at the end of the process lay the goal, foreordained and predetermined by God, in whose light the whole of history would at last make sense. The real significance of history for them lay in its end, its completion, its fulfillment in the coming Kingdom."[41]

Both of these themes are evident in Daniel 2. In Nebuchadnezzar's dream God reveals a sequence of four earthly kingdoms that is predetermined by God's permissive will (2:38). The collapse of the fourth kingdom indicates that the goal of history has been reached—the Kingdom of God. "In the time of those kings, the God of heaven will set up a kingdom that will never be destroyed, nor will it be left to another people. It will crush all those kingdoms and bring them to an end, but it will itself endure forever" (2:44).

Daniel 7 treats the same themes as well. Four beastly kingdoms will arise and dominate the world's stage. The kingdoms represented by the beasts are the same kingdoms represented by the metals in chapter 2. These kingdoms are presented before the tribunal of God's judgment and found wanting (7:10). These earthly kingdoms are then eclipsed by the Kingdom of God. "The four great beasts are four kingdoms that will rise from the earth. But the saints of the Most High will receive the kingdom and will possess it forever—yes, for ever and ever" (7:17-18).

The apocalyptic genre is characterized by a number of features. In his fine volume entitled *Apocalyptic*, Leon Morris lists thirteen of these features.[42] They are:

(1) *Revelations.* Apocalyptic visionaries typically looked to angels as the source of their information. Consequently, they did not have the same awareness of the immediate presence of God as did the great prophets.

(2) *Symbolism.* Symbolism (beasts, mountains, stars) and significant numbers (3, 4, 7, 10, 12, 70) abound.

(3) *Pessimism.* According to the visionaries, this world was in a bad state and it would get worse. Nothing but trouble could be expected for a sinful world.

(4) *The shaking of the foundations.* As a result of this profound pessimism, the visionaries were convinced that only a cataclysmic destruction could set the cosmos straight.

---

[41]Ibid., p. 137.
[42]Morris, *Apocalyptic*, pp. 34-67.

(5) *The triumph of God.* At the heart of the apocalyptic movement is the conviction of the ultimate victory of God.

(6) *Determinism.* For the apocalyptists it was clear that the course of this world's history is predetermined. This approach did give meaning to the world's agony. The apocalyptists maintained that the hand of God was in it all.

(7) *Dualism.* Evil and good are set against each other — Satan against God and the heathen nations against God's people. The nations of this world are contrasted with the kingdom of God. This age is set against the age to come.

(8) *Pseudonymity.* The apocalyptic writer attributes his work to a recognized hero of the faith, such as Ezra or Moses or Abraham or Baruch. Ascribing a work to an illustrious ancient added immensely to the respect accorded the writings.

(9) *A literary form.* Apocalyptic is a literary device, a way of getting a message across. The message conveyed arose from the author's imagination, and not from actual events of the past.

(10) *Rewritten history.* Apocalyptists take history and rewrite it in the form of prophecy.

(11) *Ethical teaching.* The apocalyptists looked for upright conduct. The hope the visionaries held out at the End was for the righteous, not all men. If the End is imminent, men cannot put off repentance.

(12) *Prediction.* The visionaries were futurists. They were vitally interested in the way God would break into this world of time and sense and bring an end to the present system.

(13) *Historical perspective.* Apocalyptic visionaries are content to abandon the present and look for the future consummation — a divine breaking in on this present historical process. The historical process they are ready to abandon.

The Book of Daniel certainly evidences many of these apocalyptic features. Apropos of (1), each major unit in Daniel 7–12 features a heavenly being offering words of explanation to Daniel (7:16; 8:15-16; 9:21; 10:5; 12:5). Symbolism (2) is obviously paramount in a book like Daniel. The Book of Daniel shares the perspective of pessimism (3). The world is in a bad state, and it can only get worse. Daniel 12:1 warns, "There will be a time of distress such as has not happened from the beginning of nations until then."

In Daniel the belief in the inevitable triumph of God (5) and determinism (6) are obvious, as has already been noted. Dualism (7) is also significantly attested in Daniel. Demonic resistance to the divine will is mentioned in 10:12-14, and again in 10:20-21. The predicted persecution of the Jews under the terrible reign of Antiochus (8:9-12) is evidence enough of heathen hatred of God's people.

Daniel 7–12 may not abound in ethical teaching (11), but two instances are integral to the texture of the book. First, in Daniel 9, as Daniel confesses his and the nation's sin, the angel Gabriel was dispatched to announce God's long-term solution to the sin problem. Second, in terms of the End, only "those who are wise" and "those who lead many to righteousness" will receive "everlasting life." The others will experience "shame and everlasting contempt" (12:2-3).

The Book of Daniel shares with the apocalyptic genre these seven characteristics. The other six are much more debatable. For example, rewritten history (10) is the assumption of late-date theorists. This is not the view of this commentary. It is a precarious argument to label a book "apocalyptic," and then to assign to it a date of composition based on this nomenclature, when there is much in the book that is not apocalyptic, or when the material can be explained from another perspective, such as prophecy.

To summarize: Daniel shares with apocalyptic literature the twin concerns of God's control and the coming Kingdom of God, as well as a number of important features or characteristics.

These affinities with the apocalyptic genre must be balanced by Daniel's affinities with earlier prophetic literature, the Wisdom literature and the Psalms. N. Porteous is right to claim: "Perhaps the wisest course is to take the Book of Daniel as a distinctive piece of literature with a clearly defined witness of its own, and to take note of the various ways in which it borrows from and is colored by the earlier prophetic literature, the Wisdom literature, and the Psalms and has its successors in the apocalypses, though these often exhibit an extravagance and a fantastic imagination which is less prominent in the Book of Daniel."[43]

Of the same opinion, Morris writes, "We should not miss the uniqueness of this book. It is like the apocalypses it is true, and there

---

[43]As cited in ibid., p. 80.

can be little doubt that many of the apocalyptists copied its form. But its essence is otherwise."[44]

Daniel's affinity with earlier prophecy is obvious. For example, both prophecy and Daniel stress God's moral control of the outcomes of history. In Isaiah 10 the prophet first bemoans the moral collapse of Judah: "Woe to those who make unjust laws, to those who issue oppressive decrees, to deprive the poor of their rights and withhold justice from the oppressed of my people, making widows their prey and robbing the fatherless" (10:1-2). As a consequence, the prophet then warns: "What will you do on the day of reckoning, when disaster comes from afar? To whom will you run for help? Where will you leave your riches? Nothing will remain but to cringe among the captives or fall among the slain" (10:3-4). Disaster will come from afar – the Assyrian army, "the rod of my [God's] anger" (10:5).

In turn, the Assyrians will come into the courtroom of the holy judge of the cosmos. His verdict: guilty! "I will punish the king of Assyria for the willful pride of his heart and the haughty look in his eyes" (10:12). The prophet then warns of Assyria's impending destruction: "Therefore, the Lord, the LORD Almighty, will send a wasting disease upon his sturdy warriors; under his pomp a fire will be kindled like a blazing flame" (10:16).

The prophet Habakkuk provides a second example of this glorious theme. He complains to God of the perversion manifest in Judean society. "The wicked hem in the righteous, so that justice is perverted" (1:4). The LORD responds to the prophet's complaint by promising judgment upon Judah – judgment in the form of the Babylonians. "Look at the nations and watch—and be utterly amazed. For I am going to do something in your days that you would not believe, even if you were told. I am raising up the Babylonians, that ruthless and impetuous people, who sweep across the whole earth to seize dwelling places not their own" (1:5-6).

In turn, the Babylonians will fall, undone by the consequences of their own sin. Five times in chapter 2 the prophet pronounces a "Woe" oracle against the Babylonians (2:6,9,12,15,19). Each pronouncement warns of impending judgment upon the moral depravity of the Babylonians. For example, hear the third oracle: "Woe to him who builds a city with bloodshed and establishes a town by

---

[44]Ibid., pp. 80-81.

crime! Has not the LORD Almighty determined that the people's labor is only fuel for the fire, that the nations exhaust themselves for nothing? For the earth will be filled with the knowledge of the glory of the LORD, as the waters cover the sea" (2:12-14).

Every Old Testament prophecy against a foreign nation understands that nation's impending calamity to be a direct result of God's moral determinism for the cosmos. The holy standards of a just God are writ large across the pages of human history.

MATTHEW 24:15

The expression "the abomination that causes desolation" occurs four times in Daniel (8:13; 9:27; 11:31; 12:11). Daniel 8:13 and 11:31 clearly refer to the desecration of the Jewish temple under Antiochus Epiphanes, who erected an altar to Zeus and sacrificed swine upon it. In Matthew 24:15 Jesus is identifying Daniel 9:27 and 12:11 (Matthew agrees with the LXX of 12:11) with certain events about to take place. In all likelihood, Jesus' identification of the latter passage is a typological fulfillment. The destruction of Jerusalem and its temple in A.D. 70 by the Romans would easily be likened to the desecration of the temple by Antiochus over two centuries earlier. The Romans erected on the temple mount their standards, which bore the image of the emperor, then offered sacrifice to them (Josephus *Wars* 6:316). John Broadus comments, "The Roman military standard, with its eagle of silver or bronze, and under that an imperial bust which the soldiers were accustomed to worship, standing anywhere in the holy city, would be a violation of the second commandment, would be abominable in the eyes of all devout Jews, would in itself desolate the holy place, according to their feeling, and would foretoken a yet more complete desolation."[45]

Since Luke writes for Gentile readers, who would not understand the Jewish expression "the abomination that causes desolation," he paraphrases Daniel. "When you see Jerusalem surrounded by armies, you will know that its desolation is near" (21:20). Jesus by this Jewish expression meant the threat to Judea and Jerusalem by

---

[45]John A. Broadus, *Commentary on Matthew* (Grand Rapids: Kregel, 1990), p. 486.

hostile armies — the Roman army that would overwhelm Jerusalem. The setting up of an abomination in the temple precinct is a direct result of the pagan attack.

LIFE OF DANIEL

We know nothing of the early life of Daniel, except what is recorded in the book that bears his name. Daniel 1:3 reports that he was one of the youths of royal or noble seed who were exiled to Babylon by Nebuchadnezzar in the third year of Jehoiakim king of Judah.

In captivity he was educated in the language and literature of the Babylonians. He was even given the Babylonian name Belteshazzar ("protect the king"). The Babylonians were grooming him for royal service. But his God, the God of Israel, had a plan for him as well. He bestowed on him the gift of understanding visions and dreams. At the end of his formal training he was found to be superior to all the Babylonian magicians and enchanters in every matter of wisdom and understanding.

Daniel's public service was in keeping with his education and divine giftedness. He interpreted King Nebuchadnezzar's dreams, as recorded in Daniel 2 and Daniel 4. In Daniel 5 he was called upon by Belshazzar to interpret the extraordinary writing on the palace wall. In the last six chapters of the book we have recorded his own visions, all of which relate to the future history of the great world empires and the final triumph of the Kingdom of God.

In addition to his duties as interpreter, Daniel also stood high in the governmental service of Nebuchadnezzar, Belshazzar, and Darius = Cyrus. He was governor over the whole province of Babylon under Nebuchadnezzar (Dan 2:48). Belshazzar made him third highest ruler in the kingdom (Dan 5:29). Darius made him one of the three presidents to whom the satraps were to give an account (Dan 6:1-3).

The last recorded vision of Daniel occurred in the third year of Cyrus (536 B.C.), when the prophet was very advanced in years. By tradition Daniel was buried in Susa, though this is admittedly difficult to substantiate.

OUTLINE OF DANIEL

I. DANIEL AND HIS FRIENDS IN NEBUCHADNEZZAR'S
COURT — 1:1-21
A. Historical Introduction — 1:1-2
B. The Introduction of Daniel and His Friends — 1:3-7
C. The Test — 1:8-16
D. The Conclusion — 1:17-21

II. GOD REVEALS NEBUCHADNEZZAR'S DREAM TO
DANIEL — 2:1-49
A. Introduction — 2:1
B. The King and His Unwise Courtiers — 2:2-12
C. Daniel and Arioch — 2:13-16
D. Daniel and His Friends Pray to God — 2:17-23
E. Daniel and Arioch — 2:24-25
F. The King and Daniel, the Wise Courtier — 2:26-45
G. Result/Nebuchadnezzar's Response — 2:46-49

III. GOD SAVES DANIEL'S FRIENDS FROM THE FIERY
FURNACE — 3:1-30
A. The Image of Gold — 3:1-7
B. The Accusation against Shadrach, Meshach, and
Abednego — 3:8-12
C. The Confrontation with Nebuchadnezzar — 3:13-18
D. Deliverance — 3:19-27
E. Nebuchadnezzar Worships God — 3:28-30

IV. NEBUCHADNEZZAR PRAISES THE MOST HIGH GOD —
4:1-37
A. Nebuchadnezzar Praises the Most High God — 4:1-3
B. Nebuchadnezzar's Dream — 4:4-18
C. Daniel's Interpretation and Its Fulfillment — 4:19-33
D. Nebuchadnezzar Praises the Most High God — 4:34-37

V. THE WRITING ON THE WALL — 5:1-31
A. The Profanation of the Temple Vessels — 5:1-4

BIBLIOGRAPHY

Archer, Gleason L. Jr. "The Aramaic of the 'Genesis Apocryphon' Compared with the Aramaic of Daniel." In *New Perspectives on the Old Testament*, pp. 160-169. Edited by J. Barton Payne. Waco, TX: Word, 1970.

_____. "Daniel." In *The Expositor's Bible Commentary*, vol. 7, pp. 1-158. Edited by Frank E. Gaebelein. Grand Rapids: Zondervan, 1985.

Arnold, B.T. "The Use of Aramaic in the Hebrew Bible: Another Look at Bilingualism in Ezra and Daniel." *Journal of Northwest Semitic Languages* 22 (1996): 1-16.

_____. "Wordplay and Narrative Techniques in Daniel 5 and 6." *JBL* 112 (1993): 479-485.

Baker, David W. "Further Examples of the *Waw Explicativum*." *VT* 30 (1980): 129-136.

Baldwin, Joyce G. *Daniel*. Tyndale Old Testament Commentaries. Downers Grove, IL: InterVarsity, 1978.

Barker, Margaret. "Slippery Words III, Apocalyptic." *ExpTim* 89 (1977–78): 324-329.

Braverman, Jay. *Jerome's Commentary on Daniel: A Study of Comparative Jewish and Christian Interpretations of the Hebrew Bible*. The Catholic Biblical Quarterly Monograph Series, no. 7. Washington: The Catholic Biblical Association of America, 1978.

Brewer, David. "Mene Mene Teqel Uparsin: Daniel 5:25 in Cuneiform." *TynBul* 42 (1991).

Butler, Paul T. *Daniel*. Bible Study Textbook Series. Joplin, MO: College Press, 1970.

Calvin, John. *Commentaries on the Book of the Prophet Daniel,* volume second. Translated by Thomas Myers. Grand Rapids: Eerdmans, 1948.

_____ . *Daniel I.* Calvin's Old Testament Commentaries, no. 20. Translated by T.H.L. Parker. Grand Rapids: Eerdmans, 1993.

Clouse, Robert C., ed. *The Meaning of the Millennium: Four Views.* Downers Grove, IL: InterVarsity, 1980.

Collins, John J. *Daniel.* Hermeneia. Minneapolis: Fortress Press, 1993.

_____ ., ed. *Apocalypse: The Morphology of a Genre.* Semeia 14. 1979.

Davies, P.R. "Daniel Chapter Two." *JTS* 27 (1976): 392-401.

Fewell, D.N. *Circle of Sovereignty: A Story of Stories in Daniel 1-6.* Sheffield: JSOT, 1988.

Gammie, J.G. "The Classification, Stages of Growth, and Changing Intentions in the Book of Daniel." *JBL* 95 (1976): 197-202.

Goldingay, John E. *Daniel.* Word Biblical Commentary. Dallas: Word, 1989.

Gooding, David W. "The Literary Structure of the Book of Daniel and Its Implications." *TynBul* 32 (1981): 43-79.

Gurney, Robert J.M. "The Four Kingdoms of Daniel 2 and 7." *Themelios* 2 (1977): 39-45.

_____ . "The Seventy Weeks of Daniel 9:24-27." *EvQ* 53 (1981): 29-36.

Hanson, Paul D. *Old Testament Apocalyptic.* Nashville: Abingdon Press, 1987.

Harrison, Roland K. *Introduction to the Old Testament.* Grand Rapids: Eerdmans, 1969.

Heaton, E.W. *The Book of Daniel.* Torch Bible Commentaries. London: SCM Press, 1956.

Hoekema, Anthony A. *The Bible and the Future.* Grand Rapids: Eerdmans, 1979.

Holt, Frank. "Alexander in the East." *Odyssey* 4 (July/August 2001): 14-23, 58.

Keil, C.F. *Biblical Commentary on the Book of Daniel.* Commentary on the Old Testament in Ten Volumes, vol. IX. Grand Rapids: Eerdmans, 1980.

Lenglet, A. "La structure litteraire de Daniel 2–7." *Biblica* 53 (1972): 169-190.

Longman, Tremper III. *Daniel.* The NIV Application Commentary. Grand Rapids: Zondervan, 1999.

Lowe, Chuck. "Do Demons Have Zip Codes?" *Christianity Today* 42 (July 13, 1998): 57.

Lucas, Ernest C. "The Origin of Daniel's Four Empires Scheme Re-Examined." *TynBul* 40 (1989): 185-202.

Luck, G. Coleman. *Daniel.* Chicago: Moody, 1958.

McComiskey, Thomas E. "The Seventy 'Weeks' of Daniel against the Background of Ancient Near Eastern Literature." *WTJ* 47 (1985): 18-45.

Metzger, Bruce M., ed. *The Oxford Annotated Apocrypha.* New York: Oxford University Press, 1977.

Millard, A.R. "Daniel and Belshazzar in History." *BAR* 11 (1985): 72-78.

_____. "Daniel 1–6 and History." *EvQ* 49 (1977): 67-73.

Montgomery, James A. *A Critical and Exegetical Commentary on the Book of Daniel.* ICC. Edinburgh: T. & T. Clark, 1959.

Morris, Leon. *Apocalyptic.* Grand Rapids: Eerdmans, 1972.

Newman, Robert C. "Daniel's Seventy Weeks and the Old Testament Sabbath-Year Cycle." *JETS* 16 (Fall 1973): 229-234.

Oswalt, John N. "Recent Studies in Old Testament Eschatology and Apocalyptic." *JETS* 24 (1981): 289-301.

Payne, J. Barton. "The Goal of Daniel's Seventy Weeks." *JETS* 21 (June 1978): 97-115.

Porteous, Norman W. *Daniel: A Commentary.* The Old Testament Library. Philadelphia: The Westminster Press, 1965.

Prinsloo, G.T.M. "Two Poems in a Sea of Prose: The Context and Content of Daniel 2.20-23 and 6.27-28." *JSOT* 59 (1993).

Pusey, E.B. *Daniel the Prophet.* New York: Funk & Wagnalls, 1885.

Rowley, H.H. *Darius the Mede and the Four World Empires in the Book of Daniel.* Cardiff: University of Wales, 1958.

Russell, D.S. *Daniel.* The Daily Study Bible. Philadelphia: The Westminster Press, 1981.

_____. *Divine Disclosure.* Minneapolis: Fortress Press, 1992.

Soesilo, Daud. "Why Did Daniel Reject the King's Delicacies? (Daniel 1:8)." *BT* 45 (1994): 441-444.

Tatford, Frederick A. *The Climax of the Ages: Studies in the Prophecy of Daniel.* London: Oliphants, 1964.

Towner, W. Sibley. *Daniel.* Interpretation. Atlanta: John Knox Press, 1984.

Unger, Merrill F. *Biblical Demonology.* Wheaton, IL: Van Kampen Press, 1953.

Wallace, Ronald S. *The Lord Is King: The Message of Daniel.* The Bible Speaks Today. Downers Grove, IL: InterVarsity, 1979.

Waltke, Bruce K. "The Date of the Book of Daniel." *BSac* 133 (Oct.-Dec. 1976): 319-329.

Walton, John H. "The Decree of Darius the Mede in Daniel 6." *JETS* 31 (1988): 279-286.

_____. "The Four Kingdoms of Daniel." *JETS* 29 (1986): 25-36.

Wenham, David. "The Kingdom of God and Daniel." *ExpTim* 98 (1987): 132-134.

Wenham, Gordon J. "Daniel: The Basic Issues." *Themelios* 2 (1977): 49-52.

Whitcomb, J.C. *Darius the Mede.* Grand Rapids: Eerdmans, 1959.

Wiseman, Donald J. *Chronicles of Chaldean Kings (626–556 B.C.)*. London: British Museum, 1956.

——————. "The Last Days of Babylon." *Christianity Today* (Nov. 25, 1957): 7-10.

Wiseman, D.J.; T.C. Mitchell and R. Joyce; W.J. Martin; and K.A. Kitchen, eds. *Notes on Some Problems in the Book of Daniel*. London: Tyndale Press, 1965.

Wolters, Al. "The Riddle of the Scales in Daniel 5." *Hebrew Union College Annual* 62 (1991): 155-177.

——————. "Untying the King's Knots: Physiology and Wordplay in Daniel 5." *JBL* 110 (1991): 117-122.

Wood, Leon. *A Commentary on Daniel*. Grand Rapids: Zondervan, 1973.

Yamauchi, Edwin M. *Greece and Babylon*. Grand Rapids: Baker, 1967.

Young, Edward J. *The Prophecy of Daniel*. Grand Rapids: Eerdmans, 1978.

Youngblood, Ronald. "A Holisitic Typology of Prophecy and Apocalyptic." In *Israel's Apostasy and Restoration*, pp. 213-221. Edited by Avraham Gileadi. Grand Rapids: Baker, 1988.

DANIEL 1

I. DANIEL AND HIS FRIENDS
IN NEBUCHADNEZZAR'S COURT (1:1-21)

A. HISTORICAL INTRODUCTION (1:1-2)

Pharaoh Neco placed Eliakim (= "God raises up"), whom he renamed **Jehoiakim** ("the LORD raises up"), on the throne in Judah (the southern kingdom) in 609 B.C., three months after the death of his father Josiah at Megiddo (2 Kgs 23:31-37). Jehoiakim's reign of eleven years (609–598), according to the author of Kings, was "evil in the eyes of the LORD" (2 Kgs 23:37).

[1]In the third year of the reign of Jehoiakim king of Judah, Nebuchadnezzar king of Babylon came to Jerusalem and besieged it. [2]And the Lord delivered Jehoiakim king of Judah into his hand, along with some of the articles from the temple of God. These he carried off to the temple of his god in Babylonia[a] and put in the treasure house of his god.

[a]2 Hebrew *Shinar*

1:1 When the Egyptian control over Syro-Palestine was broken at the battle of Carchemish in May-June 605, **Nebuchadnezzar**, king of Babylon (605–562), began to impose his will upon **Jerusalem**, the capital city of Judah (2 Kgs 24:1; 2 Chr 36:6-7). The epithet **king** is here used in a proleptic or anticipatory sense. He was not yet king at the time of this attack. On August 15/16, 605, Nabopolassar, the father of Nebuchadnezzar died. Nebuchadnezzar, the crown prince, reached the capital twenty-three days after his father's death, and ascended the throne on the same day, September 6/7, 605.[1]

---

[1]D.J. Wiseman, *Chronicles of Chaldean Kings (626–556 B.C.)* (London: British Museum, 1956), pp. 23-28.

The spelling of this foreign king's name varies in the biblical record: either Nebuchadnezzar (Daniel and the historical books) or Nebuchadrezzar (usually, Ezekiel and Jeremiah). The latter more accurately renders the Babylonian original Nabu-kudurri-uṣur = "Nabu protects the firstborn/boundary stone."

1:2 The Lord's sovereign control of human history is evident here: the **Lord delivered** (literally, "gave") Judah's king into enemy hands.[2] Nebuchadnezzar was a mere instrument of the Lord's will. The disaster took place not because of the apparent military might of Babylon or of the political weakness of Judah, but because the Lord was judging the sin of his people. The noun **Lord** (אֲדֹנָי, *'ădōnāy*), rather than "Lord" (יְהוָה, *YHWH*), emphasizes God's control.

Hezekiah had displayed the temple articles one century earlier to Babylonian emissaries (2 Kgs 20:13). Isaiah then predicted that these sacred articles would one day be seized (2 Kgs 20:17), even as now they were. In all probability the Babylonians saw the plundering of the temple of the Lord as evidence of a great victory over both Israel and over Yahweh himself. Mention here of the articles from the temple of God is also vital information for Daniel 5.

The captured articles were likely deposited in the splendid Marduk/Bel temple (cf. Jer 50:2; 51:44). When Marduk became the chief god of Babylon in the second millennium, he was given the additional name of Bel.

Shinar as a term for Babylonia "suggests a place of false religion, self-will, and self-aggrandizement" (Gen 11:1-9; Zech 5:11).[3]

B. THE INTRODUCTION OF DANIEL AND HIS FRIENDS (1:3-7)

[3]Then the king ordered Ashpenaz, chief of his court officials, to bring in some of the Israelites from the royal family and the

---

[2]Hippolytus (170–236) wrote: "These words, 'and the Lord gave,' are written, that no one, in reading the introduction to the book, may attribute their capture to the strength of the captors and the slackness of their chief" [*The Ante-Nicene Fathers*, vol. 5: *Hippolytus, Cyprian, Caius, Novatian* (Grand Rapids: Eerdmans, 1951), p. 185.

[3]John E. Goldingay, *Daniel*, Word Biblical Commentary (Dallas: Word, 1989), p. 15.

nobility— ⁴young men without any physical defect, handsome, showing aptitude for every kind of learning, well informed, quick to understand, and qualified to serve in the king's palace. He was to teach them the language and literature of the Babylonians.ᵃ ⁵The king assigned them a daily amount of food and wine from the king's table. They were to be trained for three years, and after that they were to enter the king's service.

⁶Among these were some from Judah: Daniel, Hananiah, Mishael and Azariah. ⁷The chief official gave them new names: to Daniel, the name Belteshazzar; to Hananiah, Shadrach; to Mishael, Meshach; and to Azariah, Abednego.

ᵃ4 Or *Chaldeans*

1:3-4 Commissioned by the king to spot future diplomats,[4] Ashpenaz chose men of good looks (**without any physical defect, handsome**), intellectual aptitude (**showing aptitude for every kind of learning, well informed, quick to understand**), and prior diplomatic training (**qualified to serve in the king's palace**).

These men were then to be assimilated into Babylonian society, learning the **language and literature** of the culture, imbibing in its food and drink, and receiving new names.

The native **language** of the culture was Akkadian, a Semitic language written in syllabic cuneiform. Through archaeological discovery we know something of the **literature** of that culture. Today we have examples of legal texts, historical writings, religious myths, heroic epics, wisdom material, and more.

1:5 Since food and drink are key to the plot of chapter 1, we will reserve discussion until the next section.

1:6-7 The Babylonians began the process of acculturation by giving their captives new names. Notice how these new names obliterate association with the God (-el, אֵל) or LORD (-iah, יָהּ = יְהוָה) of Israel and now associate these young men with Babylonian gods.

---

⁴Calvin wrote: "And without doubt he wished to keep them in his favor so as to entice some other Jews. Then after they had been given authority, they could (if the situation demanded) be appointed governors in Judæa and rule over their own nation, remaining nevertheless as servants of the Babylonian Empire" [D.F. Wright, ed., *Daniel I*, Calvin's Old Testament Commentaries, vol. 20 (Grand Rapids: Eerdmans, 1993), p. 25].

Hebrew Name	Meaning	Babylonian Name	Meaning[5]	Association with Babylonian deity
Daniel	God is my judge	Belteshazzar	Lady, protect the king	Lady = wife of Marduk or Bel, the patron of Babylon
Hananiah	The LORD has been gracious	Shadrach	I am very fearful	
Mishael	Who is what God is?	Meshach	I am of little account	
Azariah	The LORD is my help	Abednego	Servant of the shining one	Nabu

Rabbinic tradition and patristic literature suggest that Daniel and his three associates were eunuchs and that their captivity was in fulfillment of Isaiah 39:7: "And some of your descendants, your own flesh and blood who will be born to you, will be taken away, and they will become eunuchs in the palace of the king of Babylon."[6]

According to Plato, when the eldest son and heir to the Persian throne reaches fourteen years of life, "he is taken over by the royal tutors" (*Alcibiades* I:121). Xenophon cites sixteen or seventeen years of age as the time when young men "put themselves at the disposal of the authorities, if they are needed for any service to the state" (*Cyropaedia* I.ii.9). If these references to the Persian system of education are reliable and relevant to Babylon, then we can surmise that Daniel and his friends were teens when they began their training. Given the longevity of Daniel's career (see verse 21 and 10:1), this seems likely.

C. THE TEST (1:8-16)

⁸But Daniel resolved not to defile himself with the royal food and wine, and he asked the chief official for permission not to defile himself this way. ⁹Now God had caused the official to show

---

⁵A.R. Millard, "Daniel 1–6 and History," *EvQ* 49 (1977): 72.

⁶Jay Braverman, *Jerome's Commentary on Daniel: A Study of Comparative Jewish and Christian Interpretations of the Hebrew Bible*, The Catholic Biblical Quarterly Monograph Series, no. 7 (Washington: The Catholic Biblical Association of America, 1978), pp. 53-71.

favor and sympathy to Daniel, [10]but the official told Daniel, "I am afraid of my lord the king, who has assigned your[c] food and drink. Why should he see you looking worse than the other young men your age? The king would then have my head because of you." [11]Daniel then said to the guard whom the chief official had appointed over Daniel, Hananiah, Mishael and Azariah, [12]"Please test your servants for ten days: Give us nothing but vegetables to eat and water to drink. [13]Then compare our appearance with that of the young men who eat the royal food, and treat your servants in accordance with what you see." [14]So he agreed to this and tested them for ten days.

[15]At the end of the ten days they looked healthier and better nourished than any of the young men who ate the royal food. [16]So the guard took away their choice food and the wine they were to drink and gave them vegetables instead.

[a]10 The Hebrew for *your* and *you* in this verse is plural.

1:8 Up to this point the text has recorded no resistance to this acculturation. The youths do not object to either the formal education or to the Babylonian names. Why then do Daniel and his friends draw a line in the sand of their conscience concerning diet? In other words, why did compromise with Babylonian culture become impossible at this point? The question is not easily answered.[7]

Perhaps these young men were motivated by the dietary laws of the Old Testament (Lev 11; Deut 14:3-21). In other words, they wanted to keep *kosher*. This view seems unlikely, given that the law did not restrict any but the Nazirite from wine (Num 6:1-4), and there is no proof that these young men had taken the Nazirite vow. Additionally, according to Ezekiel 4:13, all food from Babylon or Assyria was ritually unclean (cf. Hos 9:3; Amos 7:17).

Perhaps Daniel and his friends were troubled by eating food that had first been offered to idols. Again, this seems unlikely. We have no reason to doubt that the vegetables which Daniel chose to eat had also been offered to the idols along with the meat and drink.

---

[7]Daud Soesilo, "Why Did Daniel Reject the King's Delicacies? (Daniel 1:8)," *BT* 45 (1994): 441-444.

Baldwin has suggested that eating from the king's table was tantamount to accepting a covenant-style relationship with him. "It would seem that Daniel rejected this symbol of dependence on the king because he wished to be free to fulfill his primary obligations to the God he served."[8] This view is also not convincing. Daniel and his friends may not be eating the choice meat and drink from the king's table, but they are still eating vegetables from that same table.

Daniel's rejection cannot be attributed to mere asceticism, for Daniel 10:3 presupposes that Daniel normally partook of meat and wine.

Longman suggests that the purpose of the vegetable diet was to "keep the four pious Judeans from believing that their physical appearance (and by consequence, perhaps, their intellectual gifts) were the gift of the Babylonian culture."[9] In other words, their robust appearance was a divine working.

Perhaps Daniel's abstinence insists on a limit to assimilation. Daniel did not wish to become addicted to the pleasures of court, which would have made him lose his spiritual focus. (The captive King Jehoiachin, who ate regularly at the king's table [2 Kgs 25:29], may not have been sensitive to this issue.) Calvin suggested that Daniel "was conscious of his own weakness and wanted to beware in good time lest he should be taken in the snares and fall away from godliness and the worship of God and degenerate into Chaldean customs, as if he had been brought up there and was merely one among the princes."[10]

1:9 Even though the chief official did not participate in Daniel's plan, he neither mistreated the Judean youths nor caused them trouble. This is because **God had caused the official to show favor and sympathy to Daniel**. The text literally reads, "The God gave Daniel to kindness and compassion before the chief official." The word *God* has the definite article ("the") prefixed to show that this was the work of the true God. Here, as in verse 2 and again in 17, the verb "to give" suggests divine intervention.

---

[8]Baldwin, *Daniel*, p. 83.

[9]Tremper Longman III, *Daniel*, The NIV Application Commentary (Grand Rapids: Zondervan, 1999), p. 53.

[10]Calvin, *Daniel I*, p. 31.

1:10-16 Daniel turns next to the guard whom the chief official had appointed over him. He proposes a ten-day fast. **Ten days** is long enough for the effects to be seen yet short enough not to arouse concern. The guard agrees. The test works.

In verse 15, the expression **better nourished** is used of the cows in pharaoh's dream in the Joseph story (Gen 41:2).

The guard may have agreed to the test because he could possibly have partaken of the choice food and wine apportioned to the four youths.

D. THE CONCLUSION (1:17-21)

[17]**To these four young men God gave knowledge and understanding of all kinds of literature and learning. And Daniel could understand visions and dreams of all kinds.**
[18]**At the end of the time set by the king to bring them in, the chief official presented them to Nebuchadnezzar.** [19]**The king talked with them, and he found none equal to Daniel, Hananiah, Mishael and Azariah; so they entered the king's service.** [20]**In every matter of wisdom and understanding about which the king questioned them, he found them ten times better than all the magicians and enchanters in his whole kingdom.**
[21]**And Daniel remained there until the first year of King Cyrus.**

1:17-19 At the end of their course of study, Daniel and his friends were brought before the king and, being found superior to all the other candidates, were appointed to his service. This verse ascribes this superiority to God. The use of the verb "to give" is intentional, again suggesting the sovereignty of God in Daniel's life. God directs Daniel's world by his providence. The use of the Hebrew names in verse 19 also suggests that God, and God alone, deserves the credit for the brilliance of these four youths.[11]

1:20 Daniel was additionally blessed by receiving the ability to

---

[11]Calvin's comments are apropos here. "It is God's custom to throw his enemies into amazement at his power, even when they do their utmost to flee from the light. For what was King Nebuchadnezzar's aim except to blot out any remembrance of God? That he might have about him Jews from

interpret visions and dreams (oneiromancy), just as Joseph in Genesis 37–50. This point is recorded because of what follows in chapter 2.

The superiority of these four Judeans would not endear them to those they surpassed. This jealousy becomes an important factor in chapter 3.

1:21 Daniel was in the Babylonian court for the rest of *its* days. In point of fact, according to 10:1, which attests a revelation given to Daniel in the third year of Cyrus king of Persia, Daniel outlasts his Babylonian conquerors! The chronological comments of chapter 1 suggest that Daniel lived safely through the entire seventy years of Jewish exile (606/605–536/535).

Chapter 1 has shown that "success without compromise was possible even in the midst of captivity."[12] Daniel's life testifies to the challenge of cooperating with society without compromising godliness.

Two important passages bear witness to our responsibility to seek the peace and prosperity of our societies. The first passage, Jeremiah 29:5-7, reads:

Build houses and settle down; plant gardens and eat what they produce. Marry and have sons and daughters; find wives for your sons and give your daughters in marriage, so that they too may have sons and daughters. Increase in number there; do not decrease. Also, seek the peace and prosperity of the city to which I have carried you into exile. Pray to the LORD for it, because if it prospers, you too will prosper.

Jeremiah first instructs the Judean exiles to become natural participants in their new Babylonian setting. Then he reminds them of their responsibility through prayer to the supernatural to transform that setting. Cooperate without compromise.

The second passage is 1 Peter 2:13-17.

---

noble families who would attack the religion in which they were born? This was Nebuchadnezzar's plan. But God frustrated the tyrant's purpose and made his own name to shine the brighter" (*Daniel I,* p. 44).

[12]Longman, *Daniel,* p. 56.

Submit yourselves for the Lord's sake to every authority instituted among men: whether to the king, as the supreme authority, or to governors, who are sent by him to punish those who
do wrong and to commend those who do right. For it is God's
will that by doing good you should silence the ignorant talk of
foolish men. Live as free men, but do not use your freedom as
a cover-up for evil; live as servants of God. Show proper
respect to everyone: Love the brotherhood of believers, fear
God, honor the king.

This passage begins ("submit") and ends ("honor") with concern
for the respect of rightful authority. This concern manifests itself
socially. Our lives are to be so beneficial to our social context that
they deserve commendation. The command to "fear God" precludes
compromising our integrity as we cooperate with culture.

Daniel and his friends stood against their culture when it threatened to compromise their integrity before God. In chapter 1 they
abstained from the royal diet. In chapter 3, Shadrach, Meshach, and
Abednego stood against the image of gold. In chapter 6 Daniel
stood against the evil decree against prayer. Their lives exhort us to
be fully committed to godliness, lest we be consumed by the god-
lessness of this present age.

➤ Accordingly, we must stand against every ideological expression
of the godless spirit of the age. "See to it that no one takes you captive through hollow and deceptive philosophy, which depends on
human tradition and the basic principles of this world rather than
on Christ" (Col 2:8). In fact, Paul exhorts us to take the offensive in
this ideological war. "We demolish arguments and every pretension
that sets itself up against the knowledge of God, and we take captive
every thought to make it obedient to Christ" (2 Cor 10:5).

There is no idea more insidious than philosophical naturalism.
Its explanation of human origins so devalues mankind that it leaves
us without meaning, with moral anarchy, and with existential
despair and misery. Parents, teachers, preachers should take every
opportunity to teach that human value, dignity, purpose, and hope
are based only in the biblical teaching of creation.

➤ We must stand for purity in sexual expression and against the
cultural obsession with sensuality. Paul says it succinctly in

1 Corinthians 6:13b: "The body is not meant for sexual immorality, but for the Lord, and the Lord for the body."

We were created sexual beings and God called our creation "very good." We must always remember, however, that that pronouncement was made after God had formed both Adam and Eve in his image and mandated they become one flesh. Accordingly, sexual expression is reserved for marriage. Proverbs 5:15-23 speaks of sexual satisfaction and responsibility to the marriage bond.

> Drink water from your own cistern, running water from your own well. Should your springs overflow in the streets, your streams of water in the public squares? Let them be yours alone, never to be shared with strangers. May your fountain be blessed, and may you rejoice in the wife of your youth. A loving doe, a graceful deer—may her breasts satisfy you always, may you ever be captivated by her love. Why be captivated, my son, by an adulteress? Why embrace the bosom of another man's wife? For a man's ways are in full view of the LORD, and he examines all his paths. The evil deeds of a wicked man ensnare him; the cords of his sin hold him fast. He will die for lack of discipline, led astray by his own great folly.

We must stand against every improper expression of physical passion, such as the sexualizing of children, pornography, and adultery. These degrade our humanity as men and women, empty us of any meaningful satisfaction, and tear apart the fabric of our families. "Flee from sexual immorality" (1 Cor 6:18). "Flee the evil desires of youth, and pursue righteousness, faith, love and peace, along with those who call on the Lord out of a pure heart" (2 Tim 2:22).

➤ We must stand against the seduction of materialism and serve only God. Know assuredly that Jesus told us that both the kingdom of God and money are capable of inspiring our devotion. He said, "No one can serve two masters. Either he will hate the one and love the other, or he will be devoted to the one and despise the other. You cannot serve both God and Money" (Matt 6:24).

Wealth, in and of itself, is valueless — it will bring nothing in eternity. The Bible emphatically teaches that wealth does not permit us to purchase our redemption (Ps 49:6-9; 1 Pet 1:18-19); wealth does not permit us to obtain the gift of God, the Holy Spirit (Acts 8:18-20);

wealth does not profit us in the day of wrath (Prov 11:4; cf. Job 36:19; Ezek 7:19); and, most assuredly, wealth will amount to nothing at death. Classic expressions of this are found in both testaments. In Ecclesiastes 5:15 we read, "Naked a man comes from his mother's womb, and as he comes, so he departs. He takes nothing from his labor that he can carry in his hand" (cf. Job 1:21; Ps 49:10-12). In 1 Timothy 6:7 Paul writes, "For we brought nothing into the world, and we can take nothing out of it" (cf. Jas 1:10-11; Luke 12:15-21).

If we serve money, then we have chosen to live apart from God. Wealth has tempted us to put our confidence in money rather than in God. Such was the case with the "rich ruler" (Luke 18). Even though he possessed a modicum of moral integrity, he was still far from the kingdom of God, for, you see, he had been seduced by the spirit of money. He had submitted to its power; he had been possessed by it. Money was his god.

A proper use of money is a worship of and service to Christ. Jesus taught that to the extent that we fed the hungry, gave drink to the thirsty, showed hospitality to the stranger, clothed the naked, visited the sick and imprisoned, we did it to him (Matt 25:31-46).

DANIEL 2

II. GOD REVEALS NEBUCHADNEZZAR'S DREAM TO DANIEL (2:1-49)

A. INTRODUCTION (2:1)

The outline for chapter 2, with one small variation, is that of G.T.M. Prinsloo.[1] His outline is presented here in order to see the chiastic effect.

  A. Introduction (v. 1)
    B. The king and his unwise courtiers (vv. 2-12)
      C. Daniel and Arioch (vv. 13-16)
        D. Daniel and his friends pray to God (vv. 17-23)
      C'. Daniel and Arioch (vv. 24-25)
    B'. The king and Daniel, the wise courtier (vv. 26-47)
  A'. Result (vv. 48-49)

[1]In the second year of his reign, Nebuchadnezzar had dreams; his mind was troubled and he could not sleep.

2:1 Nebuchadnezzar's second year began in March/April 603 B.C. In the spring of Nebuchadnezzar's second year, his troops were engaged in a protracted siege against a city in Syria.[2] According to Ecclesiastes 5:3, "a dream comes when there are many cares."

---

[1]G.T.M. Prinsloo, "Two Poems in a Sea of Prose: The Context and Content of Daniel 2.20-23 and 6.27-28." *JSOT* 59 (1993): 99.

[2]Wiseman, *Chronicles,* pp. 28-29.

B. THE KING AND HIS UNWISE COURTIERS (2:2-12)

[2]So the king summoned the magicians, enchanters, sorcerers and astrologers[a] to tell him what he had dreamed. When they came in and stood before the king, [3]he said to them, "I have had a dream that troubles me and I want to know what it means.[b]"

[4]Then the astrologers answered the king in Aramaic,[c] "O king, live forever! Tell your servants the dream, and we will interpret it."

[5]The king replied to the astrologers, "This is what I have firmly decided: If you do not tell me what my dream was and interpret it, I will have you cut into pieces and your houses turned into piles of rubble. [6]But if you tell me the dream and explain it, you will receive from me gifts and rewards and great honor. So tell me the dream and interpret it for me."

[7]Once more they replied, "Let the king tell his servants the dream, and we will interpret it."

[8]Then the king answered, "I am certain that you are trying to gain time, because you realize that this is what I have firmly decided: [9]If you do not tell me the dream, there is just one penalty for you. You have conspired to tell me misleading and wicked things, hoping the situation will change. So then, tell me the dream, and I will know that you can interpret it for me."

[10]The astrologers answered the king, "There is not a man on earth who can do what the king asks! No king, however great and mighty, has ever asked such a thing of any magician or enchanter or astrologer. [11]What the king asks is too difficult. No one can reveal it to the king except the gods, and they do not live among men."

[12]This made the king so angry and furious that he ordered the execution of all the wise men of Babylon.

[a]2 Or *Chaldeans*; also in verses 4, 5 and 10   [b]3 Or *was*   [c]4 The text from here through chapter 7 is in Aramaic.

2:2-3 Having apparently forgotten[3] the dream, Nebuchadnezzar

---

[3]Nebuchadnezzar retained enough of the dream so that he could later confirm the correctness of Daniel's reconstruction. Perhaps the king has not forgotten the dream but wants to test the integrity of his experts. Nebuchadnezzar may have reasoned that if the gods could reveal interpretations to the experts, then they could reveal the actual dream to the

demands that his experts — **the magicians, enchanters, sorcerers,**[4] **and astrologers** — reveal the content of the dream and the dream's meaning. This was an unreasonable and unprecedented (cf. v. 10b) demand, given that dream interpretation was based on historical precedent. Whenever a king would share the content of his dream with his experts, they, in turn, would consult their dream manuals. These manuals consisted of historical dreams and the events that followed them. Without the content of the dream, therefore, the experts had no way to anticipate the events to follow, or, if you will, to interpret it. In verses 4 and 7 the experts remind the king that interpretation is based on the content of the dream.

2:4 With the initial response of the **astrologers**, we have a language change from Hebrew to Aramaic, the *lingua franca* of the Near East at the time. The Aramaic portion of Daniel continues until 7:28 (Ezra 4:8–6:18; 7:12-26 is the other lengthy Aramaic section of the Old Testament).

The anxiety of the king, which prompted the dream, is compounded by his inability to remember the dream. The Babylonians believed that, if a man could not remember the dream he saw (it means), then his (personal) god is angry with him.

2:5-9 If the experts could not meet the king's demand, then they would be dismembered (cf. Ezek 16:40) and their homes would be ruined.

2:10-11 The experts do not receive divine revelation. They freely admit so. "**No one can reveal it to the king except the gods, and they do not live among men.**" Accordingly, they are totally unprepared for the task at hand. And this they also freely admit. "**What the king asks is too difficult.**" As a result, they know they are doomed, unless the king forgets the incident (cf. 2:9).

2:12 But he will not forget. Rather, incensed at their stall tactics, he orders their execution (cf. Prov 16:14; 19:12; 20:2). This order

---

experts. If the so-called experts could not reconstruct the king's dream, then perhaps they were frauds.

[4]The inclusion of enchanters and sorcerers in this list suggests the anticipated need to magically dispel the evil consequences of the interpreted dream.

threatens the lives of Daniel and his friends encountered in chapter 1. How will God intervene to resolve this dangerous situation?

C. DANIEL AND ARIOCH (2:13-16)

[13]**So the decree was issued to put the wise men to death, and men were sent to look for Daniel and his friends to put them to death.**
[14]**When Arioch, the commander of the king's guard, had gone out to put to death the wise men of Babylon, Daniel spoke to him with wisdom and tact.** [15]**He asked the king's officer, "Why did the king issue such a harsh decree?" Arioch then explained the matter to Daniel.** [16]**At this, Daniel went in to the king and asked for time, so that he might interpret the dream for him.**

2:13-16 The narrative does not explain how Daniel was able to have an audience with Nebuchadnezzar when he was under the threat of death. How does Daniel secure the very item — more time — which the magicians were denied? The providential care of God is always at work in this great book.

If **Arioch**, the commander of the king's guard, had already begun killing the wise men of Babylon when he came to Daniel, the granting of time to Daniel implies a stay in the execution of the remaining wise men.

Why do Daniel and his friends not know about the general order to execute all the wise men of Babylon? The text does not say. Their apparent isolation from the other experts may suggest that this story is set within the period of their three-year training. Jerome has suggested two additional possibilities: "When the king was promising rewards and gifts and great honor, they [Daniel and his friends] did not care to go before him, lest they should appear to be shamelessly grasping after the wealth and honor of the Chaldeans. Or else it was undoubtedly true that the Chaldeans themselves, being envious of the Jews' reputation and learning, entered alone before the king, as if to obtain the rewards by themselves. Afterwards they were perfectly willing to have those whom they had denied any hope of glory to share in a common peril."[5]

---

[5]Braverman, *Jerome's Commentary*, p. 26.

D. DANIEL AND HIS FRIENDS PRAY TO GOD (2:17-23)

[17]**Then Daniel returned to his house and explained the matter to his friends Hananiah, Mishael and Azariah.** [18]**He urged them to plead for mercy from the God of heaven concerning this mystery, so that he and his friends might not be executed with the rest of the wise men of Babylon.** [19]**During the night the mystery was revealed to Daniel in a vision. Then Daniel praised the God of heaven** [20]**and said:**

"**Praise be to the name of God for ever and ever;**
  wisdom and power are his.
[21]**He changes times and seasons;**
  he sets up kings and deposes them.
He gives wisdom to the wise
  and knowledge to the discerning.
[22]**He reveals deep and hidden things;**
  he knows what lies in darkness,
  and light dwells with him.
[23]**I thank and praise you, O God of my fathers:**
  You have given me wisdom and power,
you have made known to me what we asked of you,
  you have made known to us the dream of the king."

2:17-19 When the professionals told the king that divine revelation was needed to reconstruct the king's dream, they were quite right. This was the reason why Daniel and his friends prayed to God. They prayed that God would reveal the mystery of Nebuchadnezzar's dream, and, in so doing, show the reality, power, and wisdom of the one true God. Their prayer presupposes the revelatory nature of God, as had been manifest, for example, in the ministries of Israel's great prophets. For example, Amos 3:7 reads: "Surely the Sovereign LORD does nothing without revealing his plan to his servants the prophets." Likewise, Isaiah 46:10: "I make known the end from the beginning, from ancient times, what is still to come. I say: My purpose will stand, and I will do all that I please."

Daniel enlists the prayer help of his friends. In this context of prayer and faith, the Hebrew names of Daniel's colleagues are appropriately used.

2:20-23 Daniel's spontaneous hymn of thanksgiving emphasizes the power and wisdom of the one true God (cf. Job 12:13).[6] The power of God is illustrated by his control over the course of history: **he sets up kings and deposes them**. (This is precisely the point of Nebuchadnezzar's dream.)

Wisdom is a divine attribute – light dwells with him – that God had shared with the wise of this world (v. 21) and now shares with Daniel: "I thank and praise you, O God of my fathers: *You* have given me wisdom and power, *you* have made known to me what we asked of you, *you* have made known to us the dream of the king."

The epithet **God of heaven**, which is frequently used in postexilic texts (2 Chr 36:23; Ezra 1:2; 5:12; 6:9,10; 7:12,21,23; Neh 1:4,5; 2:4,20; Ps 136:26) and takes up the earlier testimony that the gods' dwelling is not with mere humanity (v. 11), bears testimony to the transcendence of God. This does not make God inaccessible (cf. v. 28). The epithet **God of my fathers** bespeaks God's immanence.

E. DANIEL AND ARIOCH (2:24-25)

[24]**Then Daniel went to Arioch, whom the king had appointed to execute the wise men of Babylon, and said to him, "Do not execute the wise men of Babylon. Take me to the king, and I will interpret his dream for him."**

[25]**Arioch took Daniel to the king at once and said, "I have found a man among the exiles from Judah who can tell the king what his dream means."**

2:24-25 Arioch claims credit for himself in discovering someone to reconstruct and interpret the king's dream: "*I* **have found a man among the exiles from Judah who can tell the king what his dream means**" (v. 25). But Arioch also expresses complete confidence in Daniel's ability to deal with the king's dream.

---

[6]Speaking of God's power and wisdom, Calvin wrote, "Let us therefore remember that God is defrauded of his just praise when these two are not kept whole – that he foresees all things, and that he governs the world so that nothing happens except by his will" (*Daniel I,* p. 68).

F. THE KING AND DANIEL, THE WISE COURTIER (2:26-45)

[26]The king asked Daniel (also called Belteshazzar), "Are you able to tell me what I saw in my dream and interpret it?" [27]Daniel replied, "No wise man, enchanter, magician or diviner can explain to the king the mystery he has asked about, [28]but there is a God in heaven who reveals mysteries. He has shown King Nebuchadnezzar what will happen in days to come. Your dream and the visions that passed through your mind as you lay on your bed are these:

[29]"As you were lying there, O king, your mind turned to things to come, and the revealer of mysteries showed you what is going to happen. [30]As for me, this mystery has been revealed to me, not because I have greater wisdom than other living men, but so that you, O king, may know the interpretation and that you may understand what went through your mind.

[31]"You looked, O king, and there before you stood a large statue—an enormous, dazzling statue, awesome in appearance. [32]The head of the statue was made of pure gold, its chest and arms of silver, its belly and thighs of bronze, [33]its legs of iron, its feet partly of iron and partly of baked clay. [34]While you were watching, a rock was cut out, but not by human hands. It struck the statue on its feet of iron and clay and smashed them. [35]Then the iron, the clay, the bronze, the silver and the gold were broken to pieces at the same time and became like chaff on a threshing floor in the summer. The wind swept them away without leaving a trace. But the rock that struck the statue became a huge mountain and filled the whole earth.

[36]"This was the dream, and now we will interpret it to the king. [37]You, O king, are the king of kings. The God of heaven has given you dominion and power and might and glory; [38]in your hands he has placed mankind and the beasts of the field and the birds of the air. Wherever they live, he has made you ruler over them all. You are that head of gold.

[39]"After you, another kingdom will rise, inferior to yours. Next, a third kingdom, one of bronze, will rule over the whole earth. [40]Finally, there will be a fourth kingdom, strong as iron—for iron

breaks and smashes everything—and as iron breaks things to pieces, so it will crush and break all the others. [41]Just as you saw that the feet and toes were partly of baked clay and partly of iron, so this will be a divided kingdom; yet it will have some of the strength of iron in it, even as you saw iron mixed with clay. [42]As the toes were partly iron and partly clay, so this kingdom will be partly strong and partly brittle. [43]And just as you saw the iron mixed with baked clay, so the people will be a mixture and will not remain united, any more than iron mixes with clay.

[44]"In the time of those kings, the God of heaven will set up a kingdom that will never be destroyed, nor will it be left to another people. It will crush all those kingdoms and bring them to an end, but it will itself endure forever. [45]This is the meaning of the vision of the rock cut out of a mountain, but not by human hands—a rock that broke the iron, the bronze, the clay, the silver and the gold to pieces.

"The great God has shown the king what will take place in the future. The dream is true and the interpretation is trustworthy."

2:26 Nebuchadnezzar's question implies disbelief, "Are you able to tell me what I saw in my dream and interpret it?"

2:27-28 Daniel's response, unlike Arioch in verse 25, is not self-seeking. Daniel does not even mention himself! Daniel publicly gives God all the glory. And, in 2:30, when Daniel does mention himself, he claims that his mediation is only for the benefit of the king.

2:29-30 This verse implies that the sleepy king was thinking of the future before he fell asleep (**your mind turned to things to come**), and that God determined to clarify that future for the king (**and the revealer of mysteries showed you what is going to happen**).

2:31-35 Nebuchadnezzar had dreamt he saw a statue (not an idol), an enormous, dazzling statue, awesome in appearance (v. 31). The statue was in human form: The head of the statue was made of pure gold, its chest and arms of silver, its belly and thighs of bronze, its legs of iron, its feet partly of iron and partly of baked clay (vv. 32-33). The statue was top-heavy, likely to topple to its ruin. To bring about this ruination, a rock appeared. The rock, moved by superhuman power, struck the statue on its feet, felling it. The fall resulted in the destruction of the iron, the clay, the bronze, the silver, and the gold of the statue.[7] A wind swept away the pieces of the statue without leaving a trace (v. 35). The rock, however, became a huge mountain and filled the whole earth (v. 35).

2:36 The **we** of this verse may be a reference to Daniel's companions (cf. vv. 17-18) or to his humility (cf. 1 Cor 2:6) — the message was not Daniel's own.

If the dream were interpreted based purely on the psychology of human fear, one could interpret the dream as follows: "The statue stood for the king, with his huge empire that he could scarcely hold, and symbolized his inadequacy in the face of threats from breakaway factions. He feared he had overreached himself and would fall. The stone which grew to fill the earth would have been a rival kingdom which supplanted his."[8]

2:37-38 Daniel's interpretation of the dream begins with the identification of Nebuchadnezzar as the **head of gold** (v. 38).[9] This identification with the most precious of metals — gold — would have been flattering. But lest pride besiege Nebuchadnezzar's mind, Daniel informs the king that his authority to rule is merely derivative. "**The God of heaven has given you dominion and power and might and glory**" (v. 37; cf. Jer 27:6; 28:14).

2:39 The **after you** of verse 39 suggests that Nebuchadnezzar will not live forever; after all, he is a mere mortal.

The adjective **another** suggests that the Neo-Babylonian Empire had been implied in the identification of Nebuchadnezzar with the "head of gold." The Neo-Babylonian Empire had been founded by Nabopolassar (626–605), the father of Nebuchadnezzar. Nebuchadnezzar was followed by Amel Marduk, the Evil-Merodach of 2 Kgs

---

[7]Keil wrote: "It is not said of the parts of the image, the head, the breast, the belly, and the thighs, that they were broken to pieces by the stone, for the forms of the world-power represented by these parts had long ago passed away, when the stone strikes against the last form of the world-power represented by the feet, but only of the materials of which these parts consist, the silver and the gold, is the destruction predicated" (*Daniel*, p. 104).

[8]Baldwin, *Daniel*, p. 92.

[9]Herodotus (1.183) reports that in the temple of Bel in Babylon there was "a solid golden statue of a man some fifteen feet high."

25:27-30 (562–560), Neriglissar (560–556), Labashi-Marduk (556), and Nabonidus (556–539), the final king of the Neo-Babylonian Empire. The Neo-Babylonian Empire would be followed by a second ("another"), **third**, and **fourth** kingdom. In other words, Daniel interprets the remaining metals as symbolic of nations rather than individual kings.[10] These kingdoms will be world empires (**will rule over the whole earth**). The identification of these kingdoms with inferior metals — silver, bronze, iron/clay — implies gradual decline.

2:40-43 The fourth kingdom is described in greater detail than either the second or third. The fourth kingdom has greater strength[11] than the previous kingdoms: **so it will crush and break all the others** (v. 40).[12] But since clay and iron do not bond together (v. 43), this kingdom is intrinsically weak.[13] "Unity is impossible and

---

[10]A number of scholars have identified individual kings with the various metals. Goldingay (*Daniel*, p. 51) suggests that the four regimes/reigns can be linked with Nebuchadnezzar and three of his Babylonian successors. P.R. Davies ["Daniel Chapter Two," *JTS* 27 (1976): 392-401] is also of the same opinion. The rock then is Cyrus. Gammie has suggested that the author of Daniel 2 understood the four metals of the image to be the first four Ptolemaic kings of Egypt [J.G. Gammie, "The Classification, Stages of Growth, and Changing Intentions in the Book of Daniel," *JBL* 95 (1976): 197-202].

[11]The greater strength of this fourth kingdom may be seen in a comparison of the longevity of these respective historical kingdoms: Neo-Babylonia: 605–539; Medo-Persia: 539–331; Greece: 331–146; Rome: 27 B.C.–A.D. 476.

[12]The interpreter of verse 40 would be wrong to think that this fourth kingdom would find the three previous kingdoms existing together. The most natural reading sees the first kingdom destroyed by the second, and the second by the third, etc. The materials of each kingdom undoubtedly passed on to the next kingdom. "The elements out of which the Babylonian world-kingdom was constituted, the countries, peoples, and civilization comprehended in it, as its external form," writes Keil, "would be destroyed by the Medo-Persian kingdom, and carried forward with it, so as to be constituted into a new external form. Such, too, was the relation between the Medo-Persian and the Macedonian world-kingdom, that the latter assumed the elements and component parts not only of the Medo-Persian, but also therewith at the same time of the Babylonian kingdom" (*Daniel*, p. 108).

[13]The expression "feet of clay" suggests a weakness in an otherwise strong person. Commenting upon the fourth kingdom, Jerome wrote: "Now the fourth empire, which clearly refers to the Romans, is the iron empire which breaks in pieces and overcomes all others. But its feet and toes are partly of iron and partly of earthenware, a fact most clearly demonstrated at the pres-

the kingdom is vulnerable because it is seeking to unite elements which will not coalesce."[14]

The translation **so the people will be a mixture** in verse 43 is literally "they shall mix through the seed of man." This is generally taken as a reference to intermarriage. This mixing, however, will fail.

2:44 Not one of these four world empires will endure forever. Each in turn collapses to its successor. By contrast the **God of heaven will set up a kingdom that will never be destroyed**. This kingdom is, of course, the rock that "became a huge mountain and filled the whole earth" (2:35).[15] Ronald Wallace has said it well: "Four outstanding and different empires will run their course before the kingdom of God finally enters the world with new dynamic power as the deciding factor in history."[16] For the idea of filling the earth, see Isaiah 6:3 and 11:9. For the idea of a mountain symbolizing God's rule, see Isaiah 2:2-3; Micah 4:1-2; Ezekiel 17:23; Psalms 2:6; 48:1-2.

The symbolism of the statue falling and its resultant destruction does not need imply that these kingdoms were contemporary. The kingdoms have appeared to be consecutive: **After you. . . . Next. . . . Finally. . . .**

2:45 The interpretation ends with an affirmation of its certainty: **The dream is true and the interpretation is trustworthy**.

About the second empire Daniel said that it was **inferior** (lit., "beneath you") to Babylon. The second, third, and fourth kingdoms lack an inner unity. This lack is borne out in the symbolism of the colossus. Babylon is represented by one head; the second kingdom by breast and arms; the third by belly and thighs; and the fourth by legs and feet.

The inferiority of the final three kingdoms did not concern size,

ent time. For just as there was at the first nothing stronger or hardier than the Roman realm, so also in these last days there is nothing more feeble, since we require the assistance of barbarian tribes both in our civil wars and against foreign nations" (Braverman, *Jerome's Commentary*, p. 32).

[14]Baldwin, *Daniel*, p. 93.

[15]David Wenham, "The Kingdom of God and Daniel," *Exp Tim* 98 (1987): 132-134. The New Testament applies the image of a stone to Christ: Matt 21:42-44//Mark 12:10-11//Luke 20:17-18; Rom 9:32-33; 1 Pet 2:4-8.

[16]Ronald S. Wallace, *The Lord Is King: The Message of Daniel*, The Bible Speaks Today (Downers Grove, IL: InterVarsity, 1979), p. 58.

because they were all larger than the first. Nor does it concern morality.[17] According to Leon Wood, it can have referred only to quality of government.[18] From Nebuchadnezzar's standpoint the restriction on the Medo-Persian king's authority to annul a law once he made it (cf. 6:12; Esther) was less desirable than his own absolute authority. Likewise, the third and fourth kingdoms, Greece and Rome, were republican in their political traditions.

Keil has proposed that the gradation of the metals corresponds to the relation of the world kingdoms to the kingdom and people of God. Since both Nebuchadnezzar (2:47; 4:3,34-35) and Cyrus=Darius (6:26-27) respected the living God, they are likened to gold and silver. On the other hand, "from the third and the fourth kingdoms the greatest persecutors of the kingdom of God, who wish utterly to destroy it (ch. Vii, viii), arise."[19] Accordingly, they are likened to bronze and iron.

The kingdom of God will be victorious, while the kingdom of man, as represented by the statue, will be vanquished. The kingdoms of men are always in revolt against the Lord (Ps 2:9). "We need not give only a political significance to this colossal statue," writes Wallace, "It can stand for our little empires, domestic, social, business, financial or ecclesiastical in the midst of which some of us sit enthroned, trying in vain to find security and satisfaction. It can stand merely for the image of our own future. But we shall never be at peace till we have really seen and acknowledged that the empire of ours, whatever it is, must give way before the coming of the kingdom of God."[20]

The kingdom that God "will set up" is historical, that is, it will emerge "in the time of those kings" (v. 44). The "historicity" of the emergence of this eternal kingdom in the birth of Jesus is emphasized quite naturally by the writers of the New Testament.

Luke prefaces his narrative about the birth of Jesus with the statement, "In those days Caesar Augustus issued a decree that a

---

[17]Calvin conjectured that morality was the issue. "Experience also shows that the world always grows worse and little by little deteriorates into vices and corruptions" (*Daniel I*, p. 86).

[18]Wood, *Daniel*, p. 68.

[19]Keil, *Daniel*, p. 264.

[20]Wallace, *The Lord Is King*, p. 60.

census should be taken of the entire *Roman* world" (2:1, emphasis mine). Matthew traces the genealogical record of Jesus from Abraham to Joseph, "the husband of Mary, of whom was born Jesus, who is called Christ" (1:16). Jesus was born during *Pax Romana* and in the genealogic line of covenant expectation. Clothed in flesh, Jesus entered human history, proclaiming the arrival of the kingdom of God. Notice how Paul ties together these great truths. "But when the time had fully come, God sent his Son, born of a woman, born under law, to redeem those under law, that we might receive the full rights of sons. Because you are sons, God sent the Spirit of his Son into our hearts, the Spirit who calls out, 'Abba, Father.' So you are no longer a slave, but a son; and since you are a son, *God has made you also an heir*" (Gal 4:4-6, emphasis mine).

G. RESULT/NEBUCHADNEZZAR'S RESPONSE (2:46-49)

[46]Then King Nebuchadnezzar fell prostrate before Daniel and paid him honor and ordered that an offering and incense be presented to him. [47]The king said to Daniel, "Surely your God is the God of gods and the Lord of kings and a revealer of mysteries, for you were able to reveal this mystery."

[48]Then the king placed Daniel in a high position and lavished many gifts on him. He made him ruler over the entire province of Babylon and placed him in charge of all its wise men. [49]Moreover, at Daniel's request the king appointed Shadrach, Meshach and Abednego administrators over the province of Babylon, while Daniel himself remained at the royal court.

2:46 Nebuchadnezzar's worship of Daniel is simply a way of honoring the God Daniel represents (cf. Acts 10:25; 14:13).[21]

2:47 The king is not committing himself to exclusive devotion to the God of Israel. As a polytheist Nebuchadnezzar can always add another deity to his pantheon.

---

[21]Calvin wrote: "Although he [Nebuchadnezzar] confesses that the God of Israel was the only God, he transfers part of his worship to a mortal man. Those who excuse this do not sufficiently consider that the heathen mix up heaven and earth; although their original impetus may be right, they slip back at once into their superstitions" (*Daniel I*, p. 109).

The title **Lord of kings** is apt in view of verse 21 and the content of the king's dream.

2:48 In keeping with the promise of verse 6, the king lavished many gifts and royal honors upon Daniel.

2:49 Daniel's friends were elevated to spheres of influence in the country districts of the province. Daniel **remained at the royal court** (literally, "at the gate of the king") as a member of the king's cabinet (cf. Esth 2:19,21; 3:2). The promotion of **Shadrach, Meshach, and Abednego** sets the stage for chapter 3.

Daniel 2 is a vivid reminder that the kingdoms of this world are at best transient. The great kingdoms of antiquity — Babylon, Persia, Greece, and Rome — are just that: ancient history. But the Kingdom of God is eternal!

The Old Testament is replete with prophecies against foreign nations: Isaiah 13–23, Jeremiah 46–51, and Ezekiel 25–32 in the Major Prophets; Amos 1–2, Obadiah, Nahum, Habakkuk 2, and Zephaniah 2 in the Minor Prophets.

In addition to giving theological justification for the disaster that is to befall these kingdoms, these prophecies remind Israel or Judah that political alliances with these mighty kingdoms are ill fated. If the days of these kingdoms are numbered, then why would any nation, especially God's people, entrust themselves to an alliance? God's people must entrust themselves exclusively to Him! In his masterful commentary on Isaiah, John N. Oswalt succinctly frames this issue: "These chapters [Isa 13–23] demonstrate the folly of trusting in nations whose doom is already sealed. God is the master of the nations. It is at his command that the armies move out to destroy one after another, both great and small. Thus, it is foolish for Israel to trust in her own system of alliances, with the necessary commitments to foreign gods, to save her. Only God, who has promised to save her, can save her."[22]

Political alliances are seductive. The great kingdoms of this world offer glory, wealth, wisdom, sophistication, and culture. But these prophecies, as well as Daniel 2, remind us that all human pride and

---

[22]John N. Oswalt, *The Book of Isaiah: Chapters 1–39* (Grand Rapids: Eerdmans, 1986), p. 299.

accomplishment are under God's judgment. Apropos of this, Oswalt, paraphrasing Isaiah, writes, "Do not trust the nations of this world. They are not preeminent. They do not hold your destiny in their hands. They, like you, are under the judgment of God — your God."[23]

The seductive glory of Babylon is mere illusion before the bar of God's judgment. Isaiah writes, "Babylon, the jewel of kingdoms, the glory of the Babylonians' pride, will be overthrown by God like Sodom and Gomorrah" (13:19).

The seductive wealth of Tyre is also mere illusion before the same bar. Isaiah characterized Tyre as the "marketplace of the nations" (23:3). Then he adds, "The LORD Almighty planned it, to bring low the pride of all glory and to humble all who are renowned on the earth" (23:9).

The seductive wisdom of Egypt is also mere illusion. Isaiah writes,

Where are your wise men now? Let them show you and make known what the LORD Almighty has planned against Egypt. The officials of Zoan have become fools, the leaders of Memphis are deceived; the cornerstones of her peoples have led Egypt astray. The LORD has poured into them a spirit of dizziness; they make Egypt stagger in all that she does, as a drunkard staggers around in his vomit. There is nothing Egypt can do—head or tail, palm branch or reed (19:12-15).

The seduction of sophistication and culture are mirages as well. "See the LORD is going to lay waste the earth and devastate it; he will ruin its face and scatter its inhabitants" (24:1).

The initial readers of Daniel 2 saw and now its contemporary readers see a breathtaking vision of God's sovereign mastery of history. When all is said and done, "The God of heaven will set up a kingdom that will never be destroyed, nor will it be left to another people. It will crush all those kingdoms and bring them to an end, but it will itself endure forever" (Dan 2:44).

---

[23]Oswalt, *Isaiah*, p. 427.

DANIEL 3

III. GOD SAVES DANIEL'S FRIENDS FROM THE FIERY FURNACE (3:1-30)

A. THE IMAGE OF GOLD (3:1-7)

¹King Nebuchadnezzar made an image of gold, ninety feet high and nine feet[a] wide, and set it up on the plain of Dura in the province of Babylon. ²He then summoned the satraps, prefects, governors, advisers, treasurers, judges, magistrates and all the other provincial officials to come to the dedication of the image he had set up. ³So the satraps, prefects, governors, advisers, treasurers, judges, magistrates and all the other provincial officials assembled for the dedication of the image that King Nebuchadnezzar had set up, and they stood before it.

⁴Then the herald loudly proclaimed, "This is what you are commanded to do, O peoples, nations and men of every language: ⁵As soon as you hear the sound of the horn, flute, zither, lyre, harp, pipes and all kinds of music, you must fall down and worship the image of gold that King Nebuchadnezzar has set up. ⁶Whoever does not fall down and worship will immediately be thrown into a blazing furnace."

⁷Therefore, as soon as they heard the sound of the horn, flute, zither, lyre, harp and all kinds of music, all the peoples, nations and men of every language fell down and worshiped the image of gold that King Nebuchadnezzar had set up.

[a]*1 Aramaic sixty cubits high and six cubits wide* (about 27 meters high and 2.7 meters wide)

3:1-3 Inspired by the identification with the head of gold in chapter 2, Nebuchadnezzar **made an image of gold, ninety feet high and**

nine feet wide.[1] The image may have represented a god, the king, or the nation.[2] The image probably was overlaid with gold leaf (cf. Isa 40:19; 41:7; Jer 10:3-4). The height of the statue, sixty cubits or about ninety feet, is surpassed in the ancient world only by the colossus of Rhodes (seventy cubits). The width may refer to the distance through the chest to the back. The mandatory attendance at the dedication of this image and the subsequent prostration before it may have been Nebuchadnezzar's attempt to demand complete loyalty to the nation.

The location of Dura is uncertain. Dura is a word that means "city wall" or "fortress." Dura must have been within easy reach of Babylon.

3:4 The three words of verse 4 — **peoples, nations and [men of every] language** — placed together denote all peoples — no one was exempt from obeying the command.

3:5-7 The penalty for not obeying the king's order was capital: **Whoever does not fall down and worship will immediately be thrown into a blazing furnace** (v. 6). Refusal to bow before the image was tantamount to treason. According to Jeremiah 29:22, the king of Babylon roasted two false prophets, Ahab and Zedekiah, in the fire. It is difficult to imagine what the furnace is likely to have looked like. Baldwin envisages a tunnel-shaped brick furnace. Keil's description resembles a beehive, with an opening on the top into which the men were thrown.

---

[1]Since chapter 3 does not give a more detailed chronological marker, we do not know how much time has elapsed since the episode of chapter 2. The Septuagint (LXX) dates the episode to Nebuchadnezzar's eighteenth year. This seems improbable. A brief period of time seems more probable.

[2]Calvin wrote: "Sometimes superstitious people spend vast sums on building temples and making idols. If anyone should ask what their motive is, their answer will come pat, that they are doing it for the honor of God. Yet there is none that does not put his own fame and reputation first. Therefore the worship of God is treated as almost nothing by the superstitious; they want rather to gain for themselves favor and esteem among men" (*Daniel I,* p. 116). Keil believes that the image was a "symbol of the world-power established by Nebuchadnezzar, so that falling down before it was a manifestation of reverence not only to the world-power, but also to its gods; and that therefore the Israelites could not fall down before the image, because in doing so they would have rendered homage at the same time also to the god or gods of Nebuchadnezzar, in the image of the world-power" (p. 120).

The identification of the musical instruments in Nebuchadnezzar's orchestra is not easy.[3] The **horn** is a wind instrument formed
from an animal's horn. The translation **flute** for the second instrument is apt, given that this noun is related to the verb "to hiss," suggesting some kind of whistling instrument. The third instrument is
either a **zither** or a **lyre**. The fourth instrument may be a four-
stringed triangular **harp**, if the identification of the Septuagint translation be trusted. The fifth instrument is generally recognized as a
stringed instrument of triangular shape. The sixth instrument may
be either a drum or a (bag)pipe.[4]

The Babylonians' love for music is well attested (Isa 14:11; Ps
137:3; Herodotus I:191).

B. THE ACCUSATION AGAINST SHADRACH,
MESHACH, AND ABEDNEGO (3:8-12)

[8]**At this time some astrologers**[a] **came forward and denounced
the Jews.** [9]**They said to King Nebuchadnezzar, "O king, live forever!** [10]**You have issued a decree, O king, that everyone who hears the
sound of the horn, flute, zither, lyre, harp, pipes and all kinds of
music must fall down and worship the image of gold,** [11]**and that
whoever does not fall down and worship will be thrown into a blazing furnace.** [12]**But there are some Jews whom you have set over the
affairs of the province of Babylon—Shadrach, Meshach and Abednego—who pay no attention to you, O king. They neither serve
your gods nor worship the image of gold you have set up."**

[a]*8 Or* Chaldeans

3:8 Some astrologers denounced Daniel's friends.[5] The expres-

---

[3]T.C. Mitchell and R. Joyce, "The Musical Instruments in Nebuchadnezzar's Orchestra," in *Notes on Some Problems*, pp. 19-27.

[4]The word for this sixth instrument may also denote ensemble playing. In
fact, the word *symphony* is derived from this Greek word [symphonia]. This
sixth word is omitted in verse 7, suggesting ensemble playing as opposed to
a specific instrument.

[5]"The three who were merely youths in chap. 1 and merely Daniel's
friends in chap. 2 are here full-grown men of importance in their own right"
(Goldingay, *Daniel,* p. 70).

sion translated **denounced** is literally "they ate their pieces." This malicious slander may have been prompted by professional jealousy or hatred on ethnic grounds (cf. Esth 5:8). We must remember that these very astrologers owed their lives to Daniel and his three friends (2:17-18,24).

3:9-12 The accusation implies ingratitude. One can hear this sense in the paraphrased words of the astrologers: "The very three men **you have set over the affairs of the province of Babylon** are treating your edict with contempt. How dare they?" This ingratitude is a personal affront. Shadrach, Meshach, and Abednego **pay no attention to *you*, O king. They neither serve *your* gods nor worship the image of gold *you* have set up**.

Where was Daniel during this episode? The text supplies no answer. Perhaps Daniel was absent due to government business. He may have been too ill (cf. 8:27; 7:28; 10:8).[6] Perhaps Daniel was in Babylon, but was not required to be present or bow to the image. Perhaps Daniel took the same stand as his friends, but the astrologers were afraid to accuse him, knowing of the king's respect for him.[7]

C. THE CONFRONTATION WITH NEBUCHADNEZZAR (3:13-18)

[13]**Furious with rage, Nebuchadnezzar summoned Shadrach, Meshach and Abednego. So these men were brought before the king,** [14]**and Nebuchadnezzar said to them, "Is it true, Shadrach, Meshach and Abednego, that you do not serve my gods or worship the image of gold I have set up?** [15]**Now when you hear the sound of the horn, flute, zither, lyre, harp, pipes and all kinds of music, if you are ready to fall down and worship the image I made, very**

---

[6]Wood, *Daniel*, p. 78.

[7]G. Coleman Luck, *Daniel* (Chicago: Moody, 1958), p. 50. Calvin adds: "It could be that they let Daniel alone for the time being, knowing that the king had exalted him. And they brought the accusation against these three, because they could be oppressed more easily and with less trouble. I think it was this craftiness that moved them not to name Daniel along with the three, lest favor towards him might soften the king's anger" (*Daniel I*, p. 127).

good. But if you do not worship it, you will be thrown immediately into a blazing furnace. Then what god will be able to rescue you from my hand?"
[16]Shadrach, Meshach and Abednego replied to the king, "O Nebuchadnezzar, we do not need to defend ourselves before you in this matter. [17]If we are thrown into the blazing furnace, the God we serve is able to save us from it, and he will rescue us from your hand, O king. [18]But even if he does not, we want you to know, O king, that we will not serve your gods or worship the image of gold you have set up."

3:13-15 Nebuchadnezzar confronts the three men with the hearsay evidence, giving them a chance to recant if their actions had been treasonous.

3:16-18 The three men are guilty; they did defy the king's edict. They would not defy, however, their God's condemnation of idolatry (Exod 20:4-6). But instead of pleading for the king's mercy, they cast themselves on the mercy of their God: **"If we are thrown into the blazing furnace, the God we serve is able to save us from it, and he will rescue us from your hand, O king. But even if he does not, we want you to know, O king, that we will not serve your gods or worship the image of gold you have set up."** These men were not uncertain as to God's ability to deliver them; they were not sure that he would choose to deliver.[8] In the words of Joyce Baldwin, "They do not doubt the power of their God to deliver them from the king's furnace, but they have no right to presume that He will do so."[9]

Their faith is matched by their submission to the Lord's will. "The young men recognized that God's will might be different from what they would find pleasant, and they were willing to have it so, without complaining."[10]

---

[8]Cyprian (200–258) wrote: "They believed that they might escape according to their faith, but they added, 'and if not,' that the king might know that they could also die for the God they worshipped. For this is the strength of courage and of faith, to believe and to know that God can deliver from present death, and yet not to fear death nor to give way, that faith may be the more mightily proved" (*Ante-Nicene Fathers,* p. 348).

[9]Baldwin, *Daniel,* p. 104.

[10]Wood, *Daniel,* p. 89. Calvin adds, "The constancy of Shadrach, Meshach,

When they declare, "**we do not need to defend ourselves**," they are "acknowledging the correctness of the indictment laid against them and declaring that there is no defense or apology that need be made. They cast themselves utterly upon God."[11]

D. DELIVERANCE (3:19-27)

[19]**Then Nebuchadnezzar was furious with Shadrach, Meshach and Abednego, and his attitude toward them changed. He ordered the furnace heated seven times hotter than usual** [20]**and commanded some of the strongest soldiers in his army to tie up Shadrach, Meshach and Abednego and throw them into the blazing furnace.** [21]**So these men, wearing their robes, trousers, turbans and other clothes, were bound and thrown into the blazing furnace.** [22]**The king's command was so urgent and the furnace so hot that the flames of the fire killed the soldiers who took up Shadrach, Meshach and Abednego,** [23]**and these three men, firmly tied, fell into the blazing furnace.**

[24]**Then King Nebuchadnezzar leaped to his feet in amazement and asked his advisers, "Weren't there three men that we tied up and threw into the fire?"**

They replied, "Certainly, O king."

[25]**He said, "Look! I see four men walking around in the fire, unbound and unharmed, and the fourth looks like a son of the gods."**

[26]**Nebuchadnezzar then approached the opening of the blazing furnace and shouted, "Shadrach, Meshach and Abednego, servants of the Most High God, come out! Come here!"**

So Shadrach, Meshach and Abednego came out of the fire, [27]**and the satraps, prefects, governors and royal advisers crowded around them. They saw that the fire had not harmed their bodies, nor was a hair of their heads singed; their robes were not scorched, and there was no smell of fire on them.**

---

and Abednego was grounded on two things: that they were entirely convinced that God was the keeper of their life and that his power would free them from imminent death if that was right; and also that they had boldly and fearlessly determined to die if God wished such a sacrifice to be offered to him" (*Daniel I,* p. 134).

[11]Young, *Daniel,* p. 90.

3:19-23 Enraged at their resolve, Nebuchadnezzar has the men **bound and thrown into the blazing furnace** (v. 21). The furnace had been stoked so that it blazed **seven times hotter than usual** (v. 19).[12] This intense heat took the lives of the men who **took up** the three (v. 22).

In verse 19, the translation **his attitude toward them changed** is literally, "the image of his face changed." This word "image" is, of course, the very same word used throughout this chapter. Longman perceptively notes, "The one who in his pride has created an image with the purpose of assuring uniform loyalty finds his own image provoked beyond his control."[13]

3:24-25 As Nebuchadnezzar looks into the furnace, he sees **four men walking around in the fire, unbound and unharmed, and the fourth looks like a son of the gods** (v. 25). Other than the ropes that had melted in the intense heat, the fire did not affect the men. **The fire had not harmed their bodies, nor was a hair of their heads singed; their robes were not scorched, and there was no smell of fire on them** (v. 27). Nebuchadnezzar stood face to face with a sheer miracle! The author of Hebrews 11 refers to those who "quenched the fury of the flames" (v. 34; cf. Isa 43:1-2; Deut 4:20).

Who or what was the identity of this fourth person? Nebuchadnezzar identifies the being first as divine (v. 25; "son of the gods" = "divine being") and then an angel (v. 28).[14] Many early Christian expositors adopted the view that this being was a preincarnate appearance of the second Person of the Trinity.[15] No certain answer

---

[12]Hippolytus wrote: "He bids the vast furnace be heated one seven times more, as if he were already overcome by them. In earthly things, then, the king was superior; but in faith toward God the three youths were superior. Tell me, Nebuchadnezzar, with what purpose you order them to be cast into the fire bound? Is it lest they might escape, if they should have their feet unbound, and thus be able to extinguish the fire?" (*Ante-Nicene Fathers*, p. 188).

[13]Longman, *Daniel*, p. 101.

[14]Calvin comments: "Here there is no doubt that God sent one of his angels to encourage the holy men by his presence lest they should give way. For it was a fearful sight, to see the furnace burning like that and themselves to be thrown into it. God, therefore, wished to relieve their anguish with this comfort and to soothe their distress by giving the angel to be their comrade" (*Daniel I*, p. 140).

[15]Hippolytus wrote: "Tell me, Nebuchadnezzar, when didst thou see the Son of God, that thou shouldst confess that this is the Son of God? And who

is possible. Young and Wood favor the position of early Christian expositors. Wood writes,

> This story affords one of the most meaningful illustrations in the Bible of God's tender care for His children. God might have effected deliverance for Shadrach, Meshach, and Abednego without sending such a personal messenger, and this would have been wonderful of itself. But He did more. He effected the deliverance by a special emissary who tangibly demonstrated God's presence with them in the trying hour. God had permitted the men to be cast into the horrifying furnace, but in doing so He had literally gone in with them.[16]

Throughout the Old Testament, the Angel of the LORD appeared to God's people. The Angel appeared to Abraham at Mamre (Gen 18), to Jacob at the Jabbok (Gen 32:30; Hos 12:4), to Moses in the burning bush (Exod 3:2), to Joshua near Jericho (Josh 5:13–6:5), to Gideon in Ophrah (Judg 6:11), and to others at various times and places. Many commentators have conjectured that this Angel is also a preincarnate appearance of Jesus Christ. If this conjecture is correct, then it is much more likely that the fourth being in the furnace was indeed the preincarnate Christ.

3:26-27 Nebuchadnezzar does not call the God of the three men the only true God, but only the **"Most High God,"** that is, the chief of the gods. This admission can be likened to the phrase he used at 2:47, "God of gods."

---

pricked thy heart, that thou shouldst utter such a word? And with what eyes wert thou able to look into this light? And why was this manifested to thee alone, and to none of the satraps about thee? But, as it is written, 'The heart of a king is in the hand of God:' the hand of God is here, whereby the Word pricked his heart, so that he might recognize Him in the furnace, and glorify Him. And this idea of ours is not without good ground. For as the children of Israel were destined to see God in the world, and yet not to believe on Him, the Scripture showed beforehand that the Gentiles would recognize Him incarnate, whom, while not incarnate, Nebuchadnezzar saw and recognized of old in the furnace, and acknowledged to be the Son of God" (*Ante-Nicene Fathers*, p. 188).

[16]Wood, *Daniel*, p. 94.

E. NEBUCHADNEZZAR WORSHIPS GOD (3:28-30)

[28]**Then Nebuchadnezzar said, "Praise be to the God of Shadrach, Meshach and Abednego, who has sent his angel and rescued his servants!** They trusted in him and defied the king's command and were willing to give up their lives rather than serve or worship any god except their own God.** [29]**Therefore I decree that the people of any nation or language who say anything against the God of Shadrach, Meshach and Abednego be cut into pieces and their houses be turned into piles of rubble, for no other god can save in this way."** [30]**Then the king promoted Shadrach, Meshach and Abednego in the province of Babylon.**

3:28 In verse 15 Nebuchadnezzar defiantly asked, "What god will be able to rescue you from my hand?" The king now has the answer — the God of Shadrach, Meshach, and Abednego. In this chapter God deals "gently" with the king's defiance. God's response in the next chapter will be for the king more humbling. Neither response is as devastating as God's response to the defiance of Sennacherib — articulated in Isaiah 36:18-20 and answered in Isaiah 37:36-37.

3:29-30 Nebuchadnezzar makes Judaism a recognized religion and threatens all who interfere with it (cf. Ezra 6:6-12). Furthermore, he promotes the three men, completely thwarting the intentions of their accusers.

The three Hebrew youths cast themselves upon the mercy of their God. The mercy of God is an expression of his kindness in times when man's perspective is bleak or desperate at best. When faced with the prospect of either three years of famine, or three months of being swept away before his enemies, or three days of the sword of the LORD — days of plague in the land, with the angel of the LORD ravaging every part of Israel, David's response is a classic expression of God's mercy. "I am in deep distress. Let me fall into the hands of the LORD, for his mercy is very great; but do not let me fall into the hands of men" (1 Chr 21:13; cf. 2 Sam 24:14).

When David was a fugitive, running from the maniacal Saul, his situation was desperate. At any number of moments he may have been handed over to or seized by King Saul. But David chose, according to Psalm 57:1, to live in the context of God's mercy. David said, "Have mercy on me, O God, have mercy on me, for in you my soul takes refuge. I will take refuge in the shadow of your wings until the disaster has passed."

The psalmists consistently cried out for the mercy of God (4:1; 6:2; 9:13; 26:11; 27:7; 30:10; 31:9; 41:5,10; 51:1; 56:1; 57:1; 86:3,16; 123:3; 142:1).

In times of greatest need then, men and women have longed for the beneficence of God, his mercy, which is great (Ps 25:6; Neh 9:31; 1 Pet 1:3) and from of old (Ps 25:6). "O LORD, be gracious to us; we long for you. Be our strength every morning, our salvation in time of distress" (Isa 33:2).

The testimonies of God's people abound with examples of how God has mercifully carried us through times of great distress — times of disease, doubt, grinding poverty, loss (2 Sam 12:22), persecution (2 Kgs 13:23), rejection, and sin. "As the eyes of slaves look to the hand of their master, as the eyes of a maid look to the hand of her mistress, so our eyes look to the LORD our God, till he shows us his mercy. Have mercy on us, O LORD, have mercy on us, for we have endured much contempt" (Ps 123:2-3).

The Bible abounds with the challenge of reflecting the mercy of God in our daily activities. "He has showed you, O man, what is good. And what does the LORD require of you? To act justly and to *love mercy* and to walk humbly with your God" (Micah 6:8). "This is what the LORD Almighty says: 'Administer true justice; *show mercy* and compassion to one another'" (Zech 7:9). "*Blessed are the merciful*, for they will be shown mercy" (Matt 5:7). "*Be merciful*, just as your Father is merciful" (Luke 6:36). "Judgment without mercy will be shown to anyone who has not been *merciful*" (Jas 2:13). "But the wisdom that comes from heaven is first of all pure; then peace-loving, considerate, submissive, *full of mercy* and good fruit, impartial and sincere" (Jas 3:17).

Like the three Hebrew youths of Daniel 3, our need compels us to cast ourselves upon the mercy of God. The author of Hebrews exhorts us to "approach the throne of grace with confidence, so that we may receive mercy and find grace to help us in our time of need" (4:16).

DANIEL 4

IV. NEBUCHADNEZZAR PRAISES
THE MOST HIGH GOD (4:1-37)

The outline for chapter 4 suggests that the material follows a chiastic presentation:

A. Nebuchadnezzar Praises the Most High God (4:1-3)
   B. Nebuchadnezzar's Dream (4:4-18)
   B'. Daniel's Interpretation and Its Fulfillment (4:19-33)
A'. Nebuchadnezzar Praises the Most High God (4:34-37)

Chapter 4 is the only chapter in Scripture composed by a pagan — Nebuchadnezzar. The king narrates the humiliation of his own pride, illustrating Job 33:14,17: "For God does speak—now one way, now another—though man may not perceive it. . . . to turn man from wrongdoing and keep him from pride."

Chapters 2 and 3 ended with Nebuchadnezzar's praise of the Lord (2:47; 3:28). The present chapter begins and ends with such praise (4:3,34-35), exhibiting a spirit of humility before the Most High God.

A. NEBUCHADNEZZAR PRAISES THE MOST HIGH GOD
(4:1-3)

¹King Nebuchadnezzar,

To the peoples, nations and men of every language, who live in all the world:

May you prosper greatly!

²It is my pleasure to tell you about the miraculous signs and wonders that the Most High God has performed for me.

[3]How great are his signs,
   how mighty his wonders!
His kingdom is an eternal kingdom;
   his dominion endures from generation to generation.

4:1-2 The placing of the sender's name — **King Nebuchadnezzar** — before that of the recipients — **to the peoples, nations and men of every language** — is standard in Neo-Babylonian letters.[1]

4:3 Since verse 3 exhibits affinities with Psalm 145:13 (cf. Ps 72:5), it was probably prepared under the influence of Daniel.

B. NEBUCHADNEZZAR'S DREAM (4:4-18)

[4]I, Nebuchadnezzar, was at home in my palace, contented and prosperous. [5]I had a dream that made me afraid. As I was lying in my bed, the images and visions that passed through my mind terrified me. [6]So I commanded that all the wise men of Babylon be brought before me to interpret the dream for me. [7]When the magicians, enchanters, astrologers[a] and diviners came, I told them the dream, but they could not interpret it for me. [8]Finally, Daniel came into my presence and I told him the dream. (He is called Belteshazzar, after the name of my god, and the spirit of the holy gods is in him.)
   [9]I said, "Belteshazzar, chief of the magicians, I know that the spirit of the holy gods is in you, and no mystery is too difficult for you. Here is my dream; interpret it for me. [10]These are the visions I saw while lying in my bed: I looked, and there before me stood a tree in the middle of the land. Its height was enormous. [11]The tree grew large and strong and its top touched the sky; it was visible to the ends of the earth. [12]Its leaves were beautiful, its fruit abundant, and on it was food for all. Under it the beasts of the field found shelter, and the birds of the air lived in its branches; from it every creature was fed.

---

[1]John J. Collins, *Daniel,* Hermeneia (Minneapolis: Fortress Press, 1993), p. 221.

¹³"In the visions I saw while lying in my bed, I looked, and there before me was a messenger,ᵇ a holy one, coming down from heaven. ¹⁴He called in a loud voice: 'Cut down the tree and trim off its branches; strip off its leaves and scatter its fruit. Let the animals flee from under it and the birds from its branches. ¹⁵But let the stump and its roots, bound with iron and bronze, remain in the ground, in the grass of the field.

"'Let him be drenched with the dew of heaven, and let him live with the animals among the plants of the earth. ¹⁶Let his mind be changed from that of a man and let him be given the mind of an animal, till seven timesᶜ pass by for him.

¹⁷"'The decision is announced by messengers, the holy ones declare the verdict, so that the living may know that the Most High is sovereign over the kingdoms of men and gives them to anyone he wishes and sets over them the lowliest of men.'

¹⁸"This is the dream that I, King Nebuchadnezzar, had. Now, Belteshazzar, tell me what it means, for none of the wise men in my kingdom can interpret it for me. But you can, because the spirit of the holy gods is in you."

ᵃ7 Or *Chaldeans*   ᵇ*13* Or *watchman*; also in verses 17 and 23   ᵇ*16* Or *years*; also in verses 23, 25 and 32

4:4-5 Basking in the glory of his accomplishments, the king was at home contented.[2] This peace of mind was soon shattered by the dream described here: **I had a dream that made me afraid**.

4:6-9 Nebuchadnezzar summons his experts, who, as in chapter 2, are unable to interpret the dream for the king.[3] Finally, Daniel comes before the king, who pleads, **Interpret it for me**. The king recognizes that Daniel is very spiritual (**the spirit of the holy gods is in you**).[4]

---

[2]For the translation *prosperous* (literally, *growing green*) the corresponding Hebrew word may denote the luxuriant growth of a tree (Ps 52:8). In view of Nebuchadnezzar's dream, this association may be significant.

[3]In all likelihood, they lacked the courage to convey that the dream meant humiliation and tragedy for the king.

[4]On the lips of Nebuchadnezzar, the plural "holy gods" undoubtedly betrays a polytheistic worldview. "Not only as a worshipper of the god of the Jews," writes Keil, "but also of the great god Bel, he had become a partaker of the spirit of the holy gods" (*Daniel*, p. 147).

If Daniel was so well known for his ability to interpret dreams, why did Daniel appear only after the **magicians, enchanters, astrologers, and diviners** failed to interpret the dream? Calvin answers this question:

> When the proud do not need outside help, they are puffed up and no-one can bear their insolence. But when they are brought to extremes they would rather lick the dust than not get the favor they need. Such, then, was the character of this king. He despised Daniel in his heart and deliberately neglected him in favor of the magi. But afterwards he saw he was still in difficulties and could get remedy from nowhere but Daniel, his last resort. So now he forgets his loftiness and speaks pleasantly to the holy prophet of God.[5]

4:10 Nebuchadnezzar was at the height of his powers (v. 4), established as the head of a world empire (2:37-38); accordingly, the tree he saw towered to heaven and provided food and shelter for all. "For the tree, mighty, reaching even to the heavens, and visible over the whole earth, is an easily recognized symbol of a world-ruler whose power stretches itself over the whole earth."[6]

The portrayal of man in his pride as a lofty tree is an Old Testament symbol (Isa 2:12-13; 10:33-34; Ezek 17:1-10; 31:3-14; Amos 2:9).

4:11-12 The growth of the tree — **it was visible to the ends of the earth** — is a common theme in the ancient world. Herodotus 7.19 relates a dream of Xerxes, who, ready to set out against Greece, "imagined himself crowned with olive, of which the branches spread all over the earth." In 1.108 Astyages the Mede dreamed "that a vine grew from his daughter's private parts and spread over Asia," prefiguring the rise of Cyrus.

4:13-17 But the dream had a second part. A **messenger** [literally, "a watcher"][7], a holy one, coming down from heaven shouted, **Cut down the tree.** The felling of the tree establishes that **the Most High is sovereign over the kingdoms of men and gives them to anyone**

---

[5]Calvin, *Daniel I,* p. 158.

[6]Keil, *Daniel,* p. 148.

[7]The being must be an angel, even though this term is nowhere else used in the Bible of an angelic figure.

he wishes and sets over them the lowliest of men (v. 17; cf. 1 Sam 2:8; Ps 113:7-8).

After the tree is felled, the stump is to be preserved and protected.[8] The iron and bronze shackle of verse 15 prevents removal and thus reassures the king (cf. Job 14:7-9).[9] "The tree with its roots is Nebuchadnezzar, who shall as king be cut down, but shall as a man remain, and again shall grow into a king."[10] The stump is personified — **let him** — yet destined to live as an animal — **let him live with the animals among the plants of the earth**. He exchanges his human mind for that of an animal for an uncertain, but limited period of time (**seven times**). "The sum of it is that King Nebuchadnezzar would for a time be despoiled not only of his empire but also of human understanding, so that he would differ in nothing from the beasts, since he was unworthy to hold even a lowly place among the common people. Although in his own eyes he had seemed to tower above the whole human race, he was so cast down that he was not even the last among mortals."[11]

4:18 After recounting the content of the dream, Nebuchadnezzar implores Daniel to interpret it.

C. DANIEL'S INTERPRETATION AND ITS FULFILLMENT (4:19-33)

[19]**Then Daniel (also called Belteshazzar) was greatly perplexed for a time, and his thoughts terrified him. So the king said, "Belteshazzar, do not let the dream or its meaning alarm you."**

Belteshazzar answered, "My lord, if only the dream applied to your enemies and its meaning to your adversaries! [20]**The tree you saw, which grew large and strong, with its top touching the sky, visible to the whole earth,** [21]**with beautiful leaves and abundant fruit, providing food for all, giving shelter to the beasts of the field, and having nesting places in its branches for the birds**

---

[8]In Isa 11:1 a stump implies the hope of restoration.

[9]This metal restraint suggests a reversal of the treatment Nebuchadnezzar had given Israel (Jer 28:14; 39:7; 52:11).

[10]Keil, *Daniel*, p. 151.

[11]Calvin, *Daniel I*, p. 165.

of the air— [22]you, O king, are that tree! You have become great and strong; your greatness has grown until it reaches the sky, and your dominion extends to distant parts of the earth.

[23]"You, O king, saw a messenger, a holy one, coming down from heaven and saying, 'Cut down the tree and destroy it, but leave the stump, bound with iron and bronze, in the grass of the field, while its roots remain in the ground. Let him be drenched with the dew of heaven; let him live like the wild animals, until seven times pass by for him.'

[24]"This is the interpretation, O king, and this is the decree the Most High has issued against my lord the king: [25]You will be driven away from people and will live with the wild animals; you will eat grass like cattle and be drenched with the dew of heaven. Seven times will pass by for you until you acknowledge that the Most High is sovereign over the kingdoms of men and gives them to anyone he wishes. [26]The command to leave the stump of the tree with its roots means that your kingdom will be restored to you when you acknowledge that Heaven rules. [27]Therefore, O king, be pleased to accept my advice: Renounce your sins by doing what is right, and your wickedness by being kind to the oppressed. It may be that then your prosperity will continue."

[28]All this happened to King Nebuchadnezzar. [29]Twelve months later, as the king was walking on the roof of the royal palace of Babylon, [30]he said, "Is not this the great Babylon I have built as the royal residence, by my mighty power and for the glory of my majesty?"

[31]The words were still on his lips when a voice came from heaven, "This is what is decreed for you, King Nebuchadnezzar: Your royal authority has been taken from you. [32]You will be driven away from people and will live with the wild animals; you will eat grass like cattle. Seven times will pass by for you until you acknowledge that the Most High is sovereign over the kingdoms of men and gives them to anyone he wishes."

[33]Immediately what had been said about Nebuchadnezzar was fulfilled. He was driven away from people and ate grass

like cattle. His body was drenched with the dew of heaven until his hair grew like the feathers of an eagle and his nails like the claws of a bird.

4:19-22 Daniel delayed to speak until encouraged by the king. The reason for the delay is obvious — this was an ominous message. Daniel wishes that the dream might be for the king's enemies. This wish clearly makes it known that the dream is unfavorable to Nebuchadnezzar.

4:23-27 Nebuchadnezzar would soon live like an animal — **you will eat grass like cattle and be drenched with the dew of heaven** — unless he renounced his sin and wickedness. Daniel "knew that the judgments of God were directed against men according to their conduct, and that punishment threatened could only be averted by repentance"[12] (cf. Jer 18:7-10; Jonah 3:4-10).

In verse 26, the word **heaven** is a surrogate for God, as Matthew's "kingdom of heaven" is a surrogate for Mark-Luke's "kingdom of God." This sense is unique in the Old Testament. This word is used here, according to Young, "to convince the king that the true Ruler is spiritual and above this earth, and that the true Power is heavenly and not earthly."[13]

4:28-33 Unwilling to break with his arrogant past,[14] Nebuchadnezzar was reduced to a beastlike existence: His body was drenched with the dew of heaven until his hair grew like the feathers of an eagle and his nails like the claws of a bird (v. 33).

Nebuchadnezzar's pride is on his lips as the Lord strikes him. "Is not this the great Babylon I have built as the royal residence, by my mighty power and for the glory of my majesty?"

Many scholars have diagnosed Nebuchadnezzar's illness as a form of *insania zoanthropica*, such as *boanthropy* or *lycanthropy*, where a human being thinks himself or herself an ox or a wolf.[15] The appropriateness of this affliction is noted by Fewell, who states, "A man

---

[12]Keil, *Daniel,* p. 156.

[13]Young, *Daniel,* p. 107.

[14]"Daniel's advice is to avoid sin and be kind. In other words, he should not fall prey to the temptation to think himself a god. In spite of his greatness, he must retain his humility" (Longman, *Daniel,* p. 120).

[15]R.K. Harrison details a clinical case of boanthropy in a British mental institution in 1946 (*Introduction,* p. 1116).

who thinks he is like a god must become a beast to learn that he is only a human being."[16]

At verse 28 the reader notes a shift to third person narration (**All this happened to King Nebuchadnezzar**). The first person is resumed again at verse 34 (**At the end of that time, I, Nebuchadnezzar**). This shift lies in the fact that during the time of illness Nebuchadnezzar was not "I."

D. NEBUCHADNEZZAR PRAISES THE MOST HIGH GOD (4:34-37)

[34]**At the end of that time, I, Nebuchadnezzar, raised my eyes toward heaven, and my sanity was restored. Then I praised the Most High; I honored and glorified him who lives forever.**

His dominion is an eternal dominion;
his kingdom endures from generation to generation.
[35]**All the peoples of the earth**
are regarded as nothing.
He does as he pleases
with the powers of heaven
and the peoples of the earth.
No one can hold back his hand
or say to him: "What have you done?"

[36]**At the same time that my sanity was restored, my honor and splendor were returned to me for the glory of my kingdom. My advisers and nobles sought me out, and I was restored to my throne and became even greater than before.** [37]**Now I, Nebuchadnezzar, praise and exalt and glorify the King of heaven, because everything he does is right and all his ways are just. And those who walk in pride he is able to humble.**

4:34a That Nebuchadnezzar could raise his eyes to heaven proves that he was still capable of response to God, despite his dementia. Looking toward heaven is an acknowledgment of God's superiority (cf. Ps 123:1). Wallace is quite right: "We come to be

---

[16]D.N. Fewell, *Circle of Sovereignty: A Story of Stories in Daniel 1–6* (Sheffield: JSOT, 1988), p. 101.

truly in our right mind when we begin to view and value everything else in the light of heavenly realities."[17]

4:34b-35 Nebuchadnezzar's song of praise is reminiscent of many OT passages:

"His dominion is an eternal dominion; his kingdom endures from generation to generation" (34)	"Your kingdom is an everlasting kingdom, and your dominion endures through all generations" (Ps 145:13a)
"All the peoples of the earth are regarded as nothing" (35a)	"Before him all the nations are as nothing" (Isa 40:17a)
"He does as he pleases with the powers of heaven and the peoples of the earth" (35b)	"Our God is in heaven; he does whatever pleases him" (Ps 115:3) "In that day the LORD will punish the powers in the heavens above and the kings on the earth below" (Isa 24:21)
"No one can hold back his hand or say to him: 'What have you done?'" (35c)	"For the LORD Almighty has purposed, and who can thwart him? His hand is stretched out, and who can turn it back?" (Isa 14:27)

4:36 Nebuchadnezzar is restored to sanity and to the greatness of his kingdom. But he has learned a valuable lesson: **Those who walk in pride he is able to humble.**

4:37 The king refers to God impersonally as the **King of heaven**, another expression unique in the OT, suggesting that Nebuchadnezzar's response falls short of true faith.[18]

---

[17]Wallace, *The Lord Is King,* p. 84.

[18]Young is led to the conclusion that the king did experience the regenerating grace of God. His conclusion is based on the following four considerations: (1) there is discernible a progress in his knowledge of God [cf. 2:47 with 3:28 and finally with 4:34-35]; (2) the king acknowledges the utter sovereignty of God with respect to his own experience [4:37b]; (3) the king utters true statements concerning the omnipotence of the true God [4:34-35]; and (4) the king would worship this God, whom he identifies as King of heaven [4:37a] (*Daniel,* p. 114). Wood adds, "No doubt, Nebuchadnezzar's knowledge of God at this point was meager, but it seems that what he had he held sincerely and that he did experience a change of heart" (*Daniel,* p. 128).

Nebuchadnezzar learned first hand of God's supremacy. This quality of God is positively affirmed in many Scriptures. "You rule over all the kingdoms of the nations. Power and might are in your hand, and no one can withstand you" (2 Chr 20:6). "Yours, O LORD, is the greatness and the power and the glory and the majesty and the splendor, for everything in heaven and earth is yours. Yours, O LORD, is the kingdom; you are exalted as head over all" (1 Chr 29:11). "Our God is in heaven; he does whatever pleases him" (Ps 115:3).

God's supremacy is demonstrated in his authority over the heavens and the earth. "The LORD does whatever pleases him, in the heavens and on the earth, in the seas and all their depths" (Ps 135:6). In Joshua 10:13 God made the sun stand still. In Isaiah 38:8 he caused the sun to recede ten steps on the stairway of Ahaz. In 1 Kings 17:6 he caused the ravens to bring food to Elijah the prophet. In Numbers 22:28 he caused a donkey to speak to a man. In Exodus 3:2 he caused a bush to be aflame yet not be consumed. In both Exodus 14:29 and Joshua 3:16 God parted the waters, allowing his people to pass through on dry ground. In Jonah 1:17 he caused a great fish to rescue his prophet Jonah from certain drowning.

God's supremacy is also manifest in the lives of men and women. God "gives all men life and breath and everything else" (Acts 17:25). In God "we live and move and have our being" (Acts 17:28). "For from him and through him and to him are all things" (Rom 11:36).

This attribute of God would be terrifying if not for his beneficent and moral use thereof. God's holy love and righteousness cast out this fear of the Sovereign and encourage us to find comfort and security in His will. "For I am convinced that neither death nor life, neither angels nor demons, neither the present nor the future, nor any powers, neither height nor depth, nor anything else in all creation, will be able to separate us from the love of God that is in Christ Jesus our Lord" (Rom 8:38-39).

Nebuchadnezzar also learned firsthand of the folly of human pride. His example bears witness to the teaching of the sage, the prophet, and Moses.

The Wisdom Literature of the Old Testament repeatedly warns against pride. "The LORD tears down the proud man's house but he keeps the widow's boundaries intact" (Prov 15:25). "Pride goes before destruction, a haughty spirit before a fall" (Prov 16:18). "A man's pride brings him low, but a man of lowly spirits gains honor" (Prov 29:23).

The Old Testament prophets also warned of the perils of pride. "The LORD Almighty has a day in store for all the proud and lofty, for all that is exalted (and they will be humbled). . . . The arrogance of man will be brought low and the pride of men humbled; the LORD alone will be exalted in that day" (Isa 2:12,17). "I will punish the world for its evil, the wicked for their sins. I will put an end to the arrogance of the haughty and will humble the pride of the ruthless" (Isa 13:11). Isaiah likens the trampling of Moab's pride to a swimmer in a dung pit. "The hand of the LORD will rest on this mountain; but Moab will be trampled under him as straw is trampled down in the manure. They will spread out their hands in it, as a swimmer spreads out his hands to swim. God will bring down their pride despite the cleverness of their hands" (25:10-11).

Even the Pentateuch warns of the price of pride. "I will break down your stubborn pride and make the sky above you like iron and the ground beneath you like bronze" (Lev 26:19).

Arnold writes, "The Book of Daniel is especially relevant for every generation of believers because it confronts pride as our ultimate problem. Sin and rebellion always find root in pride and self-absorption. So salvation must involve confession, rejection of prideful self-sufficiency, and a dependence on God (Mk. 8:34), all of which are so magnificently modeled by Daniel, his three companions, and later by the Saints of the Most High."[19]

As was noted in the Introduction ("Structure"), chapters 2–7 are chiastically organized to highlight the peril of human pride. This structure clearly declares that God humiliates the proud who fail to acknowledge him. Here, again, is that structure.

    I.   Nebuchadnezzar's vision of four kingdoms (ch 2)
      II. A miraculous rescue of Daniel's three friends (ch 3)
         III. The humiliation of Nebuchadnezzar's pride (ch 4)
         III'. The humiliation of Belshazzar's pride (ch 5)
      II'. A miraculous rescue of Daniel (ch 6)
    I'. Daniel's vision of four kingdoms (ch 7)

---

[19]Bill T. Arnold and Bryan E. Beyer, *Encountering the Old Testament* (Grand Rapids: Zondervan, 1999), p. 433.

DANIEL 5

V. THE WRITING ON THE WALL (5:1-31)

As with chapters 1, 2, and 4, chapter 5 is a court contest. Daniel can interpret a dream or vision where the "king's wise men" could not.

Belshazzar (the Babylonian Bel-shar-usur, i.e., "Bel, protect the king"), the son of Nabonidus, was vice-regent and in charge of Babylon during his father's ten-year absence from the capital city. Nabonidus had taken up residence in Teima (in modern-day Saudi Arabia) to promote his interests in the moon god Sin.[1]

The backdrop for chapter 5 is the fall of Babylon to the Persians on October 12, 539 B.C. According to the *Babylonian Chronicle*, a few days earlier Cyrus defeated Nabonidus and his army near Sippar, approximately 50 miles from the capital city.

A. THE PROFANATION OF THE TEMPLE VESSELS (5:1-4)

[1]King Belshazzar gave a great banquet for a thousand of his nobles and drank wine with them. [2]While Belshazzar was drinking his wine, he gave orders to bring in the gold and silver goblets that Nebuchadnezzar his father[a] had taken from the temple in Jerusalem, so that the king and his nobles, his wives and his concubines might drink from them. [3]So they brought in the gold goblets that had been taken from the temple of God in Jerusalem, and the king and his nobles, his wives and his concubines drank from them. [4]As they drank the wine, they praised the gods of gold and silver, of bronze, iron, wood and stone.

[a]2 Or *ancestor*; or *predecessor*; also in verses 11, 13, and 18

---

[1]Alan Millard, "Daniel and Belshazzar in History," *BAR* 11 (1985): 72-78.

5:1 Belshazzar must have anticipated an attack on the capital. Why, then, a banquet? Did he intend to encourage his leaders? Did he intend to alleviate some of the pressures his people felt? To feast today for tomorrow we die?

5:2-4 When the wine had overcome the king's senses, he ordered that the sacred vessels from the temple in Jerusalem be brought in for use. Proverbs 20:1 warns, "Wine is a mocker and beer a brawler; whoever is led astray by them is not wise."

According to Millard what was unusual for this orgy was that men used sacred vessels from a temple. Even if captured and carried off as booty, the equipment of national sanctuaries was normally treated with respect.[2] The king's impiety here portends calamitous consequences. Belshazzar's act, in the words of Longman, "is like spitting in the eye of God."[3]

Belshazzar's blasphemy is combined with idolatry. He uses God's goblets to toast "the gods of gold and silver, of bronze, iron, wood and stone."

The word **thousand** is probably a round number, suggesting the enormity of the banquet.

The word **father** in verse 2 is used in the sense "predecessor" (see the NIV footnote). Quite possibly, the word father carries here the sense "grandfather." It is thought that Belshazzar's mother, Nitocris, was the daughter of Nebuchadnezzar.

For the association of feasting in connection with the fall of Babylon, see Isaiah 21:5 and Jeremiah 51:39.

B. THE WRITING ON THE WALL (5:5-12)

[5]**Suddenly the fingers of a human hand appeared and wrote on the plaster of the wall, near the lampstand in the royal palace. The king watched the hand as it wrote. **[6]**His face turned pale and he was so frightened that his knees knocked together and his legs gave way.**

[7]**The king called out for the enchanters, astrologers**[a]** and divin- ers to be brought and said to these wise men of Babylon, "Who- ever reads this writing and tells me what it means will be clothed**

---

[2]Ibid., p. 74.
[3]Longman, *Daniel*, p. 137.

in purple and have a gold chain placed around his neck, and he will be made the third highest ruler in the kingdom."

[8]Then all the king's wise men came in, but they could not read the writing or tell the king what it meant. [9]So King Belshazzar became even more terrified and his face grew more pale. His nobles were baffled.

[10]The queen,[b] hearing the voices of the king and his nobles, came into the banquet hall. "O king, live forever!" she said. "Don't be alarmed! Don't look so pale! [11]There is a man in your kingdom who has the spirit of the holy gods in him. In the time of your father he was found to have insight and intelligence and wisdom like that of the gods. King Nebuchadnezzar your father—your father the king, I say—appointed him chief of the magicians, enchanters, astrologers and diviners. [12]This man Daniel, whom the king called Belteshazzar, was found to have a keen mind and knowledge and understanding, and also the ability to interpret dreams, explain riddles and solve difficult problems. Call for Daniel, and he will tell you what the writing means."

[a]7 Or *Chaldeans*; also in verse 11   [b]10 Or *queeen mother*

5:5 Belshazzar's impiety brought a divine response, a word written for the king alone. **Suddenly the fingers of a human hand appeared and wrote on the plaster of the wall, near the lampstand in the royal palace.** R. Koldewey, the excavator of the palace at Babylon, discovered the walls covered with a white plaster. The writing on the wall would have easily been seen then. The lampstand would also have illumined the writing surface.

5:6 As Belshazzar watched the disembodied or severed hand, a ripple of fear traversed his terrified body. The description of the king's terror details in descending order four bodily manifestations of fear: **his face turned pale**, his thoughts disturbed him (in 4:16 the heart is the seat of thought), the knots of his loins were loosened,[4] and **his knees knocked together**.

---

[4]The NIV translates the Aramaic here "his legs gave way." Al Wolters has suggested that the Aramaic refers to a loss of control over the sphincter muscles of the bladder and anus, which results in involuntary urination and

5:7-9 The king called out to the wisemen of Babylon to interpret the writing on the wall, promising great reward to the one who could. To wear purple and a gold chain are typical expressions of honor from a king (Gen 41:42-43; Esth 8:15). The status of **third highest ruler in the kingdom** is literally true. Nabonidus, the king, was first; Belshazzar, the vice-regent, was second. Belshazzar may have been offering equality in rank with two others, a member of a Triumvirate. Of course, none could. Presumably, the wisemen could read the inscription, since it was written in Aramaic, the common language of the day. They were, however, unable to determine the significance of the writing.[5]

5:10-11 The **queen** is evidently not Belshazzar's queen, since **his wives and concubines** were at the feast. According to verse 11, this lady's memory appears to go back to the early days of Nebuchadnezzar's reign. This queen is most likely to be, then, the widow of Nebuchadnezzar or the mother of Belshazzar.[6] Hence the NIV footnote, **queen mother.**[7]

---

defecation ["Untying the King's Knots: Physiology and Wordplay in Daniel 5," *JBL* 110/1 (1991): 119].

[5]In the midrash on Song of Songs (3.4), Rabbi Hiyya proposed that the letters were written downwards in threes instead of across. This was the approach taken in Rembrandt's painting "Belshazzar's Feast" (for a picture, see BAR 11 [1985]: 72-73). Rabbi Simeon ben Halafta proposed a code, the first letter of the alphabet replaced by the last, the second by the penultimate, and so on. The name of this code is atbash. The reader of Hebrew can see the coded procedure in this name (אתבש). The Sages explained that the letters of each word were written backwards. Rabbi Meir suggested that everyone could read the letters, but only Daniel could understand their significance. David Brewer has suggested that the original writing was cuneiform numerals which Daniel translated into Aramaic ["Mene Mene Teqel Uparsin: Daniel 5:25 in Cuneiform," *TynBul* 42 (1991): 313].

[6]If the queen of verse 10 is Nitocris, the daughter of Nebuchadnezzar and wife of Nabonidus, this would explain her knowledge of Nebuchadnezzar's relation to Daniel and her willingness to speak so courageously of Daniel (5:11-12). Wood suggests that "the possibility presents itself that she had been converted to a true faith in the Judean God, even as her father may have been" (*Daniel,* p. 141).

[7]The mother of the reigning king was held in high respect in the OT: 1 Kgs 15:13; 2 Kgs 24:12,15; Jer 13:18; 29:2.

5:12 This queen counsels, **Call for Daniel, and he will tell you what the writing means**. In all likelihood Daniel had been replaced as head of the wisemen when Nabonidus seized the throne accounting for the fact that Belshazzar was not well acquainted with Daniel. From Daniel 8:1,27, however, it seems clear that Daniel held some governmental post.

C. DANIEL READS THE WRITING ON THE WALL (5:13-28)

[13]So Daniel was brought before the king, and the king said to him, "Are you Daniel, one of the exiles my father the king brought from Judah? [14]I have heard that the spirit of the gods is in you and that you have insight, intelligence and outstanding wisdom. [15]The wise men and enchanters were brought before me to read this writing and tell me what it means, but they could not explain it. [16]Now I have heard that you are able to give interpretations and to solve difficult problems. If you can read this writing and tell me what it means, you will be clothed in purple and have a gold chain placed around your neck, and you will be made the third highest ruler in the kingdom."

[17]Then Daniel answered the king, "You may keep your gifts for yourself and give your rewards to someone else. Nevertheless, I will read the writing for the king and tell him what it means.

[18]"O king, the Most High God gave your father Nebuchadnezzar sovereignty and greatness and glory and splendor. [19]Because of the high position he gave him, all the peoples and nations and men of every language dreaded and feared him. Those the king wanted to put to death, he put to death; those he wanted to spare, he spared; those he wanted to promote, he promoted; and those he wanted to humble, he humbled. [20]But when his heart became arrogant and hardened with pride, he was deposed from his royal throne and stripped of his glory. [21]He was driven away from people and given the mind of an animal; he lived with the wild donkeys and ate grass like cattle; and his body was drenched with the dew of heaven, until he acknowledged that the Most High God is sovereign over the kingdoms of men and sets over them anyone he wishes.

²²"But you his son,ᵃ O Belshazzar, have not humbled yourself, though you knew all this. ²³Instead, you have set yourself up against the Lord of heaven. You had the goblets from his temple brought to you, and you and your nobles, your wives and your concubines drank wine from them. You praised the gods of silver and gold, of bronze, iron, wood and stone, which cannot see or hear or understand. But you did not honor the God who holds in his hand your life and all your ways. ²⁴Therefore he sent the hand that wrote the inscription.

²⁵"This is the inscription that was written:

MENE, MENE,⁸ TEKEL, PARSINᵇ

²⁶ "This is what these words mean:

Meneᶜ: God has numbered the days of your reign and brought it to an end.

²⁷Tekelᵈ: You have been weighed on the scales and found wanting.

²⁸Peresᵉ: Your kingdom is divided and given to the Medes and Persians."

ᵃ22 Or descendant; or successor   ᵇ25 Aramaic UPARSIN (that is, AND PARSIN)   ᶜ26 Mene can mean numbered or mina (a unit of money) ᵈ27 Tekel can mean weighed or shekel ᵉ28 Peres (the singular of Parsin) can mean divided or Persia or a half mina or a half shekel.

5:13-16 These verses repeat what is already known by the reader: Daniel's reputation (**Now I have heard that you are able to give interpretations and to solve difficult problems**), his challenge (**If you can read this writing and tell me what it means**), and the reward he can expect if he succeeds (**you will be clothed in purple and have a gold chain placed around your neck, and you will be made third highest ruler in the kingdom**).

Belshazzar seems to speak contemptuously of Daniel. He intends to put Daniel in his place by reminding him of his exilic status (v. 13). Calvin noted this, writing, "Here the king does not acknowledge his negligence but interrogates Daniel without shame — and interrogates him as if he were a prisoner."⁹

---

⁸Theodotion (the official Greek text for Daniel), the Septuagint, the Vulgate, and Josephus do not double the first word.

⁹Calvin, Daniel I, p. 222.

5:17 Daniel begins by dissociating himself from any thought of reward. "Daniel rejected the gift and the distinction promised," writes Keil, "to avoid, as a divinely enlightened seer, every appearance of self-interest in the presence of such a king, and to show to the king and his high officers of state that he was not determined by a regard to earthly advantage, and would unhesitatingly declare the truth, whether it might be pleasing or displeasing to the king."[10] If Daniel read the writing while the king was addressing him, he undoubtedly realized that such honors would be short-lived.

When Daniel responded to Nebuchadnezzar, one felt a sense of respect and concern. That sense is not felt here. Calvin wrote, "I have no doubt that he [Daniel] meant to speak roughly to the ungodly Belshazzar, a man beyond hope; but because there had been still some uprightness left in King Nebuchadnezzar and he had good hopes of him, he had treated him more gently."[11]

5:18-21 Belshazzar had mentioned his (grand)father Nebuchadnezzar (v. 13). Daniel uses this reference to the past to point out why Belshazzar now stands in great danger. If the Most High God would depose Nebuchadnezzar for arrogance, what will He do to you, Belshazzar, for profaning what had been dedicated to him?

Nebuchadnezzar's pride reflected a misguided sense of accomplishment. His success led him to think that he was sovereign, when, in reality, **the Most High God is sovereign over the kingdoms of men and sets over them anyone he wishes** (v. 21). Nebuchadnezzar ultimately acknowledged his subservience to the true sovereign. Nebuchadnezzar had been guilty of indifference. Belshazzar, on the other hand, was guilty of defiance, for he had set himself up **against the Lord of heaven**.

5:22 Belshazzar should have learned a lesson from the example of Nebuchadnezzar. Regrettably, he had not. And now he stands on the brink of disaster.[12]

---

[10]Keil, *Daniel,* p. 187.

[11]Calvin, *Daniel I,* p. 223.

[12]Calvin wrote, "For men plead ignorance to extenuate the blame for their crimes. But those who sin knowingly and willingly lack any excuse. Therefore the prophet convicts the king of manifest contumacy; as if he were saying that he had deliberately provoked the wrath of God, in that he was not unaware that a great and horrible judgment awaits all the proud, for he had

In verse 19 Daniel intimates that Belshazzar's actions were excessive for a monarch who was not the equal of Nebuchadnezzar in power. He was not an absolute monarch like his grandfather.

5:23-24 The description of the gods in this verse echoes Deuteronomy 4:28; Psalms 115:5-7; 135:15-17. The description of the true God echoes Numbers 16:22; Job 12:10; Jeremiah 10:23.

5:25-28 The three distinct words of the inscription are nouns designating weights: mina, shekel,[13] and half-mina.[14] "Since the context is one of divine judgment, and that judgment is explicitly pictured in verse 27 in terms of the scales of God's justice, nothing is more natural than to take the mina, shekel, and half-mina of the riddle to refer to the standardized weights against which precious metal was commonly weighed in antiquity."[15] These weight stones represent the standards of God's justice. Belshazzar did not measure up to the divine standards.

Daniel revocalizes the first noun to a verbal form and explains that this means that **God has numbered your kingdom**. The NIV translation has added **the days of**, assuming that Belshazzar's days are numbered. But the verbal root means "to count, reckon." What does it mean that God has "counted" or "reckoned" Belshazzar's kingdom? "Just as God's standards of justice correspond to the

---

such a clear and notable testimony in his own grandfather, which he ought to have had continually before his eyes" (ibid., p. 231).

[13]The Hebrew shekel (שֶׁקֶל) is in Aramaic tekel (תְּקֵל).

[14]"The evidence for 'Peresh' as 'half a Mina' is convincing, but not enough to exclude the possibility that it was used generally to mean a 'half' measure, and that its precise meaning depends on the context. Its position in 'Mina Mina Shekel Peresh' suggests that in Daniel it means a half Shekel" (Brewer, "Mene Mene," p. 312). The mina weighed sixty shekels. If peresh is a half-shekel, then parsin (the plural form or the dual which denotes pairs) would be two half-shekels. Many commentators have equated each of the words in the writing mene, mene, tekel, upharsin with kings of the Neo-Babylonian dynasty. In the Talmud weights are used to indicate the value or worth of people. Wiseman, for example, considers the two great rulers of the dynasty Nabopolassar and Nebuchadnezzar II as the minas and Nabonidus as the shekel with Belshazzar who only had part of the royal powers as the half-shekel [*The Zondervan Pictorial Encyclopedia of the Bible* [vol. 4], s.v. "Mene, Mene, Tekel, Upharsin."]

[15]Al Wolters, "The Riddle of the Scales in Daniel 5," *Hebrew Union College Annual* 62 (1991), p. 163 [9].

weights in one tray of the balance, so Belshazzar's kingdom corresponds to what in an ordinary business transaction was weighed against these weights in the other tray, namely the silver that was used as a payment."[16] In short, God had appraised the empire.

The second noun vocalized as a verb carries the meaning "to weigh." God is the judge who has weighed the king in his scales of justice.

The third noun vocalized as a verb carries the meaning "to assess."[17] This sense again speaks to God's activity of judicial inquiry.

In the NIV verse 26 ends, **and brought it to an end**. This statement announces God's verdict over Babylon. Wolters argues for the translation "and paid it out," giving the sense, "God has counted out Belshazzar's might like a sum of money, and has handed it over to another nation."[18]

This understanding resonates with the Jeremianic notion that God will repay Babylon for her sins against Israel. Jeremiah 25:14, for example, reads: "They themselves will be enslaved by many nations and great kings; I will repay them according to their deeds and the work of their hands" (see also 50:29; 51:6; 51:24; 51:56). The verbal root (Hebrew) translated here "repay" (שׁלם, *šlm*) is the same root (Aramaic) in Daniel 5:26.

Verse 27 reads, **You have been weighed in the scales and found wanting**. **Found wanting** suggests that Belshazzar is "too light," that is, he falls short of the required weight. The verbal root "too light" (in Hebrew and Aramaic קלל, *qll*) would be a pun on the weight stone "tekel" (תקל, *tql*).

Peres is clearly a play on the word for Persia. This final pun is the climax of God's verdict. Wolters has captured the sense: "We have already heard in general terms that God is settling accounts by paying out the kingdom which He has weighed on the scales; now we hear the name of the nation by which God will execute His sentence upon Babylon. In the final analysis, the embodiment of God's judgment over Babylon can be captured in one word: Persia!"[19]

In 1852 Edwin Arnold wrote,

---

[16]Ibid., p. 165 [11].
[17]*Zondervan Pictorial Encyclopedia*, s.v. "Mene, Mene, Tekel, Upharsin."
[18]Wolters, "Riddle," p. 172 [18].
[19]Ibid., p. 175 [21].

But thou hast mocked the Majesty of heaven;
And shamed the vessels to his service given.
And thou hast fashioned idols of thine own,—
Idols of gold, of silver, and of stone;
To them hast bowed the knee, and breathed the breath,
And they must help thee in the hour of death.
Woe for the sight unseen, the sin forgot!
God was among ye, and ye knew it not!
Hear what he sayeth now: "Thy race is run,
Thy years are numbered, and thy days are done;
Thy soul hath mounted in the scale of fate;
The Lord hath weighed thee, and thou lackest weight;
Now in thy palace porch the spoilers stand,
To seize thy scepter, to divide thy land."[20]

D. HONOR AND DEMISE (5:29-31)

[29]**Then at Belshazzar's command, Daniel was clothed in purple, a gold chain was placed around his neck, and he was proclaimed the third highest ruler in the kingdom.**

[30]**That very night Belshazzar, king of the Babylonians,[a] was slain, [31]and Darius the Mede took over the kingdom, at the age of sixty-two.**

[a]*30 Or Chaldeans*

5:29 The king fulfilled the promises he had earlier made: **Daniel was clothed in purple, a gold chain was placed around his neck, and he was proclaimed the third highest ruler in the kingdom.** Archer conjectures that the king thought that the Most High God might relent and not destroy Babylonia if his prophet became prime minister.[21] Calvin opines, "And when kings are most terrified, they always take good care to give no sign of nervousness; otherwise, they think, their authority will be undermined. So, to keep some respect among his subjects, he resolves to seem particularly secure and

---

[20]Quoted in Uriah Smith, *Daniel and the Revelation* (Mountain View, CA: Pacific Press Publishing Association, 1897), p. 114.

[21]Gleason L. Archer, Jr., "Daniel," in *The Expositor's Bible Commentary*, vol. 7, ed. by Frank E. Gaebelein (Grand Rapids: Zondervan, 1985), p. 75.

unafraid. This, without doubt, was the tyrant's purpose in ordering Daniel to be clothed with purple and royal insignia."[22]

In all likelihood, the proclamation was made to the group still in the throne room. A more formal and public announcement would have come later.

5:30-31 Belshazzar was slain that night and the government of Babylon was entrusted to Darius the Mede[23] **at the age of sixty-two**. The age of Darius the Mede may sum up the writing on the wall. If the mina is valued at sixty shekels, then a mina, a shekel, and two halves of a (shekel) come to 62 shekels. Darius is the actual person who brings to fruition the omen.[24]

In two classical sources — Herodotus and Xenophon — mention is made of a banquet which marked the end of the Neo-Babylonian Empire, just as in Daniel 5. The fall of Babylon and the Neo-Babylonian Empire is recounted by Herodotus (1.191) as follows: "By means of a cutting he diverted the river into the lake (which was then a marsh) and in this way so greatly reduced the depth of water in the actual bed of the river that it became fordable, and the Persian army, which had been left at Babylon for the purpose, entered the river, now only deep enough to reach about the middle of a man's thigh, and, making their way along it, got into the town. . . . The Babylonians themselves say that owing to the great size of the city the outskirts were captured without the people in the center knowing anything about it; there was a festival going on, and even while the city was falling they continued to dance and enjoy themselves, until hard facts brought them to their senses. This, then, is the story of the first capture of Babylon."

Xenophon (*Cyropaedia* 7.5.20-21) also mentions the (Euphrates) river and the festival. "'My friends,' said he [Cyrus], 'the river has made way for us and given us an entrance into the city. Let us, therefore, enter in with dauntless hearts, fearing nothing and remembering that those against whom we are now to march are the same men that we have repeatedly defeated, and that, too, when they were all

---

[22]Calvin, *Daniel I,* p. 235.

[23]Both Isaiah (13:17; 21:2) and Jeremiah (51:11,28) prophesy that the fall of Babylon will be associated with the Medes.

[24]Goldingay, *Daniel,* p. 112.

drawn up in battle line with their allies at their side, and when they were all wide awake and sober and fully armed; whereas now we are going to fall upon them at a time when many of them are asleep, many drunk, and none of them in battle array. And when they find out that we are inside the walls, in their panic fright they will be much more helpless still than they are now."

In the Hebrew Bible chapter 5 ends with verse 30; accordingly, verse 31 constitutes the opening of chapter 6.

God told Belshazzar, "You have been weighed on the scales and found wanting" (5:27). This negative appraisal serves as a contrast to the positive ideal to which Scripture holds government.

First, Scripture affirms that the state is an expression of God's common grace extended to all mankind. "Everyone must submit himself to the governing authorities, for there is no authority except that which God has established. The authorities that exist have been established by God. Consequently, he who rebels against the authority is rebelling against what God has instituted, and those who do so will bring judgment on themselves" (Rom 13:1-2).

Even when an official disgraces a public office, the authority of that office has still been established by God. In other words, the authority of government does not depend upon the moral leadership of its leaders. Christ reminded Pilate, the very man who, through sham legal proceedings, tried our Holy Lord, "You would have no power over me if it were not given to you from above" (John 19:11).

Second, the state is ordained to fulfill two responsibilities: to administer justice and to promote the general welfare. Regarding this dual role, Paul wrote, "For he is God's servant to do you good. But if you do wrong, be afraid, for he does not bear the sword for nothing. He is God's servant, an agent of wrath to bring punishment on the wrongdoer" (Rom 13:4).

The state is responsible for restraining evil by punishing crime and violence. It is also responsible for promoting moral standards in the community. "Submit yourselves for the Lord's sake to every authority instituted among men: whether to the king, as the supreme authority, or to governors, who are sent by him to punish those who do wrong and to commend those who do right" (1 Pet 2:13-14).

In addition to submitting to authority, Paul encourages Christians to pray for those in positions of authority. "I urge, then, first of all, that requests, prayers, intercession and thanksgiving be made for everyone—for kings and all those in authority, that we may live peaceful and quiet lives in all godliness and holiness" (1 Tim 2:1-2).

The LORD is often called "King" in the Old Testament (Deut 33:5; 1 Sam 12:12; Ps 48:2; Isa 41:21; 43:15; 44:6; Zeph 3:15). The Psalter is replete with examples extolling God as King. David appeals to God as King to hear his requests (Ps 5:1-3). God is King "for ever and ever" (Ps 10:16; 29:10). God, the King, will be praised for ever and ever (Ps 145:1-2).

The creation of mankind in the image of God necessitates that human kingship reflect divine kingship. Human kingship must be reflective of divine concerns, such as justice. Psalm 72:1 pleads, "Endow the king with your justice, O God, the royal son with your righteousness."

The king in ancient Israel would often serve as a judge, adjudicating legal questions (2 Sam 14). When Absalom was expanding his power base in Israel, at the expense of his father's reputation, he would call out to the one coming to the king for adjudication, "Look, your claims are valid and proper, but there is no representative of the king to hear you. If only I were appointed judge in the land! Then everyone who has a complaint or case could come to me and I would see that he gets justice" (2 Sam 15:3-4).

This is achieved, of course, through familiarity with the will of God, namely His Word. Deuteronomy 17:18-20 clearly spells this out: "When he takes the throne of his kingdom, he is to write for himself on a scroll a copy of this law, taken from that of the priests, who are Levites. It is to be with him, and he is to read it all the days of his life so that he may learn to revere the LORD his God and follow carefully all the words of this law and these decrees and not consider himself better than his brothers and turn from the law to the right or to the left. Then he and his descendants will reign a long time over his kingdom in Israel" (cf. 1 Sam 10:25).

When the time drew near for David to die, he summoned Solomon and charged him with the following words: "So be strong, show yourself a man, and observe what the LORD your God requires: Walk in his ways, and keep his decrees and commands, his laws and requirements, as written in the Law of Moses, so that you may prosper in all you do and wherever you go" (1 Kgs 2:2b-3).

The very justice and righteousness which characterizes God, and which is to characterize the rule of His representatives (Jer 22:16), is evidenced by the Messiah. The Messiah will reign on David's throne, establishing and upholding his kingdom "with justice and righteousness" (Isa 9:7; cf. 1:26-27). Because "righteousness will be his belt" (11:5), the Messiah "will not judge by what he sees with his eyes, or decide by what he hears with his ears; but with righteousness he will judge the needy, with justice he will give decisions for the poor of the earth" (11:3b-4; cf. Isa 42:1-4; Ps 72:2-4,12-14).

DANIEL 6

VI. DANIEL IN THE LIONS' DEN (6:1-28)

The outline followed here is that of Goldingay.[1] The structure of the chapter's content is again chiastic.

A. Introduction: Daniel's success (vv. 1-3)
    B. Darius signs an injunction but Daniel takes his stand (vv. 4-10)
        C. Daniel's colleagues plan his death (vv. 11-15)
            D. Darius hopes for his deliverance (vv. 16-18)
            D'. Darius witnesses his deliverance (vv. 19-23)
        C'. Daniel's colleagues meet with their death (v. 24)
    B'. Darius signs a decree and takes his stand (vv. 25-27)
A'. Conclusion: Daniel's success (v. 28)

Like chapter 3, this chapter details a court conflict. When Daniel was set for promotion ("the king planned to set him over the whole kingdom"), his jealous peers sought to bring about his death. Again, as in chapter 3, the God of Daniel intervenes to thwart the plot.

A. INTRODUCTION: DANIEL'S SUCCESS (6:1-3)

[1]It pleased Darius to appoint 120 satraps to rule throughout the kingdom, [2]with three administrators over them, one of whom was Daniel. The satraps were made accountable to them so that the king might not suffer loss. [3]Now Daniel so distinguished himself among the administrators and the satraps by his exceptional qualities that the king planned to set him over the whole kingdom.

---

[1]Goldingay, *Daniel*, p. 124.

6:1-3 With the emergence of the Medo-Persian Empire, the need arose to organize the far-flung rule. Accordingly, satraps, "protectors of the realm," were established, **with three administrators over them, one of whom was Daniel.** This organization was meant to minimize the king's loss of "territory due to uprisings, or in taxation due to graft."[2]

The number of satraps mentioned here compares favorably with the 127 mentioned in Esther 1:1.

B. DARIUS SIGNS AN INJUNCTION, BUT DANIEL TAKES HIS STAND (6:4-10)

[4]At this, the administrators and the satraps tried to find grounds for charges against Daniel in his conduct of government affairs, but they were unable to do so. They could find no corruption in him, because he was trustworthy and neither corrupt nor negligent. [5]Finally these men said, "We will never find any basis for charges against this man Daniel unless it has something to do with the law of his God."

[6]So the administrators and the satraps went as a group to the king and said: "O King Darius, live forever! [7]The royal administrators, prefects, satraps, advisers and governors have all agreed that the king should issue an edict and enforce the decree that anyone who prays to any god or man during the next thirty days, except to you, O king, shall be thrown into the lions' den. [8]Now, O king, issue the decree and put it in writing so that it cannot be altered—in accordance with the laws of the Medes and Persians, which cannot be repealed." [9]So King Darius put the decree in writing.

[10]Now when Daniel learned that the decree had been published, he went home to his upstairs room where the windows opened toward Jerusalem. Three times a day he got down on his knees and prayed, giving thanks to his God, just as he had done before.

6:4-5 In obedience to the law of the land Daniel was impeccable. But his first allegiance was to his God. Herein lies the tension. If his piety conflicted with the law of the state, then accusation may arise.

---

[2]Baldwin, *Daniel,* p. 128.

"We will never find any basis for charges against this man Daniel unless it has something to do with the law of his God."

6:6-7 Accordingly, the political sycophants, by appealing to the king's ego and his new authority, persuade him to enact a decree that prohibits any expression of religious devotion that does not regard Darius as the sole representative of deity. **"Anyone who prays to any god or man during the next thirty days, except to you, O King, shall be thrown into the lions' den."** Klieforth, as quoted by Keil, wrote: "All the nations subjected to the Medo-Persian kingdom were required not to abandon their own special worship rendered to their gods, but in fact to acknowledge that the Medo-Persian world ruler Darius was also the son and representative of their national gods. For this purpose they must for the space of thirty days present their petitions to their national gods only in him as their manifestation."[3]

According to verse 7 the **royal administrators** (of whom Daniel was chief) agreed in drawing up the decree. Darius must have had no reason to suspect that the other two administrators would misrepresent Daniel in this matter.

6:8-9 The decree was unalterable, **in accordance with the laws of the Medes and Persians** (cf. Esth 1:19; 8:8). Diodorus Siculus recounts how Darius III (336–331) "reproached himself for having made a serious mistake, but all his royal power was not able to undo what was done" (17.30), and Charidemus was led away to death.

6:10 In the face of the law, Daniel continued his habit of regular prayer. The Bible frequently mentions a roof chamber as a place of prayer (2 Sam 18:33; 1 Kgs 17:19; 2 Kgs 4:10; Acts 1:13; 20:8). Standing was the normal posture for prayer, but kneeling was common (1 Kgs 8:54; Ezra 9:5). **Windows open toward Jerusalem** is a literal understanding of Solomon's prayer recorded in 1 Kgs 8:35-36,

---

[3]Keil, *Daniel,* p. 211. If Darius was prohibiting prayer to any deity, he ran the risk of incurring the wrath of that deity. Any deity was acknowledged to have some degree of power. Accordingly Persian kings were tolerant of all religions. This tolerance explains how the Jews came to rebuild the temple of their God in Jerusalem. John Walton has suggested that "Darius could easily have been persuaded of the benefits of himself acting as mediator in order to urge by example that all Iranians give honor to Ahura Mazda" ["The Decree of Darius the Mede in Daniel 6," *JETS* 31/3 (1988): 286].

COLLEGE PRESS NIV COMMENTARY

41-43,48. The temple — the Most Holy Place — which symbolized the presence of God among his people, was situated in Jerusalem. "Hear my cry for mercy as I call to you for help, as I lift up my hands toward your Most Holy Place" (Ps 28:2). "But I, by your great mercy, will come into your house; in reverence will I bow down toward your holy temple" (Ps 5:7). **Three times a day** takes literally Psalm 55:17: "Evening, morning and noon I cry out in distress, and he hears my voice" (cf. Ps 119:164). Psalm 5:3 mentions the morning as a vital time for prayer. "In the morning, O LORD, you hear my voice; in the morning I lay my requests before you and wait in expectation" (cf. 88:13). Acts 10:9,30 makes reference to afternoon prayer. Psalm 42:8 alludes to evening prayer: "By day the LORD directs his love, at night his song is with me—a prayer to the God of my life."

C. DANIEL'S COLLEAGUES PLAN HIS DEATH (6:11-15)

[11]**Then these men went as a group and found Daniel praying and asking God for help. [12]So they went to the king and spoke to him about his royal decree: "Did you not publish a decree that during the next thirty days anyone who prays to any god or man except to you, O king, would be thrown into the lions' den?"**

The king answered, "The decree stands—in accordance with the laws of the Medes and Persians, which cannot be annulled."

[13]**Then they said to the king, "Daniel, who is one of the exiles from Judah, pays no attention to you, O king, or to the decree you put in writing. He still prays three times a day." [14]When the king heard this, he was greatly distressed; he was determined to rescue Daniel and made every effort until sundown to save him.**

[15]**Then the men went as a group to the king and said to him, "Remember, O king, that according to the law of the Medes and Persians no decree or edict that the king issues can be changed."**

6:11-15 Since both king (v. 12) and royal administrators (v. 15) affirm that **no decree or edict that the king issues can be changed**, Daniel faces certain death. He will be thrown into the den of lions.

In verse 13 Daniel's enemies refer to him as **one of the exiles from Judah,** rather than an "administrator." This clever subterfuge implies a political act of rebellion by a foreigner against the royal authority.

D. DARIUS HOPES FOR DANIEL'S DELIVERANCE (6:16-18)

[16]So the king gave the order, and they brought Daniel and threw him into the lions' den. The king said to Daniel, "May your God, whom you serve continually, rescue you!"
[17]A stone was brought and placed over the mouth of the den, and the king sealed it with his own signet ring and with the rings of his nobles, so that Daniel's situation might not be changed. [18]Then the king returned to his palace and spent the night without eating and without any entertainment being brought to him. And he could not sleep.

6:16 Having failed at overturning the edict and securing Daniel's release,[4] Darius has no choice but to condemn Daniel to the lions.

6:17 The lion pit presumably was a subterranean cavern with two entrances — side and top: a ramp for entrance and a hole in the roof by which the food would be fed to the occupants. A stone sealed off any avenue of escape. The sealing by both king and nobles rules out any possibility of intervention. Of course, the nobles had Daniel where they wanted him! This effectively prohibits the king from sending men to rescue his friend.

Darius' words, "May your God, whom you serve continually, rescue you," are an expression of hope rather than religious certitude.

6:18 The king could not sleep, nor did he take food or entertainment (such as music and/or female companionship).

---

[4]Wood expands this idea, writing, "He probably worked with lawyers to see if there were any possibility for setting the decree aside. Perhaps he argued that the king, who had made the law, ought to be able to set it aside; or he may have asked if there were no past cases where similar decrees had been rescinded; or he may have inquired if a man might be pardoned by the king and still satisfy legal requirements" (*Daniel,* p. 166).

E. DARIUS WITNESSES DANIEL'S DELIVERANCE (6:19-23)

[19]At the first light of dawn, the king got up and hurried to the lions' den. [20]When he came near the den, he called to Daniel in an anguished voice, "Daniel, servant of the living God, has your God, whom you serve continually, been able to rescue you from the lions?"

[21]Daniel answered, "O king, live forever! [22]My God sent his angel, and he shut the mouths of the lions. They have not hurt me, because I was found innocent in his sight. Nor have I ever done any wrong before you, O king."

[23]The king was overjoyed and gave orders to lift Daniel out of the den. And when Daniel was lifted from the den, no wound was found on him, because he had trusted in his God.

6:19-21 Daniel's answer to the king's question proves that Daniel's God is indeed **the living God** (cf. Deut 5:26; Jer 10:10; Ps 42:2).

6:22-23 Daniel attributes God's intervention to his innocence — **I was found innocent in his sight.** Daniel was truly innocent of disloyalty to the king. Verse 23 attributes the miracle to trust — **he had trusted in his God.** Psalm 34:7 reads: "The angel of the LORD encamps around those who fear him, and he delivers them" (cf. Ps 91:9-13). Both are obviously true! Hebrews 11:32-34 reads: "And what more shall I say? I do not have time to tell about Gideon, Barak, Samson, Jephthah, David, Samuel and the prophets, who through faith conquered kingdoms, administered justice, and gained what was promised; *who shut the mouths of lions*, quenched the fury of the flames, and escaped the edge of the sword; whose weakness was turned to strength; and who became powerful in battle and routed foreign armies."

Daniel was lifted out of the den through the upper entrance to speed his reunion with Darius. The king did not want to wait for the removal of the stone.

The fourth man in the furnace in chapter 3 is like the angel here in chapter 6. Additionally, just as Shadrach, Meshach, and Abednego came out of the fire with no smell of fire on them (3:27), so when Daniel comes out of the lions' den, **no wound was found on him.**

F. DANIEL'S COLLEAGUES MEET WITH THEIR DEATH (6:24)

[24]At the king's command, the men who had falsely accused Daniel were brought in and thrown into the lions' den, along with their wives and children. And before they reached the floor of the den, the lions overpowered them and crushed all their bones.

6:24 The enemies of Daniel were the ones disloyal to the crown, for they had conspired to deprive the king of his ablest administrator.[5] Accordingly, they were pushed into the darkness, caught in midair, and devoured by the ravenous lions. It was not because of lack of hunger that the lions did not consume Daniel![6]

"The righteous man is rescued from trouble, and it comes on the wicked instead" (Prov 11:8). "He who leads the upright along an evil path will fall into his own trap, but the blameless will receive a good inheritance" (Prov 28:10).

---

[5]Longman wrote: "The irony of the situation is that the administrators who urged the king to create this law were actually disloyal to Darius, working against his own desires and intentions, whereas Daniel, who finds himself under judgment of the law, is actually the most true to his subordinates" (*Daniel*, p. 166).

[6]Calvin writes: "For if anyone should say that the lions were full, or that there was some other reason why they did not devour Daniel, why, when he was taken out, should those beasts be impelled by such rage as to tear and devour not just one man but a great crowd? We assuredly see that God intended by this comparison to declare his power, lest any should object that the lions left Daniel alone because they were full fed and had no appetite for prey" (*Daniel I*, p. 269). Josephus writes, "Daniel's enemies, however, on seeing that he had suffered no harm, did not choose to believe that it was through the Deity and His providence that he had been saved, but held that the lions had been stuffed with food and therefore had not touched Daniel nor came near him, and so they told the king. But he, in his detestation of their wickedness, ordered a large quantity of meat to be thrown to the lions and, when they had eaten their fill, commanded Daniel's enemies to be cast into the den in order that he might discover whether the lions would refuse to come near them because of satiety. When the satraps were thrown to the beasts, it became evident to Darius that it was the Deity who had saved Daniel, for the lions spared no one of them but tore them all to pieces as though they were terribly famished and in need of food" (*Jewish Antiquities* X.260-262).

The solidarity of the family when punishment is meted out is attested in Persian times by Herodotus (3.119) and Ammianus Marcellinus (23.6.81).[7] Such punishment was forbidden by Deuteronomy 24:16. The number of victims is indeterminate.

G. DARIUS SIGNS A DECREE AND TAKES HIS STAND
(6:25-27)

[25]**Then King Darius wrote to all the peoples, nations and men of every language throughout the land:**

"**May you prosper greatly!**

[26]"**I issue a decree that in every part of my kingdom people must fear and reverence the God of Daniel.**

"**For he is the living God**
    and he endures forever;
his kingdom will not be destroyed,
    his dominion will never end.
[27]**He rescues and he saves;**
    he performs signs and wonders
    in the heavens and on the earth.
He has rescued Daniel
    from the power of the lions."

6:25-26a At the close of chapter 3 Nebuchadnezzar decreed that "the people of any nation or language who say anything against the God of Shadrach, Meshach and Abednego be cut into pieces and their houses be turned into piles of rubble" (3:29). Here, a more positive decree is issued: **people must fear and reverence the God of Daniel**.

6:26b-27 Darius' public proclamation first emphasizes that Daniel's God **is the living God**. If living, then active in this world. Surely chapter 6 demonstrates this truth. Darius then describes God as eternal (cf.

---

[7]Ammianus Marcellinus (c. A.D. 330–395), the last great Roman historian, wrote of the Persians: "They stand in special fear of the laws, among which those dealing with ingrates and deserters are particularly severe; and some laws are detestable, namely, those which provide that because of the guilt of a single person all his relatives are put to death."

4:3b,34). Finally, God is lauded as a deliverer and wonder-worker (cf. 4:3a). **He has rescued Daniel from the power of the lions.**

H. CONCLUSION: DANIEL'S SUCCESS (6:28)

[28]So Daniel prospered during the reign of Darius and the reign of Cyrus[a] the Persian.

[a]28 Or *Darius, that is, the reign of Cyrus*

6:28 Daniel 1:21 suggests that Daniel would outlive the Neo-Babylonian Empire. Here we are reminded of the same reality. In fact, according to 10:1, Daniel received the revelation of chapters 10–12 in the third year of Cyrus. Wallace writes, "What the chapter finally seems to be saying to us at this point is that empires rise and kings come and go, fashions and lifestyles change, but the one stable thing in the midst of all this change is Daniel himself—the man of God who does justice, and loves kindness, and walks humbly with his God."[8]

For a discussion of the identity of Darius, consult the Introduction ("Historicity").

Darius proclaimed that the God of Daniel is **the living God.** In the Old Testament this epithet, which is used fifteen times of God, suggests that He exists for his people, ready to intervene and deliver them from their enemies.

Joshua told his fellow Israelites that when the waters of the Jordan are "cut off and stand up in a heap" (Josh 3:13), then "you will know that the *living God* is among you and that he will certainly drive out before you the Canaanites, Hittites, Hivites, Perizzites, Girgashites, Amorites and Jebusites" (3:10).

When Goliath, the Philistine giant, defied the armies of the *living God* (1 Sam 17:26,36), David moved quickly to meet him in battle. Reaching into his bag and taking out a stone, David slung it and struck the Philistine on the forehead. The stone sank into the giant's forehead, and he fell face down on the ground. David then took hold of the Philistine's sword and cut off his head. When the Philistines saw that their hero was dead, they turned and ran. "So David

---

[8]Wallace, "The Lord Is King," p. 118.

triumphed over the Philistine with a sling and a stone" (17:50). The living God had indeed delivered the Israelites from the Philistines!

In 701 B.C. Sennacherib's Assyrian army attacked all the fortified cities of Judah and captured them. Hezekiah was then king of Judah. The Assyrians then turned toward Jerusalem. Beginning with a war of words, the field commander of the Assyrians proclaimed to the citizens of the capital city, "Do not listen to Hezekiah, for he is misleading you when he says, 'The LORD will deliver us.' Has the god of any nation ever delivered his land from the hand of the king of Assyria?" (2 Kgs 18:32-33).

When Hezekiah heard this, he went into the temple of the LORD and prayed these words, "Give ear, O LORD, and hear; open your eyes, O LORD, and see; listen to the words Sennacherib has sent to insult the *living God*. . . . Now, O LORD our God, deliver us from his hand, so that all kingdoms on earth may know that you alone, O LORD, are God" (2 Kgs 19:16,19; cf. 19:4; Isa 37:4,17).

That very night the angel of the LORD went out and put to death a hundred and eighty-five thousand men in the Assyrian camp. Sennacherib was forced to break camp and withdraw (2 Kgs 19:35-36). Again, the living God had defended his people from their enemies!

Darius was quite right then to refer to Daniel's God as the *living God* (6:20,26). Daniel's God had a history of saving his people from their enemies. Daniel could now be added to that wondrous history. Daniel had indeed been saved from the hungry lions!

This history becomes the basis for hope in times of trouble. In Psalm 42 the psalmist cries out, "Why must I go about mourning, oppressed by the enemy? My bones suffer mortal agony as my foes taunt me, saying to me all day long, 'Where is your God?'" (9b-10). The words of the psalmist's foes remind us of the defiance of both Goliath and Sennacherib. Not surprisingly the psalmist places his hope in the living God. "My soul thirsts for God, for the *living God*. When can I go and meet with God?" (2; cf. Ps 84:2).

Jeremiah contrasts lifeless idols with the living, active, and mighty God of Israel. "But the LORD is the true God; he is the *living God*, the eternal King. When he is angry, the earth trembles; the nations cannot endure his wrath" (10:10; cf. Deut 5:26). Walter Eichrodt wrote, "As the Living One he is the source of all life, and demonstrates the reality of his existence, in contrast to that of the lifeless, nonexistent gods of the heathen, by his incessant and marvelous activity."[9]

Jeremiah also contrasts the lifeless and fraudulent words of false prophets with the life-giving and true words of the LORD Almighty. "But you must not mention 'the oracle of the LORD' again, because every man's own word becomes his oracle and so you distort the words of the living God, the LORD Almighty, our God" (23:36).

Finally, Hosea uses the expression "sons of the *living God*" (1:10), in contrast with the expression "You are not my people," to encourage Israel to embrace her future by repenting in the present.

Coincidentally the expression *living God* also occurs fifteen times in the New Testament. Like Jeremiah 10:10, God, in contrast to idols, is "the *living* and true *God*" (1 Thess 1:9). When Paul and Barnabas healed a man lame from birth in Lystra, the citizens believed that the gods (Zeus and Hermes) had come down in human form. Accordingly, the crowd wanted to offer sacrifices to them. Paul and Barnabas responded, "We too are only men, human like you. We are bringing you good news, telling you to turn from these worthless things to the *living God*, who made heaven and earth and sea and everything in them" (Acts 14:15).

Jesus is the Christ, the "Son of the *living God*" (Matt 16:16; cf. 26:63).

Quoting Hosea 1:10, Paul calls believers "sons of the *living God*" (Rom 9:26). Paul also calls believers "the temple of the *living God*" (2 Cor 6:16) and the "church of the *living God*" (1 Tim 3:15). A believer's hope is "in the *living God*" (1 Tim 4:10).

Paul suggests that the Corinthians authenticate his ministry: "You show that you are a letter from Christ, the result of our ministry, written not with ink but with the Spirit of the *living God*, not on tablets of stone but on tablets of human hearts" (2 Cor 3:3).

Since Jesus offered himself unblemished to God, we "serve the *living God*" (Heb 9:14). Accordingly, the author of Hebrews exhorts the brothers not to turn "away from the *living God*" (3:12). Additionally, "It is a dreadful thing to fall into the hands of the *living God*" (10:31; cf. 12:22). This sense of dread before the judgment of God is also seen at Revelation 7:2; 15:7.

---

[9]Walter Eichrodt, *Theology of the Old Testament*, vol. 1 (Philadelphia: The Westminster Press, 1961), pp. 213-214.

DANIEL 7

VII. THE VISION OF THE FOUR BEASTS (7:1-28)

Chapter 7 scrolls back to the first year of Belshazzar's co-regency with his father Nabonidus.[1] Daniel 5 spoke of the last night of that reign.

A. FOUR GREAT BEASTS—7:1-8

[1]In the first year of Belshazzar king of Babylon, Daniel had a dream, and visions passed through his mind as he was lying on his bed. He wrote down the substance of his dream.

[2]Daniel said: "In my vision at night I looked, and there before me were the four winds of heaven churning up the great sea. [3]Four great beasts, each different from the others, came up out of the sea.

[4]"The first was like a lion, and it had the wings of an eagle. I watched until its wings were torn off and it was lifted from the ground so that it stood on two feet like a man, and the heart of a man was given to it.

[5]"And there before me was a second beast, which looked like a bear. It was raised up on one of its sides, and it had three ribs in its mouth between its teeth. It was told, 'Get up and eat your fill of flesh!'

[6]"After that, I looked, and there before me was another beast, one that looked like a leopard. And on its back it had four wings like those of a bird. This beast had four heads, and it was given authority to rule.

---

[1]Goldingay suggests 550/549 as the probable date, the year of Cyrus's decisive victory over Astyages, king of Media (p. 159).

[7]"After that, in my vision at night I looked, and there before me was a fourth beast—terrifying and frightening and very powerful. It had large iron teeth; it crushed and devoured its victims and trampled underfoot whatever was left. It was different from all the former beasts, and it had ten horns.

[8]"While I was thinking about the horns, there before me was another horn, a little one, which came up among them; and three of the first horns were uprooted before it. This horn had eyes like the eyes of a man and a mouth that spoke boastfully.

7:1 God speaks to Daniel through a dream, and Daniel writes down the content of that revelation. The writing down of revelation is attested in Isaiah 30:8, Jeremiah 36:2, and Habakkuk 2:2.

The vision takes place in the night, "when the darkness highlights fear and imagination is at its most vivid."[2]

7:2 Daniel's report of the vision begins with the setting. He is on the shore of the great sea, where the **four winds of heaven** are turning the waters into a turbulent frenzy. The **great sea** is a standard title for the Mediterranean Sea. Rejecting the natural reading, Young speaks of the sea as the "world-sea or great abyss, the boundless ocean."[3] The **four winds of heaven** (Jer 49:36; Ezek 37:9; Zech 6:5) represent "the heavenly powers and forces by which God sets the nations of the world in motion."[4]

By the time of Daniel, the sea was a symbol of humanity in rebellion against God and the ensuing chaos. "Oh, the raging of many nations—they rage like the raging sea! Oh, the uproar of the peoples—they roar like the roaring of great waters!" (Isa 17:12). "But the wicked are like the tossing sea, which cannot rest, whose waves cast up mire and mud" (Isa 57:20).

7:3 Out of the sea arise **four great beasts**, one after the other. Three of the beasts are bizarre: a lion with the wings of an eagle, a leopard with four heads and four wings like those of a bird, and a beast with iron teeth. Undoubtedly each of these mutant beasts evoked horror (cf. v. 7).

---

[2]Baldwin, *Daniel,* p. 140.
[3]Young, *Daniel,* p. 142.
[4]Keil, *Daniel,* p. 222.

Like chapter 2 these beasts represent "kingdoms that will arise from the earth" (v. 17). In the Old Testament, nations are symbolized by beasts: Ezekiel 29:3; 32:2; Isaiah 27:1; 51:9.

7:4 Like the colossus of chapter 2, we begin in the present. The **lion** with **the wings of an eagle** stands for Babylonia. This hybrid animal becomes humanlike — **it stood on two feet like a man, and the heart of a man was given to it** — reminiscent of Nebuchadnezzar's experience in chapter 4.[5] "The lion as king of the beasts and the eagle as king of the birds, well corresponds with gold (ch. 2), the most precious of metals. Thus, Babylon is represented by the lordliest of creatures."[6]

Jeremiah was fond of comparing Nebuchadnezzar to a lion (4:7; 49:19; 50:17,44) and an eagle (49:22; Lam 4:19; cf. Hab 1:8; Ezek 17:3). Winged lions in relief decorated the Processional Way in Babylon.

7:5 Both the lion and the eagle are predators, as is the **second beast** that rises out of the sea, the **bear** (2 Kgs 2:24; Hos 13:8; Amos 5:19). In fact, it **had three ribs in its mouth between its teeth**, the remains of the victim of a previous hunt. The Medo-Persian identification argues that the three ribs can be identified (1) with the three great victories of the Medo-Persian alliance: Lydia (fell to Cyrus in 546 B.C.), Babylon (Cyrus annexed in 539 B.C.), and Egypt (Cambyses acquired in 525 B.C.), or (2) with three chief cities of Babylon captured by the armies of Cyrus, or (3) with the threefold direction of its conquests. **Eat your fill** suggests that the beast must wholly consume the plunder it has already seized with its teeth.

The double-sided nature of the Medo-Persian Empire is symbolized by the beast **raised up on one of its sides**. The raised legs of the bear suggest a heavy, plodding progress, in contrast to the speed of the previous beast and the blazing speed of the beast to follow.

7:6 The third beast, the **leopard** with **four heads** and **four wings**, is blazingly fast (Jer 5:6; Hos 13:7). This terrifying beast points to the

---

[5]Goldingay writes, "The first of the creatures is the most human—not necessarily in the sense that it actually behaves in a more human way, but in the sense that God appoints it to a humanlike position of honor, authority, responsibility, and caring for the world (cf. 2:38; 4:17-19)" (*Daniel*, p. 162).

[6]Young, *Daniel*, p. 144.

incredible speed by which Alexander conquered the ancient Near East and extended his own kingdom. The four heads represent the four corners of the world or the fourfold division of Alexander's kingdom after his early death: Cassander ruled over the territory of Greece and Macedonia; Lysimachus over Thrace and a large part of Asia Minor; Seleucus over Syria and much of the Middle East; and Ptolemy over Egypt.

7:7 The **fourth beast** is nondescript, but exceedingly **powerful**. In the Old Testament, the horn symbolizes power (Deut 33:17; 1 Sam 2:1,10; Ps 18:2). This beast **had ten horns**, five times the natural two! This beast possessed great strength and violent power. With regard to the number ten, Calvin wrote, "We know this to be a frequent and usual form of speech in Scripture, where ten signifies many. When plurality is denoted, the number ten is used. Thus when the prophet states the fourth beast to have ten horns, he means, there were many provinces so divided, that each ruler, whether proconsul or praetor, was like a king."[7]

The beasts may be horrific, but their terror is relativized by two truths. First, each beast is followed by another. In other words, the terror of each beast is eclipsed by its successor. Second, these beasts are each controlled by a greater power — the power of God. "Oh, the raging of many nations — they rage like the raging sea! Oh, the uproar of the peoples — they roar like the roaring of great waters! Although the peoples roar like the roar of surging waters, when he rebukes them they flee far away, driven before the wind like chaff on the hills, like tumbleweed before a gale. In the evening, sudden terror! Before the morning, they are gone!" (Isa 17:12-14a).

7:8 According to 7:20, Daniel was particularly interested in the little horn of 7:8. Most readers of Daniel are, too! But since more is said of this horn later in the chapter, comment will be reserved until then.

---

[7]From this point on, quotations from John Calvin are from *Commentaries on the Book of the Prophet Daniel*, translated by Thomas Myers (Grand Rapids: Eerdmans, 1948). This reference is to page 25.

B. THE HEAVENLY COURT (7:9-14)

[9]"As I looked,

"thrones were set in place,
    and the Ancient of Days took his seat.
His clothing was as white as snow;
    the hair of his head was white like wool.
His throne was flaming with fire,
    and its wheels were all ablaze.
[10]A river of fire was flowing,
    coming out from before him.
Thousands upon thousands attended him;
    ten thousand times ten thousand stood before him.
The court was seated,
    and the books were opened.

[11]"Then I continued to watch because of the boastful words the horn was speaking. I kept looking until the beast was slain and its body destroyed and thrown into the blazing fire. [12](The other beasts had been stripped of their authority, but were allowed to live for a period of time.)

[13]"In my vision at night I looked, and there before me was one like a son of man, coming with the clouds of heaven. He approached the Ancient of Days and was led into his presence. [14]He was given authority, glory and sovereign power; all peoples, nations and men of every language worshiped him. His dominion is an everlasting dominion that will not pass away, and his kingdom is one that will never be destroyed."

7:9-10 Daniel is seeing first the divine judge. The epithet **Ancient of Days** refers to God as an old and wise judge sitting in his courtroom. The whiteness of his **clothing** symbolizes purity (Ps 51:7). The whiteness of his **hair** signals his wisdom. **Fire** depicts God's presence, particularly in judgment (Ps 18:8; 50:3; 97:3). Innumerable servants attend the supreme judge (cf. Matt 26:53).

Judgment is about to begin. The court is seated,[8] the written

---

[8]Verse 9 uses the plural "thrones." Who constituted the court? Passages like Isa 6:2; Rev 1:4 and 8:2 suggest that angels occupy these thrones.

evidence is produced. The deeds of men are recorded in books (Exod 32:32; Ps 56:8; 69:28; Isa 65:6; Mal 3:16; Luke 10:20; Rev 20:12), but here the reference is to the deeds of the four kingdoms and the little horn.

7:11-13 Then Daniel sees **one like a son of man.** This expression emphasizes the humanity of the person Daniel saw. Yet he is only *like* a human being, just as the beasts were "like" a lion (7:4), a bear (7:5), and a leopard (7:6).[9]

But this personage is seen coming with or riding the clouds of heaven, which, in Scripture, is the exclusive prerogative of God. In short, this figure represents a supernatural Person.[10] In Psalm 104:3 we read, "He [God] makes the clouds his chariot and rides on the wings of the wind" (cf. Ps 18:9-15; 97:2). In Nahum 1:3 we read, "The LORD is slow to anger and great in power; the LORD will not leave the guilty unpunished. His way is in the whirlwind and the storm, and clouds are the dust of his feet" (cf. Isa 19:1).

The humanity and deity of this Person are a mystery revealed only in the person of Jesus. The humanity of Jesus is a given. He was what every human being should be — a servant. "For even the Son of Man did not come to be served, but to serve, and to give his life as a ransom of many" (Mark 10:45).

The deity of Jesus is also a given. Jesus' use of the title "Son of Man" in association with judgment and in accompaniment with clouds confirms this truth.

---

[9]The expression "like a son of man" is a clear contrast with the beasts of the vision. In Genesis 1 "Man" was given dominion over the beasts of the earth. That rightful dominion and glory is reclaimed by this personage. According to Baldwin, "Whereas dominion had been exercised by beasts, the last of which was the epitome of destructive terror, dominion was now given to one like a mortal man. In view of the fact that the beasts stood for world-rulers who reckoned to be human, we may tentatively adopt the view that the writer is passing judgment on their inhumanity and is proclaiming that the day is coming when the reins of government will be for ever in the hands of a man worthy of the name: man as God, at creation, intended him to be" (*Daniel*, pp. 148-149). Calvin wrote, "But the vision offered to the Prophet was but a similitude; as Christ had not yet put on our flesh, this was only a prelude to his future manifestation in the flesh" (*Prophet Daniel*, p. 77).

[10]The Hebrew Anani, עֲנָנִי, "He of the clouds," continued to be a name of the Messiah (cf. Targum of First Chronicles 3:24).

In Matthew 25:31-33 Jesus refers to himself as "Son of Man" (cf. Luke 17:24). This passage in Matthew, like the one here in Daniel, associates this supernatural Person with judgment, the exclusive right of deity: "When the Son of Man comes in his glory, and all the angels with him, he will sit on his throne in heavenly glory. All the nations will be gathered before him, and he will separate the people one from another as a shepherd separates the sheep from the goats. He will put the sheep on his right and the goats on his left" (cf. Acts 17:31; Rom 2:16).

Jesus referred to his second coming in accompaniment with clouds: "In the future you will see the Son of Man sitting at the right hand of the Mighty One and coming on the clouds of heaven" (Matt 26:64; cf. Mark 13:26; Matt 24:30; Rev 1:7).

7:14 This verse emphasizes the universal — **all peoples, nations and men of every language worshiped him** — and everlasting — **His dominion is an everlasting dominion that will not pass away** — rule of the Son of Man. Jesus probably had this verse in mind when he told his disciples, "All authority in heaven and on earth has been given to me" (Matt 28:18).

The word translated **worshiped** in verse 14 is used in biblical Aramaic to refer only to the homage due to God (BDB, p. 1108). How, then, can one not identify this Person as the Second Person of the Godhead?

C. THE INTERPRETATION (7:15-28)

[15]"I, Daniel, was troubled in spirit, and the visions that passed through my mind disturbed me. [16]I approached one of those standing there and asked him the true meaning of all this.

"So he told me and gave me the interpretation of these things: [17]'The four great beasts are four kingdoms that will rise from the earth. [18]But the saints of the Most High will receive the kingdom and will possess it forever—yes, for ever and ever.'

[19]"Then I wanted to know the true meaning of the fourth beast, which was different from all the others and most terrifying, with its iron teeth and bronze claws—the beast that crushed and devoured its victims and trampled underfoot whatever was left. [20]I

also wanted to know about the ten horns on its head and about
the other horn that came up, before which three of them fell—the
horn that looked more imposing than the others and that had
eyes and a mouth that spoke boastfully. [21]As I watched, this horn
was waging war against the saints and defeating them, [22]until the
Ancient of Days came and pronounced judgment in favor of the
saints of the Most High, and the time came when they possessed
the kingdom.

[23]"He gave me this explanation: 'The fourth beast is a fourth
kingdom that will appear on earth. It will be different from all the
other kingdoms and will devour the whole earth, trampling it
down and crushing it. [24]The ten horns are ten kings who will come
from this kingdom. After them another king will arise, different
from the earlier ones; he will subdue three kings. [25]He will speak
against the Most High and oppress his saints and try to change the
set times and the laws. The saints will be handed over to him for a
time, times and half a time.[a]

[26]"'But the court will sit, and his power will be taken away and
completely destroyed forever. [27]Then the sovereignty, power and
greatness of the kingdoms under the whole heaven will be handed
over to the saints, the people of the Most High. His kingdom will
be an everlasting kingdom, and all rulers will worship and obey
him.'

[28]"This is the end of the matter. I, Daniel, was deeply troubled
by my thoughts, and my face turned pale, but I kept the matter to
myself."

[a]25 Or *for a year, two years and half a year*

7:15 Daniel repeatedly declares how troubling it is to receive a
vision and an understanding of the future course of history (7:15,28;
8:27; 10:2,10,11,15,17). **I, Daniel, was troubled in spirit, and the
visions that passed through my mind disturbed me.**

7:16-18 Daniel approached one of the "thousands upon thousands" who attended God (v. 10) in order to determine the true
meaning of the vision.

Daniel first asked a general question (v. 16), to which the angel
gave a general reply (vv. 17-18), indicating that the four beasts rep-

resented successive world empires. But the ultimate sovereignty over the world would be granted to the **saints of the Most High**.

From the earth (v. 17) does not contradict "out of the sea" of verse 3. Both locales simply indicate that these kingdoms were of earthly origin.

In the vision the kingdom is given to "one like a son of man" (v. 14), but in the interpretation section the kingdom is received by the **saints of the Most High** (v. 18). Who exactly are these saints or holy ones, that the kingdom given to the one like a son of man is received and possessed by them?

Though angels are so described in 4:17 and 8:13, this view seems untenable. The suffering and defeat implied in verses 21 and 25 are decisive against this view.

But in verse 27 the wording becomes "the saints, the people of the Most High," suggesting an identification with God's elect. Keil suggested that the saints are "the true members of the covenant nation, the New Testament Israel of God, i.e. the congregation of the New Covenant, consisting of Israel and the faithful of all nations; for the kingdom which God gives to the Son of man will, according to ver. 14, comprehend those that are redeemed from among the nations of the earth."[11]

The angel does not give additional comment regarding the first three kingdoms. Presumably, the first three beasts represent those kingdoms encountered in chapter 2.

7:19-21 Since the form of the fourth beast comprehends much more regarding the identity of the fourth world kingdom than chapter 2, Daniel asks the angel for the identity of the fourth beast.

7:23 This fourth beast signifies a fourth kingdom that would eat up and destroy the whole earth. As previously noted, Calvin understood the ten horns to represent the multitude of Roman provinces, each ruled by one who exercised the supreme power of life and death over all his subjects. The **little horn** referred then to the Caesars, "who attracted the whole government of the state to themselves, after depriving the people of their liberty and the senate of their power."[12] The reference to "three of the first horns" (v. 8) sug-

---

[11]Keil, *Daniel*, p. 239.
[12]Calvin, *Prophet Daniel*, p. 55.

gests how craftily the Caesars infringed upon and diminished the strength of both people and senate.[13]

7:24 Many commentators understand the ten horns to signify ten kings who shall arise out of that kingdom, either derivatives of the historical Roman Empire or yet future kings of a revived Roman Empire. These ten kings symbolize a past or future rebellion against the holy will of God. The futurist interpretation is based on the synchronicity between the demise of this fourth beast and the consummation of the Kingdom of God (7:9-10,13-14). Longman sees the four kingdoms in Daniel 7 as "symbolically representing the fact that evil kingdoms will succeed one another from the time of the Exile to the time of the climax of history, when God will intervene and once for all judge all evil and bring into existence his kingdom."[14]

7:25 The rule of the little horn is characterized by four traits: (1) blasphemy (**He will speak against the Most High**), (2) persecution (**oppress his saints**), (3) suppression of times, and (4) introduction of a new morality (**try to change the set times and the laws**).

The word for **against** is literally "at the side of," indicating that the little horn will attempt to raise itself as high as God, the Most High, and make pronouncements accordingly. The word for **oppress** is literally "wear out," as in a garment. This denotes continuous and unrelenting persecution. If the little horn is the Caesars, then their persecution of Christians reflects the wrath of Satan against the Church on account of the manifestation of Christ (1 Pet 2:12; 4:12-17; Revelation).

---

[13]The coalition formed between Caesar, Pompey, and Crassus in 60 B.C. has been called the "First Triumvirate." In time Caesar became dictator for life. The most famous triumvirate, often called the "Second," was that consisting of Mark Anthony, Marcus Aemilius Lepidus, and Caesar Octavian, created in 43 B.C. These men assumed a supreme authority, both at Rome and abroad. Lepidus was soon squeezed out, and the empire was uneasily divided between Octavian and Anthony until 31 B.C., when the issue was finally decided in Octavian's favor at the battle of Actium. Mark Anthony committed suicide, leaving Octavian in complete control of the Roman Empire. Perhaps the emergence of the Caesars, via the three-horned triumvirate, was foreseen in Daniel's dream. [cf. Tim J. Cornell, s.v. "Rome (history)," *The Oxford Classical Dictionary*.]

[14]Longman, *Daniel*, p. 190.

According to 2:21 "to change times" belongs exclusively to the power of God. It denotes the shaping of human history. **Times and laws** are "the foundations and main conditions, emanating from God, of the life and actions of men in the world."[15]

Commentators often identify this little horn as the Antichrist, the "lawless one" of 2 Thessalonians 2:8-9 and the "beast" of Revelation 13:1-10. This identification is based on the association of the little horn's destruction with a great judgment scene and the glorious appearance of the fullness of the Kingdom of God (7:11,26-27). Are these "end time" events preceded by the appearance of and persecution caused by the Antichrist? Many students of the Bible believe so.[16]

7:26 The defeat of the saints receives fuller treatment in 8:24. Here the downfall of the saints is brief because God will cut short the persecution (cf. Matt 24:22; Prov 10:27). The cutting short of the persecution is indicated by the interruption of the geometric sequence "one time, two times, four times." Quoting Ebrard, Keil writes, "it appears as if his tyranny would extend itself always the longer and longer: first a time, then the doubled time, then the four-fold — this would be seven times; but it does not go that length; suddenly it comes to an end in the midst of the seven times, so that instead of the fourfold time there is only half a time."[17]

The usurper's destructive rule will in turn be completely destroyed. The destruction of the fourth beast is effected through

---

[15]Keil, *Daniel,* pp. 241-242.

[16]Many older commentators, such as Adam Clarke, saw this little horn as a reference to the popes of Rome. The ten kings of 7:7 were: The Roman senate, the Greeks in Ravenna, the Lombards in Lombardy, the Huns in Hungary, the Alemans in Germany, the Franks in France, the Burgundians in Burgundy, the Saracens in Africa, the Goths in Spain, and the Saxons in Britain [*Isaiah to Malachi,* A Commentary and Critical Notes, vol. IV (New York: Abingdon Press, 1823), p. 592]. In 1970 Paul T. Butler wrote, "The fourth beast is the Roman empire in its beginning conquest of the world, tearing to pieces, devouring and stamping the residue with its feet; the ten horns is the Roman empire in its long and complete rule of the known world under successive emperors until its downfall; the little horn which grows great is the Roman Catholic papacy which succeeded the Roman empire in controlling nations and rulers" [*Daniel,* Bible Study Textbook Series (Joplin, MO: College Press, 1970), p. 274].

[17]Keil, *Daniel,* p. 244.

the destruction of the king symbolized by the small horn (v. 11). The people of the Most High, having endured these trials, will triumph.

7:27-28 The followers of the Son of Man are spoken of as **the saints, the people of the Most High**, indicating that the Son of Man is to be associated with the Most High himself. Note also that a distinction is made between the plural "saints" and the singular **him** in the final clause — **and all rulers will worship and obey him** — the one who is called "the Most High" — words not properly used for a finite human being. In spite of these clear distinctions, many commentators equate the saints with the Son of Man in verse 13.[18]

---

[18]See the discussion in Russell, *Divine*, pp. 121-123.

EXCURSUS
THE ANTICHRIST AND THE SON OF MAN

The term *antichrist* is found in the Bible only in the Johannine Epistles (1 John 2:18,22; 4:3; 2 John 7), but the idea underlying it is widespread. The prefix *anti* suggests opposition to Christ.

John assumes that at the end of this age a great enemy of God will come: "Dear children, this is the last hour; and as you have heard that the antichrist is coming, even now many antichrists have come" (1 John 2:18). In this verse, he also insists that an attitude of opposition to Christ already exists. In 1 John 2:22 John defines this attitude. "Who is the liar? It is the man who denies that Jesus is the Christ. Such a man is the antichrist — he denies the Father and the Son." John further defines this spirit in 4:2-3. "This is how you can recognize the Spirit of God: Every spirit that acknowledges that Jesus Christ has come in the flesh is from God, but every spirit that does not acknowledge Jesus is not from God. This is the spirit of the antichrist, which you have heard is coming and even now is already in the world" (cf. 2 John 7).

Summarizing John's teaching on this subject, Anthony Hoekema writes, "We may grant that the thought of a single future antichrist is not very prominent in John's epistles; his emphasis falls mostly on antichrists and anti-Christian thinking which is already present in his day. Yet it would not be correct to say that John had no room in his thinking for a future personal antichrist, since he still looks for an antichrist who is coming."[19]

Paul does not use the term *antichrist*, but the *man of lawlessness* in 2 Thessalonians 2:3-12 is the same being. This passage suggests that evil will continue right up to the end. Then evil will make its final onslaught against good. This battle will be led by the mysterious figure who owes his power to Satan. Paul is sure of the outcome. This last, supreme challenge of Satan will be crushed. "And then the lawless one will be revealed, whom the Lord Jesus will overthrow with the breath of his mouth and destroy by the splendor of his coming. The coming of the lawless one will be in accordance with the work

---

[19]Hoekema, *The Bible*, p. 198.

of Satan displayed in all kinds of counterfeit miracles, signs and wonders, and in every sort of evil that deceives those who are perishing" (2 Thess 2:8-10a; cf. Matt 24:23-24).

The Book of Revelation also knows of one empowered by Satan to oppose Christ in the last days (Rev 11:7; 13:11).

Daniel 7:25 is commonly understood to be an anticipatory description of the antichrist spoken of in the New Testament (this is obviously not the opinion of this commentator, however). Both the little horn of Daniel 7:25 and the *man of lawlessness* speak against the Most High and oppress the saints of the Most High.

The history of the interpretation of this figure is littered with false starts. Even though every individual identified with the antichrist evidenced an anti-Christian edge, these suggestions have obviously been flawed. We are still awaiting the final onslaught of the Evil One! Roman emperors, such as Nero, the papacy, or political dictators, such as Stalin or Hitler, have all been suggested. The march or continuance of human history is proof enough of the incorrectness of such identifications.

Son of Man. The prophet Ezekiel is addressed seventy times as "son of man" (e.g., 2:1; 3:1), and twenty-three times in the form, "you son of man" (e.g., 2:6,8). Daniel is once addressed as "son of man" (8:17). The Aramaic equivalent occurs in Daniel 7:13, where the "one like a son of man" is not a mere human being but someone that is compared to a human being.

[On the basis of Daniel 7:13, the expression "son of man" could be used as a messianic title. This seems clear from such works as 1 Enoch 37–71 and 4 Ezra 13 (especially vv. 32,37, and 52). John 12:34 also indicates that the Jews understood the title messianically. See Luke 22:69-70 for the functional equivalence to the title "Son of God."]

The other thirteen Old Testament occurrences are found in the second lines of poetic couplets: Numbers 23:19; Job 16:21; 25:6; 35:8; Psalms 8:4; 80:17; 146:3; Isaiah 51:12; 56:2; Jeremiah 49:18,33; 50:40; 51:43. It is clear that "son of man" is a poetic synonym for "man"/"human being."

The title "Son of Man" is used eighty-two times in the Gospels. It is also found once in Acts (7:56) and Hebrews (2:6); twice in Revelation (1:13; 14:14). In the Gospels, the title suggests a number of truths about the person of Jesus:

(1) The Son of Man came from heaven. "No one has ever gone into heaven except the one who came from heaven — the Son of Man" (John 3:13). "What if you see the Son of Man ascend to where he was before!" (John 6:62; cf. John 8:28).

(2) The Son of Man title can refer to the humanity of Jesus. "The Son of Man came eating and drinking" (Matt 11:19/Luke 7:34). The Son of Man "has no place to lay his head" (Matt 8:20/Luke 9:58).

(3) The title is used in the context of Jesus' authority over the Sabbath (Matt 12:8/Mark 2:28/Luke 6:5), his authority to forgive sins (Matt 9:6/Mark 2:10/Luke 5:24) and to judge (John 5:27; 9:35-39).

(4) Jesus associates the title with Isaiah's Servant of the Lord who brings redemption. "For even the Son of Man did not come to be served, but to serve, and to give his life as a ransom for many" (Mark 10:45; cf. Matt 20:28; Luke 19:10).

(5) The Son of Man will be betrayed (Matt 26:24,45/Mark 14:21,41/ Luke 9:44; 22:22,48), suffer unto death (Matt 17:12; 26:2; Mark 9:12), and be raised from the dead (Matt 17:9/Mark 9:9). "The Son of Man is going to be betrayed into the hands of men. They will kill him, and on the third day he will be raised to life" (Matt 17:22b-23a). "We are going up to Jerusalem, and the Son of Man will be betrayed to the chief priests and the teachers of the law. They will condemn him to death and will turn him over to the Gentiles to be mocked and flogged and crucified. On the third day he will be raised to life!" (Matt 20:18-19/ Mark 10:33-34; cf. Mark 8:31; 9:31; Luke 9:22; 18:31-33; 24:7; John 12:23-36; 13:31-32).

(6) The resurrected Son of Man has ascended to the right hand of God where he sits on a glorious throne. "But from now on, the Son of Man will be seated at the right hand of the mighty God" (Luke 22:69; cf. Acts 7:56). "I tell you the truth, at the renewal of all things, when the Son of Man sits on his glorious throne, you who have followed me will also sit on twelve thrones, judging the twelve tribes of Israel" (Matt 19:28; cf. 25:31).

(7) The Son of Man will come again in eschatological glory, often using the motif of coming with the clouds (Matt 24:30; 26:64; Mark 13:26; 14:62; Luke 21:27), or simply coming (Matt 10:23; 16:27-28; 24:27,39,44; Mark 8:38; Luke 10:40; 17:22-30; 18:8; John 1:51).

(8) The Son of Man comes as judge, bringing judgment upon those who denied him (Matt 13:37-42; Luke 9:26), but salvation and eternal life for those who believed (Luke 12:8). "For the Son of Man is going to come in his Father's glory with his angels, and then he will reward each person according to what he has done" (Matt 16:27). "At that time they will see the Son of Man coming in a cloud with power and great glory. When these things begin to take place, stand up and lift up your heads, because your redemption is drawing near" (Luke 21:27-28). "Do not work for food that spoils, but for food that endures to eternal life, which the Son of Man will give you" (John 6:27; cf. John 3:14; 6:53-54).

(9) One reference (Luke 6:22) links Christian suffering with our submission to the Son of Man. "Blessed are you when men hate you, when they exclude you and insult you and reject your name as evil because of the Son of Man."

In Mark 8:31 the title "Son of Man" is substituted for the title "Messiah" which Peter has just used. This substitution holds together better the ideas of transcendent majesty (#6 above) and vicarious suffering (#4 above), ideas suited to Jesus' salvific purpose.

DANIEL 8

VIII. THE RAM, GOAT, AND LITTLE HORN (8:1-27)

A. THE RAM AND THE GOAT (8:1-8)

[1]In the third year of King Belshazzar's reign, I, Daniel, had a vision, after the one that had already appeared to me. [2]In my vision I saw myself in the citadel of Susa in the province of Elam; in the vision I was beside the Ulai Canal. [3]I looked up, and there before me was a ram with two horns, standing beside the canal, and the horns were long. One of the horns was longer than the other but grew up later. [4]I watched the ram as he charged toward the west and the north and the south. No animal could stand against him, and none could rescue from his power. He did as he pleased and became great.

[5]As I was thinking about this, suddenly a goat with a prominent horn between his eyes came from the west, crossing the whole earth without touching the ground. [6]He came toward the two-horned ram I had seen standing beside the canal and charged at him in great rage. [7]I saw him attack the ram furiously, striking the ram and shattering his two horns. The ram was powerless to stand against him; the goat knocked him to the ground and trampled on him, and none could rescue the ram from his power. [8]The goat became very great, but at the height of his power his large horn was broken off, and in its place four prominent horns grew up toward the four winds of heaven.

8:1-2 Though this vision is dated to the third year of Belshazzar's reign, neither he nor Babylon is important to the context. This vision follows by two years (7:1) the one recorded in chapter 7 (**the one that had already appeared to me**), but is dependent upon it.

This vision is set in **Susa**, one of the great cities of the Persian Empire (Neh 1:1), a little over two hundred miles east of Babylon. Daniel was in Susa only in vision. The **Ulai** was an artificial canal that passed by Susa on the northeast.

8:3-4 In chapter 8 only two animals appear in a vision, suggesting a narrower scope than chapters 2 and 7. The first animal is a **ram with two horns** of unequal length. According to verse 20, the two horns represent the kings of Media and Persia. The longer horn is Persia, which eclipsed Media. (The bear at 7:5, "raised up on one of its sides," parallels this greater horn.) This ram gored every beast that stood in its way — **west, north, and south**. These three directions correspond to the three ribs in the mouth of the bear (7:5). Persia's conquests in the east were not vital to her status as a world power, and are therefore not mentioned. Verse 4 summarizes the two hundred years of Persia's world dominance (cf. Isa 41:2-3). Daniel is passing judgment in noting that this empire did as it **pleased and became great**.

8:5 The second animal, a shaggy **goat**, introduced in verse 5 and identified in verse 21, is Greece. Again, according to verse 21, the "prominent horn between his eyes" is the "first king," the founder of the empire, namely, Alexander the Great. The speed of this goat — **crossing the whole earth without touching the ground** — parallels the winged leopard at 7:6.

8:6-8 The goat charged the ram, shattering its two horns, knocking it to the ground, and trampling upon it. Coming from the west — that is from Macedonia and Greece — in 334 Alexander launched an unprovoked invasion, and within three years had decisively routed the Persian imperial forces. But at the height of the goat's power, its prominent horn was broken off. Alexander died of a sudden fever at Babylon in 323, at the age of thirty-three. "The sight and sound of horns breaking off typifies the brittle nature of political might."[1] In turn, four horns replace the broken horn. In other words, four kings take over the empire of Alexander the Great. Here, these four horns are passed over without comment. The four-headed beast at 7:6 is an obvious parallel to these four prominent horns.

---

[1]Baldwin, *Daniel,* p. 156.

B. THE LITTLE HORN (8:9-14)

⁹**Out of one of them came another horn, which started small but grew in power to the south and to the east and toward the Beautiful Land. ¹⁰It grew until it reached the host of the heavens, and it threw some of the starry host down to the earth and trampled on them. ¹¹It set itself up to be as great as the Prince of the host; it took away the daily sacrifice from him, and the place of his sanctuary was brought low. ¹²Because of rebellion, the host ᴸof the saints,ᵃ and the daily sacrifice were given over to it. It prospered in everything it did, and truth was thrown to the ground.**

¹³**Then I heard a holy one speaking, and another holy one said to him, "How long will it take for the vision to be fulfilled—the vision concerning the daily sacrifice, the rebellion that causes desolation, and the surrender of the sanctuary and of the host that will be trampled underfoot?"**

¹⁴**He said to me, "It will take 2,300 evenings and mornings; then the sanctuary will be reconsecrated."**

ᵃ*12 Or rebellion, the armies*

8:9 The conflict between the ram and the goat is but a prelude to the focus of chapter 8 — the small horn of verse 9, Antiochus IV Epiphanes (cf. 1 Macc 1:10; Josephus *Antiquities* x. 276).[2] This horn comes out of one of the four horns of verse 8, namely, the Seleucids.[3]

This horn grew in several directions: **to the south and to the east and toward the Beautiful Land**. The south is Egypt (11:5; 1 Macc 1:16-19). The east is Babylon, and particularly Elymais and Armenia (1 Macc 3:31,37; 6:1-4). The **Beautiful Land** is, of course, the land of God's promise, Palestine (cf. 11:16,41; Jer 3:19; Ezek 20:6,15).

---

[2]Antiochus IV Epiphanes, born 215 B.C., ruler 175–163, was the son of Antiochus III (the Great). His attempt to hellenize Palestine led to the cessation of the sacrifices in the Temple of the Lord. The Maccabean revolt led to the reconsecration of the Temple. On the coinage of the later years of his reign, he called himself Theos Epiphanes, "God Manifest."

[3]At the death of Alexander the Great, his kingdom would, in time, be divided amongst Cassander, who ruled over the territory of Greece and Macedonia, Lysimachus, who ruled over Thrace and a large part of Asia Minor, Seleucus, who ruled over Syria and much of the Middle East, and Ptolemy, who ruled over Egypt.

8:10 The little horn **grew until it reached the host of the heavens**. One of the names for God in the Old Testament is "God of Hosts." Since a "host" is a multitude or a large number, the name "God of Hosts" suggests that God is Lord of a) the angelic realm (Gen 32:1; Ps 103:20-21); b) the sun, moon, and stars (Deut 17:3; Jer 33:22); and c) the tribes/divisions/people of Israel (Exod 7:4; 12:41; 1 Sam 17:45).

The host of heaven is here the whole body of the stars of heaven. Daniel sees the horn grow so great in height that it is able to reach the stars with the hand, throw some of the stars to the ground, and trample upon them. But what does this mean? The words of the angel in verse 24 show that by the stars we are to understand the people of God. Keil writes, "As in heaven the angels and stars, so on earth the sons of Israel form the host of God. . . . As God, the King of this people, has His throne in heaven, so there also Israel have their true home, and are in the eyes of God regarded as like unto the stars. This comparison serves, then, to characterize the insolence of Antiochus as a wickedness against Heaven and the heavenly order of things."[4]

The nexus between *stars* and the people of God is a reminder of God's promise to Abraham: "I will surely bless you and make your descendants as numerous as the stars in the sky and as the sand on the seashore" (Gen 22:17; cf. 15:5; 26:4; Exod 32:13; Deut 1:10; 10:22; 28:62; 1 Chr 27:23; Neh 9:23).

8:11 This horn also raised itself up against the Prince of the host, namely, God Himself. Antiochus did this by forbidding the permanent practices of worship and desecrating the place of worship, the sanctuary. First Maccabees 1:45-46 narrates the historical fulfillment of Daniel's vision: "to forbid burnt offerings and sacrifices and drink offerings in the sanctuary, to profane Sabbaths and feasts, to defile the sanctuary and the priests." "The rebellion that causes desolation" of verse 13 (cf. 11:31; 12:11) was an altar to Olympian Zeus erected on Yahweh's altar of burnt offerings.

8:12 This verse summarizes the two-pronged attack of Antiochus against God's people and the entire temple ritual. This attack is the consequence of Antiochus's rebellion against God. **Truth**, the word of God, as far as it is embodied in proper worship, was thrown to

---

[4]Keil, *Daniel,* p. 297.

the ground, just as the host of heaven was. First Maccabees again provides historical commentary on Daniel's vision: "The books of the law which they found they tore to pieces and burned with fire. Where the book of the covenant was found in the possession of any one, or if any one adhered to the law, the decree of the king condemned him to death" (1:56-57).

8:13-14 Daniel overhears one angel (**holy one**) ask another, **"How long will it take for the vision to be fulfilled?"** The angelic response to the question is directed toward Daniel — **He said to me**. The answer **2,300 evenings and mornings** is enigmatic.

Two approaches to this enigma are popular. The first understands 2,300 as referring to the total number of days, approximately six and one-third years. This period of time approximates the length of Antiochus's reign of terror in Palestine. The second understands 2,300 as referring to the total number of sacrifices: 1,150 morning sacrifices and 1,150 evening sacrifices. This approach reduces the timetable to a little more than three years. This interval of time approximates the length of Antiochus's control of Jerusalem and of the temple.

The second approach seems doubtful, since "evening and morning" in the creation account (Gen 1) constituted not the half day but the whole day.

Should the number 2,300 be taken literally or symbolically? If literally, then the reign of terror will last six-plus years, ending with the reconsecration of the temple. If the number is understood symbolically, then we conclude that the oppression of the people by the little horn was to continue not fully a period of seven years.[5] Either

---

[5]Keil adds, "The time of the predicted oppression of Israel, and of the desolation of the sanctuary by Antiochus, the little horn, shall not reach the full duration of a period of divine judgment, shall not last so long as the severe oppression of Israel by the Midianites, Judg. vi. 1, or as the famine which fell upon Israel in the time of Elisha [2 Kings viii. 1], and shall not reach to a tenth part of the time of trial and of sorrow endured by the exiles, and under the weight of which Israel was mourned" (*Daniel*, p. 307). Calvin comments, "Christ therefore wished to hold up a light to direct all the elect through the approaching darkness under the tyranny of Antiochus, and to assure them that in the very depths of it they would not be deserted by the favor of God" (*Prophet Daniel*, p. 108).

way, the end point is the same — "the sanctuary will be reconsecrated." Verse 14 is thus predicting the rededication of the temple by Judas Maccabaeus on 25 Chislev (or 14 December) 164 B.C. (1 Macc 4:36-61). The celebration of this event is called Hanukkah.[6]

C. THE INTERPRETATION (8:15-27)

[15]While I, Daniel, was watching the vision and trying to understand it, there before me stood one who looked like a man. [16]And I heard a man's voice from the Ulai calling, "Gabriel, tell this man the meaning of the vision."

[17]As he came near the place where I was standing, I was terrified and fell prostrate. "Son of man," he said to me, "understand that the vision concerns the time of the end."

[18]While he was speaking to me, I was in a deep sleep, with my face to the ground. Then he touched me and raised me to my feet.

[19]He said: "I am going to tell you what will happen later in the time of wrath, because the vision concerns the appointed time of the end.[a] [20]The two-horned ram that you saw represents the kings of Media and Persia. [21]The shaggy goat is the king of Greece, and the large horn between his eyes is the first king. [22]The four horns that replaced the one that was broken off represent four kingdoms that will emerge from his nation but will not have the same power.

[23]In the latter part of their reign, when rebels have become completely wicked, a stern-faced king, a master of intrigue, will arise. [24]He will become very strong, but not by his own power. He will cause astounding devastation and will succeed in whatever he

---

[6]First Maccabees 4:52-56 reads: "Early in the morning on the twenty-fifth day of the ninth month, which is the month of Chislev, in the one hundred and forty-eighth year [164 B.C.], they rose and offered sacrifice, as the law directs, on the new altar of burnt offering which they had built. At the very season and on the very day that the Gentiles had profaned it, it was dedicated with songs and harps and lutes and cymbals. All the people fell on their faces and worshiped and blessed Heaven, who had prospered them. So they celebrated the dedication of the altar for eight days, and offered burnt offerings with gladness; they offered a sacrifice of deliverance and praise."

does. He will destroy the mighty men and the holy people. ²⁵He will cause deceit to prosper, and he will consider himself superior. When they feel secure, he will destroy many and take his stand against the Prince of princes. Yet he will be destroyed, but not by human power.

²⁶The vision of the evenings and mornings that has been given you is true, but seal up the vision, for it concerns the distant future."

²⁷I, Daniel, was exhausted and lay ill for several days. Then I got up and went about the king's business. I was appalled by the vision; it was beyond understanding.

ᵃ*19* Or *because the end will be at the appointed time*

8:15-16 Daniel saw a supernatural being in human likeness, who was being addressed as Gabriel ("man of God") by a voice from above the waters of the canal, to interpret the vision to Daniel. In the Old Testament, only in the book of Daniel are angels named (cf. 10:13; Luke 1:19,26; Jude 9).

8:17 Gabriel's approach caused Daniel to fall down in fear. Gabriel responded by saying, **Understand that the vision concerns the time of the end**. The word "end" does not necessarily mean the end of all things. Here, it must refer to the question asked in verse 13: "How long will it take for the vision to be fulfilled?"

8:18-22 The **time of wrath** is God's verdict on those who rebel against him and fail to repent. Daniel may rest assured that there is a time appointed for the end of Antiochus's rebellion and the vindication of the sanctuary.

8:23-25 These verses provide additional detail concerning the character and rebellion of Antiochus. He is determined and unyielding (**stern-faced**), cunning (**master of intrigue, he will cause deceit to prosper**), arrogant (**he will consider himself superior**), and violent (**he will destroy many**).[7] His rebellion against God (**the Prince of princes**) will cause astounding devastation and bring about the

---

[7]First Maccabees 1:29-30 reveal the cunning violence of Antiochus: "Two years later the king sent to the cities of Judah a chief collector of tribute, and he came to Jerusalem with a large force. Deceitfully he spoke peaceable

deaths of powerful, political enemies (**the mighty men**) and the saints of God (**the holy people**).

Yet, in spite of his success, **he will be destroyed**. Second Maccabees 9 gives a gruesome account of the death of Antiochus. He was first seized with sharp internal tortures (v. 5). He fell out of his chariot, and the fall was so hard as to torture every limb of his body (v. 7). Finally, his flesh rotted away (v. 9). Antiochus's death is attributed to divine causation: **Yet he will be destroyed, but not by human hands.**

8:26 Since this vision had no immediate application, it could be sealed up, preserved for use in a distant time (cf. 12:9).

8:27 The influence of this vision so agitated Daniel that **he lay ill for several days**. Once recuperated he was able to return to the king's business in Babylon. But he still brooded over the vision (**I was appalled by the vision**). Daniel may have been puzzled (**It was beyond understanding**) by the permissive will of the Lord, allowing the time of brutal oppression under the little horn.

During the reign of Antiochus Epiphanes, "truth was thrown to the ground" (8:12). From the perspective of premodern belief, this is an apt description of the emergence of modernism and now postmodernism.

The term *premodern* refers to that period of thought in which biblical revelation and tradition were the foundations of human knowledge. This period corresponds roughly to the first fifteen centuries of the Common Era.

The term *modernism* refers to that period of intellectual history in which human reason became the basis for all knowledge (roughly 1500 to 1968). Rene Descartes's famous dictum, "I think, therefore I am," elevated self-knowledge to the measure of truth. This deifying of human reason meant that biblical revelation was no longer needed.

Modernism also championed the belief that the self was sovereign (autonomous) and self-sufficient. The individual did not need others. Immanuel Kant said,

---

words to them, and they believed him; but he suddenly fell upon the city, dealt it a severe blow, and destroyed many people of Israel."

Enlightenment is man's emergence from his self-imposed nonage. Nonage is the inability to use one's own understanding without another's guidance. This nonage is self-imposed if its cause lies not in lack of understanding but in indecision and lack of courage to use one's own mind without another's guidance. Dare to know! "Have the courage to use your own understanding," is therefore the motto of the enlightenment.[8]

Modernism also asserted the inevitability of societal evolution — society would always get better.

Postmodernism (1968–   ) is skeptical of modernity's assumptions about truth, the self, and progress. Two World Wars and the Great Depression crippled our confidence in the inevitability of progress. Adolf Hitler proved that the autonomous self could be destructive. He did what *he* wanted to do. Do we now know that communities must hold individuals accountable? Confidence in human reason has also proved elusive. Science has not solved all of our problems. What do we worry about? I suspect the answers that come immediately to our minds include crime, violence, gender and racial tensions, the breakup of marriages and families, and poverty. Will science ever resolve these issues?

The modernist discovered objective truth through the scientific method. For the postmodernist, however, truth is what one believes to be true. The sayings "Whatever" and "To each his own" could be mottoes of postmodernism. Since preference has replaced objective truth, we define reality as we choose.

The modernist's self-sufficient self has been replaced by community. Truth is now relative to the community in which we associate. In other words, each person's understanding of truth is now influenced by the community (Christian, Jewish, homosexual, the poor) in which he or she is involved.

Faith in human progress once reigned, but now human misery shapes the postmodern outlook on the future. Suspicion, mistrust, insecurity have replaced modernity's utopian dream.

Truth has indeed been thrown to the ground. Neither mod-

---

[8]Immanuel Kant, "What Is Enlightenment?" in *The Enlightenment: A Comprehensive Anthology*, ed. Peter Gay (New York: Simon & Schuster, 1973), p. 384.

ernism nor postmodernism has it right. The scientific method is essential to our pursuit of better understanding the world in which we live, but it cannot relegate God and his Word to the periphery of our cosmos. And truth is not a preference. Jesus' claims are true whether any community believes them or not.

Since God creates each and every person in his image, the self is sacred. But since the self is created, it can logically never be autonomous or self-sufficient. And just as there is plurality in the Godhead, so we have been created for community.

The pervasive influence of sin (Rom 3:23; 6:23) makes any discussion of an earthly utopia an absurdity. Society has certainly made great strides forward in medicine and technology. But human engineering will never heal or program the human heart to love one's neighbor. Until each person and community repents of sin and is saved by the blood of Jesus, we will endure human misery.

In the August 6, 2001, issue of *Time* magazine, Roger Rosenblatt, essayist, writes,

> What I do know is that the world is a pitiless and dangerous place. In 20 years of observing portions of it, I have seen, or seen the aftermath of, children blown apart by car bombs in Beirut; kindergartners slaughtered in a schoolroom in Israel; hunted young men dying of starvation in Sudan; other young men and women hacked to death with machetes in Rwanda, their bodies hoisted like logs over waterfalls and carried into muddy rivers; still others decapitated in Cambodia, with kids forced to do the decapitating.[9]
>
> This is what people will do to one another. Given who they are and their individual circumstances, they will do absolutely anything to one another. The accumulation of this knowledge leaves one revulsed, heartbroken and, in some dark way, amazed. But it does not leave one with much to say.

Come, Lord Jesus.

---

[9]This commentary was in production at the time of the September 11, 2001 terrorist attack on Washington and New York City. Man's inhumanity to man continues unabated.

DANIEL 9

IX. DANIEL'S PRAYER OF REPENTANCE AND THE PROPHECY OF THE SEVENTY WEEKS (9:1-27)

A. DANIEL'S PRAYER OF REPENTANCE (9:1-19)

¹In the first year of Darius son of Xerxesª (a Mede by descent), who was made ruler over the Babylonianᵇ kingdom—²in the first year of his reign, I, Daniel, understood from the Scriptures, according to the word of the LORD given to Jeremiah the prophet, that the desolation of Jerusalem would last seventy years. ³So I turned to the Lord God and pleaded with him in prayer and petition, in fasting, and in sackcloth and ashes.

⁴I prayed to the LORD my God and confessed:

"O Lord, the great and awesome God, who keeps his covenant of love with all who love him and obey his commands, ⁵we have sinned and done wrong. We have been wicked and have rebelled; we have turned away from your commands and laws. ⁶We have not listened to your servants the prophets, who spoke in your name to our kings, our princes and our fathers, and to all the people of the land.

⁷"Lord, you are righteous, but this day we are covered with shame—the men of Judah and people of Jerusalem and all Israel, both near and far, in all the countries where you have scattered us because of our unfaithfulness to you. ⁸O LORD, we and our kings, our princes and our fathers are covered with shame because we have sinned against you. ⁹The Lord our God is merciful and forgiving, even though we have rebelled against him; ¹⁰we have not obeyed the LORD our God or kept the laws he gave us through his servants the prophets.

[11]**All Israel has transgressed your law and turned away, refusing to obey you.**

"Therefore the curses and sworn judgments written in the Law of Moses, the servant of God, have been poured out on us, because we have sinned against you. [12]**You have fulfilled the words spoken against us and against our rulers by bringing upon us great disaster. Under the whole heaven nothing has ever been done like what has been done to Jerusalem.** [13]**Just as it is written in the Law of Moses, all this disaster has come upon us, yet we have not sought the favor of the LORD our God by turning from our sins and giving attention to your truth.** [14]**The LORD did not hesitate to bring the disaster upon us, for the LORD our God is righteous in everything he does; yet we have not obeyed him.**

[15]**"Now, O Lord our God, who brought your people out of Egypt with a mighty hand and who made for yourself a name that endures to this day, we have sinned, we have done wrong.** [16]**O Lord, in keeping with all your righteous acts, turn away your anger and your wrath from Jerusalem, your city, your holy hill. Our sins and the iniquities of our fathers have made Jerusalem and your people an object of scorn to all those around us.**

[17]**"Now, our God, hear the prayers and petitions of your servant. For your sake, O Lord, look with favor on your desolate sanctuary.** [18]**Give ear, O God, and hear; open your eyes and see the desolation of the city that bears your Name. We do not make requests of you because we are righteous, but because of your great mercy.** [19]**O Lord, listen! O Lord, forgive! O Lord, hear and act! For your sake, O my God, do not delay, because your city and your people bear your Name."**

[a]*1 Hebrew Ahasuerus*　　[b]*1 Or Chaldeans*

9:1-3 Darius was named in 5:31 and in chapter 6. **Xerxes** (Hebrew = Ahasuerus) I (486–465/4 B.C.) is the king mentioned in the book of Esther. Accordingly, this name must be recognized as an ancient Achaemenid royal title,[1] much like the term *Pharaoh* in

---

[1]Wiseman, *Chronicles,* p. 15.

Egypt. Daniel has in mind the first year of the Persian Empire — 539 B.C.

According to Jeremiah 25:11 and 29:10, **the desolation of Jerusalem would last seventy years**. Three options for counting the seventy years of exile are evident. The first option begins with the Babylonian incursion of Judah in 605, the year of Jeremiah 25:11, and the year of Daniel's deportation to Babylon (Dan 1:1, 6). Sixty-six years later, in 539, Cyrus/Darius (Isa 44:28; 45:13) issued a decree that allowed the Jews to return to Palestine and thus end their exile in captivity (cf. 2 Chr 36:22-23; Ezra 1:1-4). The number 70 is thus an approximation, not an exact computation.

The second option begins with 587, the year of the destruction of Jerusalem and the temple (2 Chr 36:19-20), and ends in 516, when the restoration of the Temple was complete (Ezra 6:15; Zech 1:12).

The third option identifies the seventy years with Babylon's period of power. Seventy years after Babylon had captured and destroyed Assyria, Babylon herself was conquered by Cyrus (609-539B.C.).[2]

Given the urgency of Daniel's prayer in verses 4-19, he undoubtedly sensed that the seventy years of Jeremiah had just about run their course. This, of course, favors the first and third options above. The second option cannot explain why Daniel now gives himself over to prayer.

Fasting, sackcloth, and ashes were all outward signs of Daniel's humiliation and penitence.

9:4-19 In this prayer, Daniel's petition is found in verses 17 and 18. He asks God **to look with favor on your desolate sanctuary** and to **see the desolation of the city that bears your name**. In short, Daniel petitions God to forgive Israel, ending Israel's exile and returning her to Jerusalem and to the temple.

Daniel's petition is based upon the **great mercy** of God, not Israel's merit. In point of fact, mercy presupposes sin — Israel's sin. Daniel's great grief over Israel's sin is the haunting sense of this prayer.

Since all Israel has transgressed (v. 11), including Daniel, he consistently speaks in the plural: we . . . we . . . we . . . . This "all Israel"

---

[2]R.J.M. Gurney, "The Seventy Weeks of Daniel 9:24-27," *Evangelical Quarterly* 53 (1981): 30.

includes **our kings, our princes and our fathers, and . . . all the people of the land** (v. 6; cf. vv. 7,8).

Daniel uses a myriad of expressions for Israel's total defection from the holy will of God: **we have sinned** (vv. 5,11,5), **[we have] done wrong** (vv. 5,15), **we have been wicked** (v. 5), **[we] have rebelled** (vv. 5,9), **we have turned away** (vv. 5,11), **we have not listened/obeyed** (vv. 6,10,11,14), **we are covered with shame because of our unfaithfulness/because we have sinned** (vv. 7,8), **all Israel has transgressed** (v. 11), and **our sins [and iniquities]** (vv. 13,16).

Due to Israel's total disregard for the will of God, He **poured out** (v. 11) on her the punishment he had promised. Leviticus 26:14,31-33 forewarned Israel that the wages of sin is death: "But if you will not listen to me and carry out all these commands, . . . I will turn your cities into ruins and lay waste your sanctuaries, and I will take no delight in the pleasing aroma of your offerings. I will lay waste the land, so that your enemies who live there will be appalled. I will scatter you among the nations and will draw out my sword and pursue you. Your land will be laid waste, and your cities will lie in ruins" (cf. Deut 28:15-68; 30:17-18).

In addition to God's mercy, Daniel also reflects on other characteristics of God: **great and awesome** (v. 4; cf. Neh 1:5), **love** (v. 4), **righteous** (vv. 7,14,16), and **forgiving** (v. 9,19).

God's revelation of himself in the past, especially in the events associated with the Exodus, is the basis for Daniel's future hope. It is as if Daniel were saying, "As you brought us out of exile in Egypt, do so now out of Babylon" (vv. 15-16).

Like Moses in his prayer of intercession (Exod 32:12-13), Daniel was concerned about God's reputation (vv. 18-19). **For your sake, O my God, do not delay** (v. 19; cf. Jer 32:20; Isa 63:11-14). With the collapse of both Jerusalem and the temple, the nations may have assumed that Judah's God was either powerless or a delusion. Little did the nations understand that it was God who brought Israel under Babylonian control (cf. Lam 2:2-5).

B. GABRIEL'S RESPONSE (9:20-23)

[20]**While I was speaking and praying, confessing my sin and the sin of my people Israel and making my request to the LORD my**

God for his holy hill—[21]while I was still in prayer, Gabriel, the man I had seen in the earlier vision, came to me in swift flight about the time of the evening sacrifice. [22]He instructed me and said to me, "Daniel, I have now come to give you insight and understanding. [23]As soon as you began to pray, an answer was given, which I have come to tell you, for you are highly esteemed. Therefore, consider the message and understand the vision:

9:20-23 As soon as Daniel began to pray, **Gabriel**, who was mentioned previously at 8:16, was dispatched with an answer to Daniel's petition. The Lord's response came swiftly. Gabriel is here called **the man**, corresponding to his description in 8:15.

The reason why God immediately answered the prayer is that Daniel was a man **highly esteemed** (literally, "most desired").

The time of the evening sacrifice was the time of evening prayer.

C. THE PROPHECY OF THE SEVENTY WEEKS (9:24-27)

[24]"Seventy 'sevens'[a] are decreed for your people and your holy city to finish[b] transgression, to put an end to sin, to atone for wickedness, to bring in everlasting righteousness, to seal up vision and prophecy and to anoint the most holy.[c]
[25]"Know and understand this: From the issuing of the decree[d] to restore and rebuild Jerusalem until the Anointed One,[e] the ruler, comes, there will be seven 'sevens,' and sixty-two 'sevens.' It will be rebuilt with streets and a trench, but in times of trouble. [26]After the sixty-two 'sevens,' the Anointed One will be cut off and will have nothing.[f] The people of the ruler who will come will destroy the city and the sanctuary. The end will come like a flood: War will continue until the end, and desolations have been decreed. [27]He will confirm a covenant with many for one 'seven.'[g] In the middle of the 'seven'[g] he will put an end to sacrifice and offering. And on a wing of the temple he will set up an abomination that causes desolation, until the end that is decreed is poured out on him.[h]"[i]

[a]*24* Or *'weeks'*; also in verses 25 and 26   [b]*24* Or *restrain*   [c]*24* Or *Most Holy Place*; or *most holy One*   [d]*25* Or *word*   [e]*25* Or *an anointed one*; also in verse 26   [f]*26* Or *off and will have no one*; or *off, but not for himself*

^g27 Or *'week'*　　^h27 Or *it*　　ⁱ27 Or *And one who causes desolation will come upon the pinnalce of the abominable temple, until the end that is decreed is poured out on the desolated city*

9:24 Daniel prayed for the restoration of God's people. God's response to that prayer is found here in these verses. God's answer, in short, is: as far as the true people of God are concerned, a period of **seventy sevens** has been decreed by God for accomplishing their salvation.[3]

Seventy sevens is enigmatic. The Hebrew reads literally, "sevens seventy." How long is a seven? Commentators have almost universally understood a seven to denote seven years. Accordingly, seventy sevens is 490 years. In light of Leviticus 25:8 — "Count off seven Sabbaths of years — seven times seven years — so that the seven Sabbaths of years amount to a period of forty-nine years" — this conclusion seems certain.

But are the 490 years to be taken literally or symbolically? Commentators who take the number arithmetically (or literally) tend to use it to pinpoint in time the ministry of Jesus Christ (see footnote 7, below). The symbolic approach will be treated later.

Verse 24 employs six infinitives ("to . . .") to intimate what shall happen by the conclusion of (or within) the seventy sevens. The first three infinitives treat of the taking away of sin; the last three of the bringing in of everlasting righteousness with its consequences.

To **restrain** (so the NIV footnote) transgression means to hem it in, so that it can no longer spread about (cf. Zech 5:8). The second infinitive, **to seal up sin** (in NIV **to put an end to sin**), suggests that sin shall be guarded securely under a seal. The third infinitive, **to atone for wickedness**, speaks of forgiveness. The first two describe the cessation of sinful activity, whereas the third suggests that God removes the consequences of sinful behavior.

The fourth infinitive, **to bring in everlasting righteousness**, clearly speaks of a righteousness that shall never cease. **To seal up**

---

[3]Calvin writes, "For the Prophet here compares God's grace with his judgment; as if he had said, the people have been punished by an exile of seventy years, but now their time of grace has arrived; nay, the day of their redemption has dawned, and it shone forth with continual splendor, shaded, indeed, with a few clouds, for 490 years until the advent of Christ" (*Prophet Daniel*, p. 200).

vision and prophecy suggests the authentication of prophecy by its fulfillment. The final infinitive predicts the appointment of a new place or person of God's presence among his people.

Fourteen times in the Old Testament the expression "*the* Holy of Holies" is used of the most holy place of the tabernacle or temple (Exod 26:33,34; Num 4:4,19; 18:10; 1 Kgs 6:16; 7:50; 8:6; 1 Chr 6:34 [49 in English]; 2 Chr 3:8,10; 4:22; 5:7; Ezek 41:4). This expression is definite. It is *the* Holy of Holies. But in Daniel 9:24, the definite article is missing.

The expression without the definite article is never used in the OT of a person. It is used in association with altars (Exod 29:37; 30:10; 40:10); the bread set before the LORD (Lev 24:9); everything devoted to the LORD (Lev 27:28); all the "furniture" of the tabernacle (Exod 30:29; 1 Chr 23:13); the grain (Lev 2:3,10; 6:10 [Eng. 17];10:12), guilt (Lev 7:1,6; 14:13), and sin offerings (Lev 6:18,22 [Eng. 6:25,29];10:17); incense (Exod 30:36); offerings for priests and Levites (Num 18:9); the temple precinct (Ezek 43:12; 48:12); and the sanctuary (Ezek 45:3).

The evidence of the previous paragraph suggests that the sixth infinitive ("to anoint the most holy") refers to the temple or to the temple cultus. But such a conclusion is contrary to the teaching of Jesus, who stated that he would replace the Temple once and for all (Matt 12:6).

The superlative "Holy of Holies" or "the holiest" is certainly true of Jesus. At his birth, he was announced as "the holy one" (Luke 1:35). The devils knew Jesus as "the Holy One of God" (Luke 4:34; Mark 1:24). In the preaching of the early church, the "Holy One" was a title used of Jesus (Acts 3:14; 4:27,30; 1 John 2:20).

The anointing of Jesus as "the holiest" denotes the communication of the Spirit to Christ. When Jesus was baptized, the Spirit of God descended like a dove upon him (Matt 3:16), fulfilling such OT prophecies as Isaiah 11:2; 61:1 (cf. Ps 45:7).

9:25-27 In order to understand the prophecy that follows, one important question must be raised. Given that we are to interpret this passage messianically,[4] does the termination of the seventy

---

[4]The non-Messianic approach is represented in the International Critical Commentary by James A. Montgomery [*A Critical and Exegetical Commentary on the Book of Daniel* (Edinburgh: T. & T. Clark, 1959)]. He holds that the

sevens coincide with the First or the Second Advent (Coming) of Jesus Christ? In other words, are the six infinitives fully accomplished at the First or the Second Coming of our Lord? The answer to this question affects, as the following will demonstrate, the interpretation of the whole prophecy.

The following chart summarizes the views of E.J. Young, who believes the passage focuses upon the First Advent of Jesus,[5] and C.F. Keil, who believes the passage culminates with Jesus' Second Coming.[6] The differences in detail are telling. Both interpreters understand the numbers symbolically.

BIBLICAL TEXT (NRSV)	YOUNG	KEIL
From the time that the word went out to restore and rebuild Jerusalem until the time of an anointed prince, there shall be seven sevens	The **word** is the Edict of Cyrus (Ezra 1:1-4), dated to c. 539 B.C., allowing God's people to "[re]build the temple of the LORD, the God of Israel, the God who is in Jerusalem" (Ezra 1:3).[7]	The **word** is the Edict of Cyrus (Ezra 1:1-4), dated to c. 539 B.C., allowing God's people to "[re]build the temple of the LORD, the God of Israel, the God who is in Jerusalem" (Ezra 1:3).

initial seven sevens runs from Jerusalem's destruction (586) to Babylon's fall to Cyrus, the anointed prince (539). The sixty-two sevens run from then to the time of the high priest, Onias III, the anointed one, who was murdered in 171. The last seven encompasses the rule of Antiochus IV. The restoration of the temple was the symbol of God's victory over the forces of evil (See also the commentaries by John J. Collins [Hermeneia], John E. Goldingay [Word Biblical Commentary], E.W. Heaton [Torch Bible], Norman W. Porteous [Old Testament Library], and W. Sibley Towner [Interpretation]). This view is also represented in the notes to the 1993 *Harper Collins Study Bible*. The obvious difficulty with this view is that Antiochus did not destroy the city and the sanctuary (9:26).

[5]Paul T. Butler wrote, "The N.T., especially the treatise to the Hebrews, represents all these transactions (v. 24) as having been fulfilled at the first advent – in the great climactic event of the plan of God's redemption at Calvary" [*Daniel*, Bible Study Textbook Series (Joplin, MO: College Press, 1970), p. 346]. In his exposition Calvin suggests two points must be held as fixed: "First, the seventy weeks begin with the Persian monarchy, because a free return was then granted to the people; and secondly, they did not terminate till the baptism of Christ, when he openly commenced his work of satisfying the requirements of the office assigned him by his father" (*Prophet Daniel*, p. 209).

[6]Thomas E. McComiskey opines that this prophecy spans the period from

	YOUNG	KEIL
	An **anointed prince** is literally, "an anointed one, who at the same time is a prince." In the OT both priests and kings were anointed. Accordingly, this person must be seen as a priest-prince. Only Jesus, the Christ [= "the anointed one"], is both priest and king in one person (cf. Ps 110:4; John 4:25).	An **anointed prince** is literally, "an anointed one, who at the same time is a prince." In the OT both priests and kings were anointed. Accordingly, this person must be seen as a priest-prince. Only Jesus, the Christ [= "the anointed one"], is both priest and king in one person.
	From the Edict of Cyrus to the First Advent of Jesus is **seven sevens and sixty-two sevens.**[8] Young's reading here is crucial in understanding the difference between his view and that of Keil. Young understands the sixty-two sevens as leading up to the First Advent, whereas Keil sees them as leading up to the Second.	From the Edict of Cyrus to the First Advent of Jesus is **seven sevens.**

Cyrus to Antichrist ["The Seventy 'Weeks' of Daniel against the Background of Ancient Near Eastern Literature," *WTJ* 47 (1985): 18-45].

[7]Since the Edict of Cyrus says nothing about the restoration of the city of Jerusalem as such, commentators have suggested other decrees or edicts. In 457, the seventh year of Artaxerxes I, he issued a decree to Ezra (7:12-26; 9:9), allowing Jews to do "whatever the God of heaven has prescribed . . . . for the temple of the God of heaven" (7:23). If the numbers of this passage are to be understood literally, and if the edict of Artaxerxes is the proper starting point, and if we remember that we gain a year as we move from 1 B.C. to A.D. 1, then sixty-nine sevens later, we come to A.D. 27, the probable year of the beginning of our Lord's ministry [R.J.M. Gurney, "The Seventy Weeks of Daniel 9:24-27," *EvQ* 53 (1981): 33]. In 445 King Artaxerxes commissioned Nehemiah (Neh 2:5-8) to fortify the city. Again, if

BIBLICAL TEXT	YOUNG	KEIL
and for sixty-two weeks it shall be built again with streets and moat, but in a troubled time.	The end of the **seven sevens** corresponds with the period of Ezra and Nehemiah. The **sixty-two sevens**, therefore, cover the age of Ezra and Nehemiah to the time of Christ. God's people suffered oppression during the times of Ezra and Nehemiah (Neh 4:1; 6:1; 9:36,37).	During the **sixty-two weeks**, restoration and building shall advance amid the oppressions of the times. Keil understands here a reference to the Kingdom of God, which shall be built up during this long period, although amid severe persecutions.
After the sixty-two weeks, an anointed one shall be cut off and shall have nothing	The **anointed one** is Jesus Christ, who is **cut off** by His death upon the Cross of Calvary (cf. Isa 53:8). Having been forsaken by man and God, the Christ, hanging on the cross, had **nothing**, nothing but the guilt of sin of all those for whom he died.	**After the sixty-two weeks**, that is, in the seventieth seven, the **Anointed One shall be cut off**, so that he shall lose his place and function as Messiah.
And the troops of the prince who is to come shall destroy the city and the sanctuary	The **prince who is to come** is Titus Vespasianus, who destroyed the **city** of Jerusalem and the **sanctuary** of God in A.D. 70.	**The prince who is to come** is the Antichrist, who shall wage war against the kingdom of God throughout this entire seven.

the numbers of this passage are to be understood literally, this date does not square with the ministry or death of Jesus.

[8]The Jewish scholars who were responsible for transmitting the consonantal text of the Old Testament are called Masoretes. They were also responsible for supplying vowel points and accent marks, some of which function like marks of punctuation. After **seven sevens** the Masoretes placed an accent called Athnach, which typically marks the principal break in a sentence. To conjoin **seven sevens** with **sixty-two sevens**, therefore, goes against the respected thinking of the Masoretes.

BIBLICAL TEXT	YOUNG	KEIL
Its [His] end shall come with a flood, and to the end there shall be war. Desolations are decreed.	The city of Jerusalem shall be destroyed.	**Flood** is here the figure of the desolating judgment of God upon the Antichrist.
He[9] shall make a strong covenant with many for one week, and for half of the week he shall make sacrifice and offering cease; and in their place shall be an abomination that desolates, until the decreed end is poured out upon the desolator.	Jesus the Christ causes a **covenant** (the "New Covenant") to prevail for **many**. By his death he effectively abolishes the need for **sacrifice and offering** (cf. Heb 9:25,26; 10:8,9). Since the Messiah had effectively caused sacrifice to cease, Titus would come to destroy the temple, which had become an abomination.[10] Upon the ruins of the temple a determined full end pours out.	The Antichrist will impose on the people **a strong covenant** that they should follow him and give themselves to him as their God. Borne on the wings of idol-abominations, the Antichrist shall carry on a desolating rule, till the firmly decreed judgment shall pour itself upon him as one desolated.

Neither Young nor Keil interpret the numbers arithmetically. This is seen clearly in Keil's understanding of the sixty-two sevens — a long period of time between Jesus' First Advent and the appearance of Antichrist. Young sees two crucial events happening in what is presumably the final seven. Those two events — the crucifixion of Jesus and the destruction of Jerusalem — are historically separated by four decades.

These two events so dominate this paragraph (9:25-27), if Young is correct, that verse 27 echoes the content of verse 26. Notice the parallelism of thought here.

---

[9]Normally the last antecedent is to be taken as the subject of the following verb. This rule implies that the "he" here is the "prince" of verse 26.

[10]Calvin suggested that the destruction of city and sanctuary signified that God inflicted "dreadful vengeance upon the Jews for their murder of his Christ" (*Prophet Daniel*, p. 223).

BIBLICAL TEXT	YOUNG	KEIL
After the sixty-two weeks, an anointed one shall be cut off and shall have nothing (26a).	In A.D. 70 Titus destroyed the building (temple) which Jesus' death had rendered obsolete.	He shall make a strong covenant with many for one week, and for half of the week he shall make sacrifice and offering cease (27a).
And the troops of the prince who is to come shall destroy the city and the sanctuary (26b).	The crucifixion of Jesus fulfilled the Old Testament sacrificial system and thereby rendered obsolete the temple and its altar.	And in their place shall be an abomination that desolates, until the decreed end is poured out upon the desolator (27b).

A popularly held view of Daniel's Seventy Weeks is called the *Parenthesis Interpretation*. Advocates of this view assert that the seventieth week does not follow immediately upon the sixty-ninth week. Rather, a long parenthesis, that is, an indefinite interval of time, interrupts these two weeks. The prophetic clock stopped with the death of Jesus on the cross (end of the 69th week) and will commence again (beginning of 70th week) when the Antichrist leads a great army against the people of God.[11]

The ninth chapter started with seventy years decreed for Babylon. The chapter ends with Jerusalem given seventy times seven years. The Jews and Jerusalem had only seventy weeks (of years) to go!

Daniel was a man of prayer. Chapter 9 is proof enough. His intercession for Israel in this chapter is beyond compare. In this section, consider further aspects of prayer in the Old Testament as you contemplate your own prayer life.

Prayer is speech between man and God (Jonah 4:2). Moshe Greenberg has demonstrated that Old Testament prayer is formulated in patterns analogous to interhuman speech. "This means,"

---

[11]This view is represented in the commentaries by Archer, Luck, and Wood, to name a few. This view is most often associated with Dispensationalism [cf. O.T. Allis, *Prophecy and the Church* (Philadelphia: Presbyterian and Reformed, 1945), pp. 111-123].

according to Greenberg, "that the biblical narrators all portrayed speech between man and God on the analogy of speech between humans. Such a procedure accords perfectly with the personal conception of God in the Scriptures; the only analogy available for intercourse with him was the human-personal."[12]

Through prayer man expresses his dependence upon God: "Therefore let everyone who is godly pray to you while you may be found; surely when the mighty waters rise, they will not reach him. You are my hiding place; you will protect me from trouble and surround me with songs of deliverance" (Ps 32:6-7).

Through prayer sinful man confesses his moral failures. Speaking on behalf of Israel, Daniel prayed, "We have sinned and done wrong. We have been wicked and have rebelled; we have turned away from your commands and laws. . . . O Lord, we and our kings, our princes and our fathers are covered with shame because we have sinned against you" (Dan 9:5,8).

The confession of the sinner brings the needed forgiveness from God, which restores the divine-human relationship. "If my people, who are called by my name, will humble themselves and pray and seek my face and turn from their wicked ways, then will I hear from heaven and will forgive their sin and will heal their land" (2 Chr 7:14; cf. 6:21).

Man also entreats God through prayer. "Listen to my cry for help, my King and my God, for to you I pray. In the morning, O LORD, you hear my voice; in the morning I lay my requests before you and wait in expectation" (Ps 5:2-3).

The uncertainties of life were often the catalyst for prayer. Hannah pleaded for a new life, a child (1 Sam 1:10-11,27). Hezekiah pleaded that his life would be prolonged (2 Kgs 20:1-11), as did Jonah (2:2). Hezekiah and Isaiah pleaded with God in prayer to deliver his people from the life-threatening Assyrian menace (2 Chr 32:20-21).

"If a man sins against the LORD," Eli queries his sons, "who will intercede for him?" (1 Sam 2:25). The question implies a negative response. And yet the Old Testament is replete with examples of

---

[12]Moshe Greenberg, *Biblical Prose Prayer* (Berkeley: University of California Press, 1983), p. 36.

men interceding with God on behalf of sinful Israel: Moses (Num 11:1-2; 21:6-7; Deut 9:25-26), Samuel (1 Sam 7:5; 12:19), Hezekiah (2 Chr 30:18-20), Jeremiah (37:3; 42:2,20), Daniel (9:20), and Nehemiah (1:6). On other occasions the intercession was for an individual. Abraham interceded for Abimelech and his family (Gen 20:7,17); Moses prayed for his brother Aaron (Deut 9:20); a "man of God" prayed on behalf of Jeroboam (1 Kgs 13:6); Job prayed for his "friends" (42:8-9).

God's relationship with His people compels him to deliver his wayward family. Likewise, as Moses or Samuel interceded with God for wayward Israel, they did so because they also were committed to relationship with God's people. And just as God had blessed them, so they sought to bring God's blessing of forgiveness to his people. Vriezen writes, "The strongly personal relation with God that underlies this act of intercession and atonement is characteristic of the prophetic religion which springs from a very personal relation with God. It demonstrates to how great an extent Yahweh is known in Israel as a personal God, who wants to avail Himself of the service of men in the intercourse with the world."[13]

---

[13]Th. C. Vriezen, *An Outline of Old Testament Theology* (Oxford: Basil Blackwell, 1962), p. 295.

DANIEL 10

X. THE VISION OF A HEAVENLY MESSENGER
(10:1–11:1)

¹In the third year of Cyrus king of Persia, a revelation was given to Daniel (who was called Belteshazzar). Its message was true and it concerned a great war.ᵃ The understanding of the message came to him in a vision.

²At that time I, Daniel, mourned for three weeks. ³I ate no choice food; no meat or wine touched my lips; and I used no lotions at all until the three weeks were over.

⁴On the twenty-fourth day of the first month, as I was standing on the bank of the great river, the Tigris, ⁵I looked up and there before me was a man dressed in linen, with a belt of the finest gold around his waist. ⁶His body was like chrysolite, his face like lightning, his eyes like flaming torches, his arms and legs like the gleam of burnished bronze, and his voice like the sound of a multitude.

⁷I, Daniel, was the only one who saw the vision; the men with me did not see it, but such terror overwhelmed them that they fled and hid themselves. ⁸So I was left alone, gazing at this great vision; I had no strength left, my face turned deathly pale and I was helpless. ⁹Then I heard him speaking, and as I listened to him, I fell into a deep sleep, my face to the ground.

¹⁰A hand touched me and set me trembling on my hands and knees. ¹¹He said, "Daniel, you who are highly esteemed, consider carefully the words I am about to speak to you, and stand up, for I have now been sent to you." And when he said this to me, I stood up trembling.

¹²Then he continued, "Do not be afraid, Daniel. Since the first day that you set your mind to gain understanding and to humble

yourself before your God, your words were heard, and I have come in response to them. [13]But the prince of the Persian kingdom resisted me twenty-one days. Then Michael, one of the chief princes, came to help me, because I was detained there with the king of Persia. [14]Now I have come to explain to you what will happen to your people in the future, for the vision concerns a time yet to come."

[15]While he was saying this to me, I bowed with my face toward the ground and was speechless. [16]Then one who looked like a man[b] touched my lips, and I opened my mouth and began to speak. I said to the one standing before me, "I am overcome with anguish because of the vision, my lord, and I am helpless. [17]How can I, your servant, talk with you, my lord? My strength is gone and I can hardly breathe."

[18]Again the one who looked like a man touched me and gave me strength. [19]"Do not be afraid, O man highly esteemed," he said. "Peace! Be strong now; be strong."

When he spoke to me, I was strengthened and said, "Speak, my lord, since you have given me strength."

[20]So he said, "Do you know why I have come to you? Soon I will return to fight against the prince of Persia, and when I go, the prince of Greece will come; [21]but first I will tell you what is written in the Book of Truth. (No one supports me against them except Michael, your prince. [11:1]And in the first year of Darius the Mede, I took my stand to support and protect him.)

[a]1 Or *true and burdensome*   [b]16 Most manuscripts of the Masoretic Text; one manuscript of the Masoretic Text, Dead Sea Scrolls and Septuagint *Then something that looked like a man's hand*

10:1-2 The **third year** of Cyrus was 537 B.C. The name **Belteshazzar** had been given to Daniel nearly seventy years earlier by Nebuchadnezzar (1:7). The message that Daniel received was "true and burdensome" (cf. NIV footnote).

10:3-4 The **first month** of the year (v. 4) was traditionally a time for feasting. The Passover was celebrated on the fourteenth day; the Feast of Unleavened Bread was celebrated from the fifteenth to the twenty-first days. But on this occasion Daniel denied himself: **no meat or wine touched my lips** (v. 3). Anointing oneself with oils was a sign of rejoicing (Ps 45:7; Amos 6:6; 2 Sam 14:2). Apparently the vegetable diet of chapter 1 had not applied to the whole of Daniel's career in foreign service.

The **great river** in the Bible was usually the Euphrates. The Tigris is only here in the Bible described as the great river.

10:5-6 As Daniel looks up he sees a man, dressed like a priest in linen (Lev 6:10; cf. Ezek 9:2,3,11; 10:2,6,7; Mark 16:5) and wearing a belt of gold. The humanity of this messenger is emphasized in verses 16 and 18. But this man is glorious. **His body was like chrysolite, his face like lightning, his eyes like flaming torches, his arms and legs like the gleam of burnished bronze, and his voice like the sound of a multitude.**[1]

10:7-9 Daniel's unidentified companions fled and hid themselves (cf. Acts 9:7), leaving Daniel without human help (**So I was left alone**). Based on Daniel's description — **my face turned deathly pale and I was helpless** — his trance experience — **I fell into a deep sleep, my face to the ground** — was not one to envy.

10:10-12 The combination of touch and command enabled Daniel to get to his feet. The messenger spoke of Daniel as one **highly esteemed**. (The Servant of the Lord [Isa 42:1] was also one in whom the Lord delighted.) This is evident from the fact that this messenger had been sent in response to Daniel's prayer (v. 12; cf. 9:23).

10:13 But why a three-week delay if Daniel's prayer had been heard at the beginning? The **prince of the Persian kingdom** was to blame. A representative of Persia in the heavenly realm is intended here. In verse 20 Greece has an angelic counterpart, and in verse 21 Michael (Jude 9), one of the chief princes, belongs to Israel. This glimpse into spiritual warfare anticipates Paul's description of spiri-

---

[1]A similar description of Jesus in Rev 1:13-15 has led many a commentator to identify this messenger as a preincarnate appearance of the eternal Son. Eugene H. Merrill, for example, writes, "Though many scholars identify this 'man' clothed in linen as an angel, perhaps Gabriel or Michael, the extravagance of the description and the comparison with other texts, particularly in the New Testament (cf. Rev, 1:13-16; 2:18), make certain that this Being is none other than divine" [Merrill, "A Theology of Ezekiel and Daniel," in *A Biblical Theology of the Old Testament*, ed. Roy B. Zuck (Chicago: Moody Press, 1991), p. 388.

tual forces of evil in the heavenly realms (Eph 6:12; cf. Rev 12:7). The connection between rebellious earthly powers and evil cosmic powers is seen in Isaiah 24:21-22: "In that day the LORD will punish the powers in the heavens above and the kings on the earth below. They will be herded together like prisoners bound in a dungeon; they will be shut up in prison and be punished after many days."[2]

10:14 The **vision** of this verse is the revelation of chapter 11.

10:15-17 Despite the touch of verse 10, Daniel in verse 15 is again prostrate and, in addition, **speechless**. The messenger touches Daniel a second time (v. 16), this time on the lips, and gives him the power of speech.

10:18-19 A third time the supernatural messenger touches Daniel, strengthening and encouraging him.

10:20 The heavenly warfare is directed first against Persia and then Greece, because each in turn will have power over God's people. The supernatural messenger and Michael are the only two who support Israel in this warfare. In spite of the persecution that will befall Israel, especially under Antiochus IV Epiphanes (cf. ch. 8 and 11), God's people will survive. The revelation of chapter 11 gives unshakable assurance that, "desperate as the situation will be, God is so fully in control as to be able to disclose the sequence of events before they happen."[3]

10:21 The **Book of Truth** contains the course of future history as shaped by God (Mal 3:16; Ps 139:16; Rev 5:1).

11:1 The **first year** of Darius was that year in which royal orders were given which allowed God's people to return to Jerusalem. Though this order had appeared to be nothing more than Persian foreign policy, "Michael had been strengthened, his people had been set free to return to their land, all because God's favor was once again towards them. Spiritual factors prove to be all-important in human history."[4]

---

[2]Chuck Lowe, "Do Demons Have Zip Codes?" *Christianity Today* 42 (July 13, 1998): 57.

[3]Baldwin, *Daniel,* p. 182.

[4]Ibid., p. 182.

Michael was and would be locked in battle with Satan's deputies to Persia and Greece. Michael's victory over satanic foes must have paved the way for Queen Esther to thwart Haman, who wanted to obliterate the entire Jewish race. Michael's victory over satanic foes would pave the way for the death of Antiochus IV Epiphanes and the reconsecration of the temple for the worship of Almighty God.

Merrill Unger writes,

> Human and superhuman agencies in the government of the earth were interacting. Satan as the prince of the power of the air and his evil spirit subordinates were clashing with God's holy angels. The attempt was being made to thwart the purpose of God for his earthly people; they knew full well that the divine plan invoked challenge to their sway in the world system. In this instance this was true in a preeminent sense; for Daniel was about to be given a momentous vision, looking forward to the Second Advent . . . , which would ultimately spell the doom of Satan's rule through human governments.[5]

Daniel 10 reveals a connection between rebellious earthly powers and evil cosmic forces. In other words, there is a direct correlation between evil government and governors and demonic influence.

Demonic influence is also evident in the worship of idols. Deuteronomy 32:17 suggests that worship offered to idols is in reality offered to the demonic. This same point is made in Psalm 106:36-38. "They worshiped their idols, which became a snare to them. They sacrificed their sons and their daughters to demons. They shed innocent blood, the blood of their sons and daughters, whom they sacrificed to the idols of Canaan, and the land was desecrated by their blood."

This is also Paul's perspective. He warns the Corinthians, "The sacrifices of pagans are offered to demons, not to God, and I do not want you to be participants with demons" (1 Cor 10:20; cf. Rev 9:20).

In the New Testament demon possession is related to a number of physical maladies: blindness (Matt 12:22), dumbness (Matt 9:32-

---

[5]Merrill F. Unger, *Biblical Demonology* (Wheaton, IL: Van Kampen Press, 1953), p. 195.

33; Luke 11:14), epilepsy (Matt 17:14-18; Luke 9:37-43), and sickness (Luke 4:40-41).

In each and every case above, Jesus brought healing to the possessed person, clearly indicating that he had power over the demonic realm (see also Matt 4:24; 8:16,32; 15:21-28; Mark 1:32-34,39; 5:1-20; 7:24-30; Luke 4:33-36; 8:26-39; 13:32). There were even occasions when the disciples exhibited the same authority (Luke 10:17).

It is this authority over the demonic realm that gives Paul reason to exult. "For I am convinced that neither death nor life, neither angels nor demons, neither the present nor the future, nor any powers, neither height nor depth, nor anything else in all creation, will be able to separate us from the love of God that is in Christ Jesus our Lord" (Rom 8:38-39).

According to Paul demonic influence is also evident in false or heretical teaching (1 Tim 4:1). Paul warns the Colossians, "See to it that no one takes you captive through hollow and deceptive philosophy, which depends on human tradition and the basic principles of this world rather than on Christ" (Col 2:8). In Colosse Paul is confident that the truth of the gospel will prevail over heretical (demonic) teaching because Christ, "having disarmed the powers and authorities, he made a public spectacle of them, triumphing over them by the cross" (2:15).

DANIEL 11

XI. THE TIMES AND THE END OF TIME (11:2–12:13)

A. THE PERSIAN EMPIRE (11:2)

[2]"Now then, I tell you the truth: Three more kings will appear in Persia, and then a fourth, who will be far richer than all the others. When he has gained power by his wealth, he will stir up everyone against the kingdom of Greece.

11:2 The standpoint of Daniel is the reign of Cyrus (10:1). Cyrus (539–530) was followed by Cambyses (530–522), Gaumata (522), Darius I Hystaspes (522–486), Xerxes (486–465), Artaxerxes I Longimanus (465–424), Xerxes II (424), Sogdianos (424–423), Darius II Nothus (423–404), Artaxerxes II Mnemon (404–358), Artaxerxes III Ochus (358–338), Arses (338–336), and Darius III Codomannus (336–331). In other words, approximately 200 years and thirteen kings would pass before Persia's dominance would come to an end.

Daniel 11:2 speaks of three kings and then a fourth. If Daniel intends these numbers to be taken literally, then the three kings would be (1) Cambyses, (2) the impostor Gaumata or Bardiya, who passed himself off as Cyrus's younger son, Smerdis, and (3) Darius I Hystaspes. The fourth king is then Xerxes, who, without any just cause, invaded areas controlled by Greeks. After he had burned Athens, his fleet was battered at the Battle of Salamis in 480 and his army crushed the following year at the battle of Plataea. This Greek-Persian conflict begun in earnest by Xerxes ended with Alexander the Great.

If Daniel is employing the familiar Hebraism x / x + 1 (Prov 30:15,18,21,29; Amos 1:3,6,9,11,13; 2:1,4,6), he emphasizes not the number of kings to be expected, but that Persian wealth will invite attack from all, even Greece.[1]

B. THE GREEK EMPIRE (11:3-4)

[3]Then a mighty king will appear, who will rule with great power and do as he pleases. [4]After he has appeared, his empire will be broken up and parceled out toward the four winds of heaven. It will not go to his descendants, nor will it have the power he exercised, because his empire will be uprooted and given to others.

11:3 By 330 Alexander III (the Great) had conquered Persia. But in 323 he was dead and, in time, his kingdom would be split into four and ruled, not by his descendants (Alexander IV was his son), but by Alexander's four leading generals (7:6; 8:8), the *Diadochoi* ("Successors").

11:4 Philip III, Alexander's half-brother, and Alexander IV were murdered in 317 and 311 respectively, fulfilling the prophecy of verse 4: **It will not go to his descendants.**"[2]

In the material that follows (11:5-45), the kings of the North (Seleucids) and the kings of the South (Ptolemies) are descendants of two of the Diadochoi, Seleucus and Ptolemy. The Seleucids had their power base in Syria, while the Ptolemies had their base in Egypt. Judah was caught in the middle.

C. SOUTH VERSUS NORTH (11:5-20)

[5]"The king of the South will become strong, but one of his commanders will become even stronger than he and will rule his own kingdom with great power. [6]After some years, they will become allies. The daughter of the king of the South will go to the king of the North to make an alliance, but she will not retain her power, and he and his power[a] will not last. In those days she will be hand-

---

[1]Baldwin, *Daniel*, p. 185.

[2]An alleged son of Alexander, named Herakles, appeared briefly on the scene in 309, but he too was murdered (Collins, *Daniel*, p. 378).

ed over, together with her royal escort and her father[b] and the one who supported her.

[7]"One from her family line will arise to take her place. He will attack the forces of the king of the North and enter his fortress; he will fight against them and be victorious. [8]He will also seize their gods, their metal images and their valuable articles of silver and gold and carry them off to Egypt. For some years he will leave the king of the North alone. [9]Then the king of the North will invade the realm of the king of the South but will retreat to his own country. [10]His sons will prepare for war and assemble a great army, which will sweep on like an irresistible flood and carry the battle as far as his fortress.

[11]"Then the king of the South will march out in a rage and fight against the king of the North, who will raise a large army, but it will be defeated. [12]When the army is carried off, the king of the South will be filled with pride and will slaughter many thousands, yet he will not remain triumphant. [13]For the king of the North will muster another army, larger than the first; and after several years, he will advance with a huge army fully equipped.

[14]"In those times many will rise against the king of the South. The violent men among your own people will rebel in fulfillment of the vision, but without success. [15]Then the king of the North will come and build up siege ramps and will capture a fortified city. The forces of the South will be powerless to resist; even their best troops will not have the strength to stand. [16]The invader will do as he pleases; no one will be able to stand against him. He will establish himself in the Beautiful Land and will have the power to destroy it. [17]He will determine to come with the might of his entire kingdom and will make an alliance with the king of the South. And he will give him a daughter in marriage in order to overthrow the kingdom, but his plans[c] will not succeed or help him. [18]Then he will turn his attention to the coastlands and will take many of them, but a commander will put an end to his insolence and will turn his insolence back upon him. [19]After this, he will turn back toward the fortresses of his own country but will stumble and fall, to be seen no more.

[20]"His successor will send out a tax collector to maintain the

royal splendor. In a few years, however, he will be destroyed, yet not in anger or in battle.

ª6 Or *offspring*   ᵇ6 Or *child* (see Vulgate and Syriac)   ᶜ17 Or *but she*

11:5 The **king of the South** is Ptolemy I Soter (322–285), who had taken Egypt from the point of Alexander's death. Seleucus I Nicator (312–280), also one of the four Diadochoi, fled to Egypt, seeking refuge from Antigonus, who had captured Babylonia in 316. Seleucus became one of Ptolemy's generals. In 312 Ptolemy and Seleucus defeated Antigonus at Gaza. Seleucus then recovered Babylon, and, eventually, captured the rest of Antigonus's empire. In wresting control from Antigonus, Seleucus became **even stronger** than Ptolemy I.

11:6 About 250 Ptolemy II Philadelphus (285–246) attempted to ally himself with the Seleucid empire by marrying his daughter Berenice to Antiochus II Theos (261–246), who had divorced his wife Laodice. After two years this marriage failed; Antiochus II went back to Laodice, who then had him killed, along with his son by Berenice, Berenice herself, and a number of her Egyptian attendants. Berenice was not able to **retain her power** against her rival Laodice.

11:7-9 In retaliation for the death of his sister (Berenice), nephew, and his kingdom's subjects, Ptolemy III Euergetes (246–221), who had succeeded his father, invaded the Seleucid empire (**forces of the king of the North**), gained control of its capital city, Antioch, and plundered its wealth (**their valuable articles of silver and gold**). He also succeeded in putting to death Laodice, the murderess of his sister. He did not press for total conquest of the empire. In fact, he left the throne there to Seleucus II Callinicus (246–226), son of Antiochus II by Laodice. In 242 Seleucus II retreated from an invasion of Egypt, his army decimated (**but will retreat to his own country**). Seizing a nation's gods was a symbol of subjugation.

11:10 Seleucus II was succeeded by his sons, Seleucus III Soter Cerannus (226–223) and Antiochus III Magnus (223–187). In 219 the latter recaptured Seleucia, a fortified port on the Mediterranean. He also invaded Palestine and captured a large part of it.

11:11-12 In 217 Ptolemy IV Philopator (221–203) engaged Antiochus III in battle at Raphia, the Egyptian stronghold on the border with Palestine. According to the Greek historian Polybius (*Histories* 5.79), Antiochus III lost 14,000 men in that battle. Ptolemy IV did not press his advantage and made peace with Antiochus III.

11:13 Fourteen years passed (**and after several years**) before Antiochus III would again invade the Ptolemaic kingdom. This time he would do so in alliance with Philip V of Macedon.

11:14 Ptolemy IV, who died mysteriously, was succeeded by his infant son Ptolemy V Epiphanes (203–181). Agathocles, a chief minister under Ptolemy IV, actually ruled the country. His oppressive rule fostered insurrection (**many will rise against the king of the South**). He was himself assassinated.

11:15 In light then of Antiochus's new resolve and Egypt's inner turmoil, the forces of the South were powerless to stand. In 199 Antiochus defeated the Egyptians at Paneas (Caesarea Philippi) and in 198 at Sidon (**a fortified city**). After a century of Ptolemaic rule, Palestine now came under the control of the Seleucids.

11:16 Verse 14 acknowledges that these events were felt by the Jewish community (**your own people**). **The violent men** may be pro-Egyptian Jews who clearly backed a loser (**but without success**). The **fulfillment of the vision** is vague. Perhaps it is a reference to this prophecy now being fulfilled.

11:17 Since Antiochus had gained control of Palestine, he was in a position to invade Egypt and put an end to the Ptolemaic Empire. Fearing Roman intervention, he hoped to undermine Egypt through betrothing his daughter Cleopatra to Ptolemy V.[3] But Cleopatra became perfectly loyal to her husband and encouraged an alliance with Rome, which frustrated her father's dream of possessing Egypt (**He will give him a daughter in marriage in order to overthrow the kingdom, but his plans will not succeed or help him**).[4]

---

[3] If Cleopatra should give birth to a son, that boy could claim both crowns — Ptolemaic and Seleucid. Antiochus hoped that such a scenario would create a favorable situation for his eventual control of the region.

[4] Cleopatra gave birth to Ptolemy VI Philometor (181–146). Because Cleopatra had become sympathetic to the Ptolemaic empire, the birth of this boy

11:18 Antiochus turned his attention to the **coastlands**, attacking Macedon, Thrace, and Greece. In 191 he was defeated by the Romans at Thermopylae and in 190 at Magnesia. He became a vassal to Rome. Antiochus IV, his younger son, was taken to Rome as a hostage.

11:19 Antiochus returned to Syria, the core of his empire. He was assassinated in 187, attempting to pillage the temple of Bel in Elymais.

11:20 Seleucus IV Philopator (187–175), Antiochus's successor, was trapped beneath the burden of tribute imposed on his father's empire. He appointed Heliodorus as finance minister to maintain Rome's **royal splendor**. Seleucus died in 175, assassinated in a plot engineered by Heliodorus and Seleucus's younger brother Antiochus IV (2 Macc 3).

D. ANTIOCHUS IV EPIPHANES (11:21-45)

[21]"He will be succeeded by a contemptible person who has not been given the honor of royalty. He will invade the kingdom when its people feel secure, and he will seize it through intrigue. [22]Then an overwhelming army will be swept away before him; both it and a prince of the covenant will be destroyed. [23]After coming to an agreement with him, he will act deceitfully, and with only a few people he will rise to power. [24]When the richest provinces feel secure, he will invade them and will achieve what neither his fathers nor his forefathers did. He will distribute plunder, loot and wealth among his followers. He will plot the overthrow of fortresses—but only for a time.

[25]"With a large army he will stir up his strength and courage against the king of the South. The king of the South will wage war with a large and very powerful army, but he will not be able to stand because of the plots devised against him. [26]Those who eat from the king's provisions will try to destroy him; his army will be

---

was of little consequence for Antiochus's plan. When Ptolemy V died in 181, Cleopatra was appointed as queen regent.

swept away, and many will fall in battle. [27]The two kings, with their hearts bent on evil, will sit at the same table and lie to each other, but to no avail, because an end will still come at the appointed time. [28]The king of the North will return to his own country with great wealth, but his heart will be set against the holy covenant. He will take action against it and then return to his own country.

[29]"At the appointed time he will invade the South again, but this time the outcome will be different from what it was before. [30]Ships of the western coastlands[a] will oppose him, and he will lose heart. Then he will turn back and vent his fury against the holy covenant. He will return and show favor to those who forsake the holy covenant.

[31]"His armed forces will rise up to desecrate the temple fortress and will abolish the daily sacrifice. Then they will set up the abomination that causes desolation. [32]With flattery he will corrupt those who have violated the covenant, but the people who know their God will firmly resist him.

[33]"Those who are wise will instruct many, though for a time they will fall by the sword or be burned or captured or plundered. [34]When they fall, they will receive a little help, and many who are not sincere will join them. [35]Some of the wise will stumble, so that they may be refined, purified and made spotless until the time of the end, for it will still come at the appointed time.

[36]"The king will do as he pleases. He will exalt and magnify himself above every god and will say unheard-of things against the God of gods. He will be successful until the time of wrath is completed, for what has been determined must take place. [37]He will show no regard for the gods of his fathers or for the one desired by women, nor will he regard any god, but will exalt himself above them all. [38]Instead of them, he will honor a god of fortresses; a god unknown to his fathers he will honor with gold and silver, with precious stones and costly gifts. [39]He will attack the mightiest fortresses with the help of a foreign god and will greatly honor those who acknowledge him. He will make them rulers over many people and will distribute the land at a price.[b]

[40]"At the time of the end the king of the South will engage him in battle, and the king of the North will storm out against him with

chariots and cavalry and a great fleet of ships. He will invade many
countries and sweep through them like a flood. [41]He will also
invade the Beautiful Land. Many countries will fall, but Edom,
Moab and the leaders of Ammon will be delivered from his hand.
[42]He will extend his power over many countries; Egypt will not
escape. [43]He will gain control of the treasures of gold and silver
and all the riches of Egypt, with the Libyans and Nubians in submission. [44]But reports from the east and the north will alarm him,
and he will set out in a great rage to destroy and annihilate many.
[45]He will pitch his royal tents between the seas at[c] the beautiful
holy mountain. Yet he will come to his end, and no one will help
him.

[a]30 Hebrew *of Kittim*　　[b]39 Or *land for a reward*　　[c]45 Or *the sea and*

11:21 Since the defeat of Antiochus III at Magnesia, Antiochus IV
Epiphanes (175–163) had been a political hostage in Rome. But in 175
Demetrius I, the oldest son of Seleucus IV, was sent to Rome to replace
Antiochus IV as hostage there. Antiochus IV took power as guardian
to and co-regent with Antiochus, the younger son of Seleucus IV. In
170 Antiochus died leaving Antiochus IV to rule alone.

11:22-24 A prince of the covenant is the high priest Onias III,
replaced in 175 because of his Egyptian sympathies by Jason from
the pro-Syrian Tobiad party.[5] The Tobiads, who had emigrated from
across the Jordan River some years before, benefited from this synergism by being beneficiaries of Antiochus's liberality on the basis of
plunder (v. 24; 1 Macc 3:30). Jason and Onias were brothers. The
Tobiads wanted to hellenize Jerusalem. Second Maccabees 4:7b-10
comments on these events: "Jason the brother of Onias obtained the
high priesthood by corruption, promising the king at an interview
three hundred and sixty talents of silver and, from another source
of revenue, eighty talents. In addition to this he promised to pay one

---

[5]Archer is representative of those commentators who see Ptolemy VI
Philometor as the "prince of the covenant." Antiochus made a treaty of
friendship with Ptolemy VI aimed at uniting the Ptolemaic and Seleucid
dynasties under his authority. The alliance aided Ptolemy VI's attempt to
dislodge his younger brother Physcon from power. The alliance wore so
thin that Philometor made peace with Physcon ("Daniel," pp. 136-137).

hundred and fifty more if permission were given to establish by his authority a gymnasium and a body of youth for it, and to enrol the men of Jerusalem as citizens of Antioch. When the king assented and Jason came to office, he at once shifted his countrymen over to the Greek way of life."

11:25-26 These verses turn to Antiochus's campaign against the South. In 170 an Egyptian army set off to recapture Palestine. Antiochus defeated this army, entered Egypt, took Ptolemy VI prisoner, and occupied much of Egypt. In the words of 1 Maccabees 1:17-19: "So he invaded Egypt with a strong force, with chariots and elephants and cavalry and with a large fleet. He engaged Ptolemy king of Egypt in battle, and Ptolemy turned and fled before him, and many were wounded and fell. And they captured the fortified cities in the land of Egypt, and he plundered the land of Egypt."

According to 25b-26a Ptolemy will be the victim of treachery. Goldingay summarizes the possibilities of this treachery: "Perhaps the reference is to people who betrayed Pelusium [a border fortress] to Antiochus, or perhaps to Ptolemy's advisers who brought about the Egyptian defeat by urging the attack on Palestine, his capture by urging him to flee from Antiochus, and his deposition by then crowning his brother as Ptolemy VII in Alexandria in 169 B.C."[6]

11:27 Antiochus IV and Ptolemy VI will then unite (**sit at the same table**) to regain the throne for the latter, as a Seleucid puppet. Each king is clearly motivated by his own interests, but neither will achieve the ultimate purpose (**but to no avail, because an end will still come at the appointed time**).

11:28 During a visit to Jerusalem in 169, Antiochus IV confiscated some of the temple treasury. The **holy covenant** denotes the holy land and the covenant people. First Maccabees 1:21-23 reads: "He arrogantly entered the sanctuary and took the golden altar, the lampstand for the light, and all its utensils. He took also the table for the bread of the Presence, the cups for drink offerings, the bowls, the golden censers, the curtain, the crowns, and the gold decoration on the front of the temple; he stripped it all off. He took the silver and the gold, and the costly vessels; he took also the hidden treasures which he found."

---

[6]Goldingay, *Daniel,* p. 301.

11:29-30a In the meantime, the two Ptolemies (VI and VII) agreed to reign jointly. So in 168 Antiochus invaded again. The Roman consul Gaius Popillius Laenas (**ships of the western coastlands**[7] **will oppose him**) intercepted Antiochus and ordered him out of Egypt. He drew a circle round him and ordered him to respond before stepping out of it. Antiochus withdrew and returned via Judea.

11:30b-31 Responding to a rumor that Antiochus had died in Egypt, Jason, whom Antiochus had earlier deposed in favor of Menelaus (2 Macc 4:23-29), returned to Jerusalem and led a rebellion against the latter and the Tobiad ruling party (2 Macc 5:5-10).

Antiochus put down the rebellion and reestablished the authority of the Tobiad priesthood. Again, in the words of 2 Maccabees: "When news of what had happened reached the king, he took it to mean that Judea was in revolt. So, raging inwardly, he left Egypt and took the city by storm. And he commanded his soldiers to cut down relentlessly every one they met and to slay those who went into the houses. Then there was killing of young and old, destruction of boys, women, and children, and slaughter of virgins and infants. Within the total of three days eighty thousand were destroyed, forty thousand in hand-to-hand fighting; and as many were sold into slavery as were slain" (5:11-14).

In addition to this **fury** (v. 30), he stopped the daily temple sacrifice (Num 28:2-8) and set up the **abomination that causes desolation** (v. 31; cf. 8:11-13). The abomination was, of course, the heathen altar erected on the altar of burnt offering (1 Macc 1:54).

11:32 Menelaus and his followers, "those who forsake the holy covenant" (v. 30), did not object to either the ransacking of the temple or of the faith. Instead, they sided with the tyrant who had put them in power.

11:33-34 These verses suggest that God's people would endure the sword (1 Macc 2:9,31-38), fire (2 Macc 6:11; 7:1-41), captivity (1 Macc 3:41), and being plundered (1 Macc 1:31).

The persecuted would be comforted (**receive a little help**) by the discerning (**those who are wise**) coming to share their commitment

---

[7]"Western coastlands" is literally *kittim*. Kittim is an ancient name for Cyprus (Isa 23:1). Here it is used of the islands and coastlands west of Palestine (cf. Num 24:24).

(1 Macc 2:42). Martyrdom would test how real the commitment to the resistance really was. Some, however, joined the resistance from insincere motives (**and many who are not sincere will join them**).

11:35 The persecution has its purpose in God's plan (**they may be refined, purified, and made spotless**), and He will bring it to its appointed end (**it will come at the appointed time**).

Mattathias led a group of heroic patriots in the struggle for independence against Antiochus IV and the Seleucid Empire (cf. Zech 9:13; Heb 11:33-35). He was the father of five sons: John Gaddis, Simon Thasi, Judas Maccabaeus, Eleazar Avaran, and Jonathan Apphus. Their victory is commemorated in the festival known as Hanukkah (1 Macc 4; John 10:22). In turn a strong Jewish kingdom was founded by John Hyrcanus (134-104) and enlarged by his son Alexander Jannaeus (103-76).

11:36-39 These verses evaluate Antiochus's religious attitudes.[8] His egotism (vv. 36,37) was reflected in the title Epiphanes, "[God] Manifest," his use on coins of the title "God," his plundering of temples and suppressing of other religions. In light then of this self-glorification, he came into sharp conflict with the **God of gods**, the God of Israel (cf. 1 Macc 1:24).

When Antiochus replaced Apollo with Zeus as the god of the dynasty, he **show[ed] no regard for the gods of his fathers** (vv. 37, 38). **The one desired by women** is possibly a deity favored in Egypt — Adonis or Dionysus, who was slighted by Antiochus's politics.

Antiochus's favorable treatment of Tobiad leadership is example enough of how he **honore[d] those who acknowledge[d] him** (v. 39; cf. 1 Macc 3:36).

The reference to **fortresses** in verse 39 finds a possible parallel in 1 Maccabees: "Then they fortified the city of David with a great strong wall and *strong towers*, and it became their *citadel*. And they stationed there a sinful people, lawless men" (1:33-34a). Later, speaking of the citadel, from it Gentiles "used to sally forth and defile the environs of the sanctuary and do great damage to its purity" (14:36).

Antiochus's success (cf. 8:4; 11:3,16) is permitted **until the time of wrath is completed** (v. 36).

---

[8]Calvin opines that verses 36-45 relate to the Roman Empire.

11:40-45 Since the expression **at the time of the end** (v. 40) was used at verse 35 in connection with Antiochus, the reference here applies to the end of the reign of Antiochus. Verses 40-45 summarize the career of and depict then the doom of Antiochus.[9] At the moment of his triumph (vv. 42-43), Antiochus will be called away by disturbing reports (v. 44; cf. 2 Kgs 19:7). In a fury, he will march north and east (where the Parthian threat loomed large) and meet his end (v. 45).

Since Antiochus died at Tabae in Persia, verse 45 only suggests that he would pitch his royal tents between the sea [Mediterranean] and the beautiful holy mountain [Jerusalem], not die there.

Daniel 11 predicted a time of religious persecution for God's people. Persecution is also an important theme in the New Testament.

Like the prophets (Matt 5:12; Acts 7:52), Jesus was persecuted (John 5:16). Jesus suggests that his followers will also be persecuted: "All men will hate you because of me" (Matt 10:22; cf. 23:33-36; Luke 11:47-51; 21:12-19). "If they persecuted me, they will persecute you also" (John 15:20). Paul echoes this thought: "In fact, everyone who wants to live a godly life in Christ Jesus will be persecuted" (2 Tim 3:12). Jesus calls the persecuted one "blessed" (Matt 5:10,11), perhaps because "great is your reward in heaven" (Matt 5:12). Paul exhorts us to "bless those who persecute you; bless and do not curse" (Rom 12:14). Jesus also demands that we "pray for those who persecute" us (Matt 5:44).

---

[9]Most conservative commentators relate verses 40-45 to the Antichrist. But there is nothing in the text to indicate a change of subjects. Less than conservative commentators point to v. 40 as a transition from *ex eventu* prophecy to real and erroneous prediction. These commentators assume that v. 45 suggests that Antiochus would die in the Holy Land, which, if Polybius be believed, would be mistaken. Polybius writes, "In Syria, King Antiochus, wishing to provide himself with money, decided to make an expedition against the sanctuary of Artemis in Elymais. On reaching the spot he was foiled in his hopes . . . and on his retreat he died at Tabae in Persia, smitten with madness as some people say. Owing to certain manifestations of divine displeasure when he was attempting this outrage on the above sanctuary" (31.9). But does v. 45 necessarily say that Antiochus will die between the Mediterranean and Jerusalem? I do not think so.

Christians were persecuted by Saul (Acts 8:1; 22:4-5; 26:9-11; 1 Cor 15:9; Gal 1:13,23; Phil 3:6; 1 Tim 1:13). Paul was himself persecuted (Acts 13:50; 1 Cor 4:12; 2 Cor 4:9; Gal 5:11; 2 Tim 3:11).

The persecution of Christians advanced the proclamation of the gospel: "Now those who had been scattered by the persecution in connection with Stephen traveled as far as Phoenicia, Cyprus and Antioch, telling the message only to Jews. Some of them, however, men from Cyprus and Cyrene, went to Antioch and began to speak to Greeks also, telling them the good news about the Lord Jesus. The Lord's hand was with them, and a great number of people believed and turned to the Lord" (Acts 11:19-21).

The persecution of Christians also resulted in a greater awareness of the power of Christ. "Therefore I will boast all the more gladly about my weaknesses, so that Christ's power may rest on me. That is why, for Christ's sake, I delight in weaknesses, in insults, in hardships, in persecutions, in difficulties. For when I am weak, then I am strong" (2 Cor 12:9b-10).

Persecution also resulted in greater faith (2 Thess 1:3-4), endurance (Rom 5:3; Jas 1:2), and comfort (2 Cor 1:5).

DANIEL 12

E. RESURRECTION (12:1-4)

[1]"At that time Michael, the great prince who protects your people, will arise. There will be a time of distress such as has not happened from the beginning of nations until then. But at that time your people—everyone whose name is found written in the book—will be delivered. [2]Multitudes who sleep in the dust of the earth will awake: some to everlasting life, others to shame and everlasting contempt. [3]Those who are wise[a] will shine like the brightness of the heavens, and those who lead many to righteousness, like the stars for ever and ever. [4]But you, Daniel, close up and seal the words of the scroll until the time of the end. Many will go here and there to increase knowledge."

[a]3 Or *who impart wisdom*

12:1 Michael, who was previously mentioned in 10:13,21, is the **great prince** who delivers God's people from the midst of suffering. **The book** is the book of the living, as in Psalm 69:28.

12:2 "A time of distress" implies heavy loss of life, both godly and ungodly. These dead will **sleep in the dust of the earth**. The word "sleep" implies a temporary state from which we normally awake. In other words, the word "sleep" prepares us for the thought of a general resurrection (cf. Isa 26:19; Job 14:13-15; 19:25-27; Matt 25:46; John 5:28,29). Paul wrote to the Romans, "I consider that our present sufferings are not worth comparing with the glory that will be revealed in us" (8:18). **Everlasting life** versus **everlasting contempt**; these are humanity's ultimate destinies.

12:3 The **wise** are those who give attention to the truth of God's word (9:13). They are also those **who lead many to righteousness**, that is, encourage others to faith (11:33). As the wise **shine like the brightness of the heavens** or **like the stars for ever and ever**, they help others see the glory of God.[1]

12:4 Close up keeps the words safe until the time they are needed or fulfilled. **Seal the words** preserves them intact. These words contain the truth as to the future and, accordingly, are the only true source of knowledge. Amos 8:12 is apropos here: "Men will stagger from sea to sea and wander from north to east, searching for the word of the LORD, but they will not find it."

F. FINAL WORDS (12:5-13)

⁵**Then I, Daniel, looked, and there before me stood two others, one on this bank of the river and one on the opposite bank. ⁶One of them said to the man clothed in linen, who was above the waters of the river, "How long will it be before these astonishing things are fulfilled?"**

⁷**The man clothed in linen, who was above the waters of the river, lifted his right hand and his left hand toward heaven, and I heard him swear by him who lives forever, saying, "It will be for a time, times and half a time.ᵃ When the power of the holy people has been finally broken, all these things will be completed."**

⁸**I heard, but I did not understand. So I asked, "My lord, what will the outcome of all this be?"**

⁹**He replied, "Go your way, Daniel, because the words are closed up and sealed until the time of the end. ¹⁰Many will be purified, made spotless and refined, but the wicked will continue to be wicked. None of the wicked will understand, but those who are wise will understand.**

¹¹**"From the time that the daily sacrifice is abolished and the abomination that causes desolation is set up, there will be 1,290 days. ¹²Blessed is the one who waits for and reaches the end of the 1,335 days.**

---

[1]Calvin wrote, "The sons of God, who being devoted entirely to God and ruled by the spirit of prudence, point out the way of life to others, shall not only be saved themselves, but shall possess surpassing glory far beyond anything which exists in this world" (*Prophet Daniel*, p. 377).

[13]"As for you, go your way till the end. You will rest, and then at the end of the days you will rise to receive your allotted inheritance."

[a]7 Or *a year, two years and half a year*

12:5-7 Two additional heavenly figures appear (v. 5), and one raises the question, **How long will it be before these astonishing things are fulfilled?** (v. 6; cf. 8:13-14). The root translated "astonishing things" is used for the deeds of Antiochus in 8:24 and 11:36. Daniel's heavenly messenger, the one clothed in linen, raises both hands in solemn oath and answers, **It will be for a time, times, and half a time. When the power of the holy people has been finally broken, all these things will be completed** (v. 7).

Raising both hands in oath emphasizes the truth here affirmed. Typically both God (Deut 32:40) and man (Gen 14:22) raise one hand in oath (cf. Rev 10:5-6). Perhaps the two figures are present to bear witness to the oath spoken in verse 7.

Deliverance will come at an unlikely time —**when the power of the holy people has been finally broken** (11:21-45). When evil seems to have become overpowering, it will be slowed and then stopped (**Time, times, and half a time**).[2]

12:8-10 Wanting to know more, Daniel asks, **My lord, what will the outcome of all this be?** The celestial messenger responds by affirming that since the revelation is closed up and sealed, Daniel should leave the matter alone. Additionally, the wise understand that the suffering of God's people serves the positive goal of preparing them for God's presence. In contrast, the wicked will continue to be wicked, not suspecting that in the end they will be overwhelmed by God's presence.

---

[2]Calvin writes, "Time means a long period, times, a longer period, and a half means the end or closing period. The sum of the whole is this: many years must elapse before God fulfills what his Prophet had declared. Time therefore signifies a long period; times, double this period; as if he had said, while the sons of God are kept in suspense so long without obtaining an answer to their petitions, the time will be prolonged, nay, even doubled. . . With respect to the half of a time, this is added for the comfort of the pious, to prevent their sinking under the delay, because God does not accomplish their desire" (*Prophet Daniel,* p. 383).

12:11-12 Both **1,290** and **1,335** days are approximately three and one-half years, roughly the time of the desecration of the temple under Antiochus's reign of terror. But this reign has its appointed end. Blessed are the wise who endure this evil time (cf. Matt 24:13). Perhaps the numerical difference between these two numbers suggests the subsequent death of Antiochus, that is, his death follows in point of time the desecration of the Temple.

12:13 Daniel is told twice to **Go your way** (vv. 9,13). In other words, "Keep on living." And when living is done (**You will rest**), then Daniel **will rise to receive [his] allotted inheritance**. The picture of death as rest is found in Isaiah 57:2; Job 3:13,17.

In the Old Testament two men — Enoch and Elijah — did not experience physical death. They are the exception to the truth of Hebrews 9:27: "Man is destined to die once." Eight times in Genesis 5 the refrain, "and then he died," is sounded, a reminder that death is the rule for mortal man. But in Genesis 5:24 we read, "Enoch walked with God; then he was no more, because God took him away." The contrast drawn between Enoch and the other persons mentioned in Genesis 5 is obvious. Elijah, the great prophet of God who defied the Baalism of his day, was also exceptional. According to 2 Kings 2:11 Elijah was taken up alive into heaven in a whirlwind.

Two Old Testament figures did not once experience death. At least three figures experienced it twice. Through the power of God, Elijah restored to life the once dead son of the widow of Zarephath (1 Kgs 17:20-21). Elisha restored to life the dead son of a woman from Shunem (2 Kgs 4:20,35). Presumably both these boys would become men and, in time, die for a second time. In 2 Kings 13 contact with the bones of the deceased Elisha brought a dead man's body back to life (13:21). Again, presumably, this once dead man would later die.

Death is clearly the appointed end for the life of man "under the sun." But the Old Testament expands our horizon and enables us to see a life beyond. The Old Testament Scriptures express a belief in a general resurrection. Isaiah 26:19 proclaims: "But your dead will live; their bodies will rise. You will dwell in the dust, wake up and shout for joy. Your dew is like the dew of the morning; the earth will give birth to her dead." Isaiah 25:7-8 proclaim: "On this mountain he will destroy the shroud that enfolds all peoples, the sheet that covers all nations; he will swallow up death forever. The Sovereign LORD will wipe away the tears from all faces; he will remove the disgrace of his people from all the earth."

Like the three examples above, to say nothing of the New Testament examples of Lazarus (John 11:44) and Eutychus (Acts 20:9-10), Jesus died and was resurrected. But unlike these examples, Jesus did not die a second time. In this great drama, God had conquered death. In Jesus' death, resurrection, and ascension into the heavens, death had been defeated once and for all, for all the peoples of the earth. Speaking to John on the isle of Patmos, Jesus said, "I am the First and the Last. I am the Living One; I was dead, and behold I am alive for ever and ever! And I hold the keys of death and Hades" (Rev 1:17-18; cf. Rom 6:14; 1 Cor 15:12-57; 1 Thess 4:14; Rev 21:4).

Daniel 12:2 has taught us that our earthly lives are just a precursor to eternity: "Multitudes who sleep in the dust of the earth will awake: some to everlasting life, others to shame and everlasting contempt." The New Testament also calls persons not to live as though this world is the end. Christians are expected to endure hardships, contradictions, and unanswered questions because of what is laid up for us beyond death (Rom 8:18-25; 1 Cor 15:20-28; Heb 12:1-3; Rev 2:7,10,11,17,26-29; 14:13).

The resurrection of Jesus empowers our lives in the daily struggle against sin. His resurrection gives us perspective on the vanity and futility of this world. His resurrection is God's confirmation of the atoning work of the cross. His resurrection challenges us to live now in the light of eternity, and it generates a sure and certain hope. Those are truths for this life! Words cannot begin to express the riches Christ's resurrection will bring us in eternity!

Psalm 33:8-22 is a fitting conclusion to this study of Esther and Daniel. Listen to the words of the psalmist and appreciate how they serve as commentary for these great books of Scripture!

> Let all the earth fear the LORD;
>   let all the people of the world revere him.
> For he spoke, and it came to be;
>   he commanded, and it stood firm.
> The LORD foils the plans of the nations;
>   he thwarts the purposes of the peoples.

But the plans of the LORD stand firm forever,
  the purposes of his heart through all generations.

Blessed is the nation whose God is the LORD,
  the people he chose for his inheritance.
From heaven the LORD looks down
  and sees all mankind;
from his dwelling place he watches
  all who live on earth—
he who forms the hearts of all,
  who considers everything they do.
No king is saved by the size of his army;
  no warrior escapes by his great strength.
A horse is a vain hope for deliverance;
  despite all its great strength it cannot save.
But the eyes of the LORD are on those who fear him,
  on those whose hope is in his unfailing love,
to deliver them from death
  and to keep them alive in famine.

We wait in hope for the LORD;
  he is our help and our shield.
In him our hearts rejoice,
  for we trust in his holy name.
May your unfailing love rest upon us, O LORD,
  even as we put our hope in you.